Oriole Park Branch
7454 W. Balmoral Ave.
Chicago, IL 60656

E
159
.E69
2004

Chicago Public Library

R0401552915

DISC

ORIOLE

Marilyn Monroe dyed here : more location

Praise for *James Dean Died Here*
A BookSense 76 Selection

DATE DUE

FEB 1 4 2005
MAR 0 5 2005
MAR 2 6 2005

DEMCO 38-296

"*James Dea*
present."

"The where
momentou
slapped th

"Who says /
appealing."

"Chris Eptir
American I
the young i
the hangar

"Chris Eptin
toes to the
the 600-pl
take a stup

"Just in tim
650 pilgrir
The Loca
profound

"Want to I
burial gro

"This bool

"With sw
Location
their Am
are stick
a spirite
most ex

...culture past and

...entity, from the
(where Zsa Zsa

...ctoids are most

often hysterical
the spot where
unch house, and

...ed"

ting couch pota-
are represented,
gain lose $40 to

...cation of about
Dean Died Here:
...id, trashy and

on the Indian
in here, Baby!"

ied Here: The
those who like
. Whether you
an Died Here is
...untry's

Oriole Park Branch
7454 W. Balmoral Ave.
Chicago, IL 60656

DISCARD

D1468874

Praise for *James Dean Died Here*
A BookSense 76 Selection

"Takes you on road trips all over the country. . . . This book is a lot of fun!"
— National Public Radio's "The Savvy Traveler"

"Take a cross-country trip with this offbeat guide to America's historical and pop culture landmarks. Patty Hearst's bank, the site of Ritchie Valen's plane crash, the spot where George Washington crossed the Delaware, and the *Brady Bunch* house are among the listings. Full of photos, Epting's book is a guilty pleasure for the celebrity obsessed and offers an intriguing peek into the quirks of Americana."
— *Bookline*

"Looking for a good read? *James Dean Died Here* fits the bill."
— *Westways*

"*James Dean Died Here* is a pure gas of a book . . . The detail is impressive, the prose is straightforward but dryly humorous, and whenever Epting deals with things I know about firsthand, the book is absolutely accurate."
— *Palm Beach Post*

"An interesting curiosity quencher"
— *College and Research Libraries News*

"An interesting reference to take along when hitting the road this summer"
— *Detroit News*

"This offbeat travelogue provides the armchair traveler or road warrior tourist with all the information needed to visit America's pop culture sites of significance."
— *Chapter 11 Newsletter*

"Guilty fun! No other book will tell you which grate in New York City lifted Marilyn Monroe's skirt in *The Seven Year Itch* or from which marina in California The Minnow left for a 'three-hour tour.'"
— *Willamette Weekly*

Marilyn Monroe Dyed Here

More Locations of America's Pop Culture Landmarks

Chris Epting

S A N T A
M O N I C A
P R E S S

Copyright ©2004 by Chris Epting

All rights reserved. This book may not be reproduced in whole or in part or in any form or format without written permission of the publisher.

SANTA

MONICA

PRESS

Published by:
Santa Monica Press LLC
P.O. Box 1076
Santa Monica, CA 90406-1076
1-800-784-9553
www.santamonicapress.com
books@santamonicapress.com

Printed in the United States

Santa Monica Press books are available at special quantity discounts when purchased in bulk by corporations, organizations, or groups. Please call our Special Sales department at 1-800-784-9553.

ISBN 1-891661-39-6

Library of Congress Cataloging-in-Publication Data

Epting, Chris, 1961-
  Marilyn Monroe dyed here : more locations of America's pop culture landmarks / Chris Epting.
    p. cm.
  ISBN 1-891661-39-6
  1. Historic sites--United States--Guidebooks. 2. Popular culture--United States--History.
  3. United States--Guidebooks. 4. United States--History, Local. I. Title.
  E159.E69 2004
  306'.0973--dc22
                            2004005595

Book and cover design by Ohmontherange
Interior production by Future Studio

Front cover image: Don't go looking for this star on Hollywood Boulevard — alas, it only exists in cyberspace!

R0401552915

Oriole Park Branch
7454 W. Balmoral Ave.

Table of Contents

"Twenty years from now you will be more disappointed by the things that you didn't do than by the ones you did do. So throw off the bowlines. Sail away from the safe harbor. Catch the trade winds in your sails. Explore. Dream. Discover."
— Mark Twain

"The everyday kindness of the back roads more than makes up for the acts of greed in the headlines."
— Charles Kuralt

"Hey, ho — let's go!"
— The Ramones

Well, here we go again — off to find those places where something notable happened. Something monumental . . . something lesser-known but still significant . . . something truly offbeat or shocking or melodramatic or sad or glorious or accidental . . . *something*.

Just to re-visit the purpose and inspiration of my pop-culture mission: I stated in the Introduction of this book's predecessor, *James Dean Died Here*, that I believed that no other country is as fascinated with pop culture as America. I still believe that, which brings me back again to this path of discovery.

In *James Dean Died Here*, I also shared this definition I had come upon: "Pop Culture: Those series of activities and events that are, more or less, equivalent to national identity." The simplicity of the statement still holds true, and thus once again provides a context for all of the events you are about to encounter. And finally, beyond researching merely the details of a pop culture event, my primary mission continues to be to locate the precise (or as close to exact as can be had) spot where each one of these events took place. After all, the "where" of an event still seems to be the most elusive detail in our collective consciousness.

Often we know *all* of the facts of a famous or infamous event — except for that part about how to stand in the place where it happened, whether we want to or not. As a reporter mentioned to me last year, "I may not visit all of these places, but that's okay — I just love knowing they exist, that they have an address."

So for me, as a fan of history, the most interesting challenge continues to be trying to put each event in its place. Literally. Once you do that, I think it brings you closer to the event — makes it more real, lets you imagine what it was like that particular day.

This time around, in addition to locating hundreds of familiar pop culture landmarks, I wanted to push the idea further. Many obvious spots were covered in *James Dean Died Here*, like where the Hindenberg crashed, where Marilyn Monroe's dress famously billowed up, where the *Brady Bunch* house is, etc. But in this volume, I wanted to dig deeper and reveal some things that are perhaps not as well known — but still relevant and just as (if not more) compelling.

So that is what this book does — goes the extra mile, so to speak. Oh, there are still many of the ultra-famous events. The big-ticket pop culture events with which we all are familiar: Elvis getting a haircut (and where he got his first guitar). Truman holding up that famous newspaper headline. Where Jesse James was killed (and the wall where the bullet hole is still visible). Where Marilyn Monroe married Joe DiMaggio. The room where the very first Academy Awards ceremony was held. George Washington's headquarters. J.F.K.'s birthplace. Seabiscuit's stable. And hundreds more.

But then there are the places whose magic lies in the fact that, while still pivotal in the scope of pop culture history, they are not that well known. Like the place where an attempt was made on Lincoln's life . . . years before Booth killed him. Or where Teddy Roosevelt was also shot (and survived; he even gave a speech with the bullet in him!). Where the mythical Johnny Appleseed first planted his famous (and very real) trees. Where the first black NBA player took the court. Where Blackbeard the Pirate met his fate. Where Dylan first performed as "Dylan." The McDonald's where the infamous (and expensive) coffee spill occurred. Where a brunette actress named Norma Jeane Baker, soon to be Marilyn Monroe, first became a blonde. And on and on and on. This is where I think you'll have the most fun with this book — learning the details that are layered in the stuff you didn't know about before.

Subject-wise, I've included some categories that were either not covered in *James Dean Died Here,* or perhaps only had one entry. For example, in the previous book, I wrote about the famous Crossroads where Robert Johnson may have met the Devil. Now, you'll learn about the true birthplace of the blues: where W.C. Handy first heard a mysterious slide player at the spot "Where the Southern Crosses the Dog" (and many other vital Blues landmarks along the Delta). I originally covered where Martin Luther King was shot, but did you know that, years before, he had actually been stabbed in a Harlem department store while on a book tour? (There are many other M.L.K. sites in this book, along with a section dedicated to Civil Rights landmarks.)

I have included an extensive chapter on many great works of literature. Did you know that you can actually stand in the rooms where Poe, Steinbeck, Cather, Wharton, Faulkner, and Hemingway (among others) penned their classics and lived their lives?

There's also a new section on food (within the "Americana" chapter), featuring the exact spots where potato chips, Toll House Cookies, ice cream cones, the hot fudge sundae, the Egg McMuffin, and the Cobb Salad first came into being.

Plus, throughout the book are special sidebar "tours" dedicated to sites relating to Bob Dylan, Frank Sinatra, Elvis Presley, Marilyn Monroe, Bonnie and Clyde, and more. All of our country's famous and infamous — the gifted, the tortured, the visionary . . . our most storied heroes and villains, right where they did what they did.

And once again, everything is organized by topic (with a state-by-state index in the back).

Whether you're familiar with the specific events or not, I hope you'll see how (and why) they fit into the American pop culture pantheon. If you don't find a specific event in this volume, perhaps check *James Dean Died Here.* If it's not there, well . . . there's always the next sequel.

So on that note, I'll simply thank you for picking up this book and becoming part of the experience. After *James Dean Died Here* came out, I was put in touch with many like-minded fans of this type of history, which actually helped me decide to do the sequel as soon as possible — hey, when others are enthusiastic about something you're doing, it's a great motivator. It's been wonderful getting to meet and correspond with many of you; the shared experience is a real bonus and I hope that with this book, the fire continues to be fed with your observations, thoughts, and impressions on what I've compiled, photographed, and written about.

And whether you pack it in the car when hitting the road . . .
Or you find yourself reading it by the beach or the pool . . .
Whether you're perusing it at work or on a plane or a train or in a dorm or a library . . .
Or just sinking into the couch or a good easy chair . . .
Wherever, however, whenever . . .
Get ready to cover a lot of ground . . .
And a lot of pop culture history.

Chris Epting
May 2004

PS — The author and publisher kindly request that you respect the sanctity and/or privacy of the locations listed in this book.

Comments, questions, or suggestions for upcoming editions? Write the author at:
Chris@chrisepting.com and visit www.chrisepting.com for even more pop culture history.

This book is dedicated with love and devotion to my family.

Americana: The Weird and the Wonderful

Appleseed, Johnny

13th Street and Franklin Avenue
Franklin, Pennsylvania

Johnny Appleseed was the name given to John Chapman, an American pioneer who planted large, mythical numbers of apple trees along the early frontier. As a result of his deeds, Johnny became a folk hero and inspired many novels, short stories and poems.

Chapman was born in Leominister, Massachusetts on September 26, 1774. From 1797 until his death, he traveled alone from western Pennsylvania through Ohio, Indiana and Illinois, planting orchards as the settlers moved westward. He eventually owned about 1,200 acres of orchards.

In Pennsylvania, Chapman lived along French Creek in Venango County between 1797 and 1804. Records indicate that one of his first nurseries was near here, which is why the Pennsylvania Historical and Museum Commission placed a historical marker at this spot to commemorate the time Chapman spent in Franklin. Throughout the country, other markers can be found noting the sites where Johnny Appleseed planted his trees.

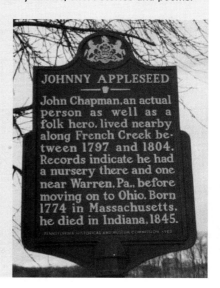

Blackbeard

Ocracoke Island, North Carolina

Ocracoke Island, accessible only by water or air, is part of Hyde County. It is one of the barrier islands of the Outer Banks of North Carolina.

The notorious pirate known as *Blackbeard* was killed by Lt. Robert Maynard on November 21, 1718, here off the coast of Ocracoke, North Carolina. Infamously (and according to legend), after Maynard killed Blackbeard, he severed his head and attached it to the bowsprit of his ship, *The Ranger.*

For several years leading up to the event, pirates had made peaceful commerce almost impossible along the North Carolina Coast. The most vicious pirate was Captain Drummond, who used the name "Edward Teach" or "Thatch," but who is remembered by the nickname "Blackbeard." He roamed from the Caribbean to the Virginia Capes robbing ships before being killed here in the bloody duel that marked the end of large scale piracy on the Atlantic Coast.

Bonneville Salt Flats

Near Wendover, Utah
Directions: Take I-80 West from Salt Lake City. Take Exit 4 just before the Utah-Nevada state line. Follow the directions to the Bonneville Raceway.

The Bonneville Salt Flats is a salt deposit left by the receding of ancient Lake Bonneville. This deposit covers about 159 square miles extending some nine miles along U.S. Highways 40 and 50 and the Western Pacific Railroad. In 1912, this area was tested as a racetrack and has since proved to be the greatest automobile speedway in the world. In 1931, Ab Jenkins of Salt Lake City famously broke all former world speed records. In the years that followed, especially the 1950s and 1960s, the salt flats were a motorsports Mecca, and today, hundreds of competitors still arrive twice every year to attempt to break records.

Bridge of Sighs

The Virginia Street Bridge
Reno, Nevada

From about 1906 until the 1960s, Reno was known as the "Divorce Capital of the World," and the Virginia Street Bridge (which crosses the Truckee River) was the main symbol of this fact. Upon receiving their final decree from the judge at the nearby Washoe County Courthouse, divorcees would head over to the Virginia Street Bridge – also known as the "Bridge of Sighs" – to toss their wedding rings into the Truckee River.

Bridgeville, the eBay town

Bridgeville, California

This Northern California town was sold to someone who bid $1,777,877 on eBay in late December 2002. While San Jose-based eBay provided the venue for the auction, the bidding was private and the buyer's name was not immediately made public. Tracing its heritage to 1865, Bridgeville is about 82 acres in size and has its own ZIP Code (95526). It also came with a backhoe, which the seller noted would be needed to make numerous repairs.

Brodie, Steve

Brooklyn Bridge
New York City, New York

Steve Brodie was a Brooklyn bookmaker who gained immediate fame and a measure of immortality by allegedly jumping off the Brooklyn Bridge on July 23, 1886, and surviv-

ing the fall. Skeptics claimed that Brodie had not, in fact, jumped from the bridge, but that a dummy was used as he hid under a pier. Brodie fervently denied this, and in any case he gained the publicity he was seeking, and a tavern he opened shortly after in the Bowery became a Mecca for sightseers. The original address of the bar is: 114 Bowery (Lower East Side).

Buffalo Bill

The Sheridan Inn
5th Street and Broadway
Sheridan, Wyoming
307-674-5440

The Sheridan Inn opened in May of 1893. Shortly after the opening, famed Wild West personality Buffalo Bill Cody leased the building's interior. It was from here, on the front porch, that Cody actually hired his Wild West Show performers for his famous touring show. In 1964, The Sheridan Inn was given landmark status by the National Park Service, and is one of the 17 National Historic Landmarks in Wyoming. Today, tours of the building are available, either via guided tours for all three floors, or self-guided tours of the first floor. Note: It is no longer possible to stay here.

Captain Kidd

Gardiners Island
Long Island, New York

In 1699, Scottish sea captain William "Captain" Kidd buried a large amount of his treasure here on Gardiners Island, a half-mile inland from its western coastline. Kidd marked the burial spot with a large pile of rocks (called a "cairn"). The vine-covered cairn still stands on the island, near a granite marker that was erected in the 19th century to mark the spot. While part of the famous pirate's treasure was recovered, many believe that some is still buried.

Cell Phone Call (First Wireless)

57th Street and Fifth Avenue (approximate location)
New York City, New York

On April 4, 1973, the first public telephone call was placed on a portable cellular phone by a gentleman named Martin Cooper, then the General Manager of Motorola's Communications Systems Division. It was the incarnation of his vision for personal wireless communication – distinct from cellular car phones – which initially pushed this technology. That first call, placed to Cooper's rival at AT&T Corp.'s Bell Labs, caused a fundamental technology and communications market shift toward the person and away from the place.

"Champ"

Lake Champlain
Lake Champlain, New York

Lake Champlain, on the border between New York, Vermont and extending a little north into Quebec, is the home of a creature (or creatures) collectively known as "Champ." Reports of the sea monster started showing up in newspapers around 1873, and to date, over 300 sightings have been recorded of this, America's version of the Loch Ness Monster. Described as something resembling a "Pleasiasaur," Champ supposedly has a long neck, bulky body, four fins and a long tail.

Interestingly, Lake Champlain is very similar to the Loch Ness lake. It is long, deep, narrow and cold. Scientists have discovered that both bodies of water have an underwater wave called a "seiche" that can periodically push debris from the bottom of the lake up to the surface, producing a strange effect. Some skeptics think this may explain many of the monster sightings.

Christo and Jeanne-Claude

Biscayne Bay
Miami, Florida

In 1983, renowned artists Christo and Jean Claude, the leading figures in environmental art, produced the project entitled "Surrounded Islands, Biscayne Bay, Greater Miami, Florida, 1980-83." The artwork consisted of 11 islands in Biscayne Bay near Miami, Florida, being surrounded by wide collars of floating pink polypropylene fabric.

It wasn't the first time that the two artists had made a splash in America with a large-scale temporary outdoor installation. In 1976, their project entitled "Running Fence, Sonoma and Marin Counties, California, 1972-76" involved stringing a nylon fence across the northern California landscape, from Cotati to the Marin coast. The work, which used some 2.5 million square feet of nylon cloth, was an 18-foot-tall fabric wall extending for nearly 25 miles. Both "Surrounded Islands" and "Running Fence" were designed to be ephemeral, and thus were erected for only a short time before being disassembled.

Coldest Day (North America)

Snag Airport
Yukon, Canada

On February 3, 1947, the temperature dropped to 81 degrees below zero, making this the coldest day ever recorded in North America.

Coldest Day (United States)

Prospect Creek, Alaska

It was 80 degrees below zero here on January 23, 1971, making this the coldest temperature ever recorded in the United States.

Dean, James

James Dean Died Here documented several sites surrounding Dean's last day alive, leading up to his fatal crash. These included where he awoke that day, where he picked up his car, where he made his last stop, and, of course, where the crash occurred. Here are a few others sites related to that last day, along with some other memorable James Dean landmarks.

Birthplace

Corner of 4th Street and McClure Street
Marion, Indiana

At this corner stood the house where James Byron Dean was born at 2:00 A.M. on February 8, 1931. A stone with a plaque and a star in the sidewalk now commemorate the spot where the house, known as "The Seven Gables," once stood. Each September 30th, to commemorate the day Dean was killed, the town honors its favorite son with a festival. Note: The nearby Fairmount Historical Museum (203 East Washington Street) holds the James Dean Memorial Gallery where you can see the actual speeding ticket issued to Dean just before his fatal crash, as well as the Lee Rider jeans he wore in *Giant*.

Dean, James

Villa Capri

6735 Yucca Street
Hollywood, California

This former Rat Pack haunt was also a favorite of James Dean, and it was here that he ate his last supper on the evening of September 29th, the night before he was killed. Dean would always come and go through the back door, which is still visible on the left. These days the building houses a radio station, with an original menu from the building's restaurant days hanging on the wall.

Gas Station

14325 Ventura Boulevard
Sherman Oaks, California

Early on the afternoon of September 30, 1955, James Dean stopped here to fill his Porsche with gas one last time before he and his crew hit the freeway and headed north.

Photographer Sanford Roth, who was documenting the trip with Dean (and would go on to take the famous accident pictures), shot a memorable photo of the actor right here at the pump, posed near his car after he'd filled it with gas. Today, a flower shop occupies the old gas station building, but the structure where the pumps were located remains virtually unchanged.

Dean, James

Tip's Restaurant

Castaic Junction
Intersection of I-5 and SR-126 West
Newhall, California

Once a thriving intersection, this is where Tip's Restaurant was located in the 1950s, and it was here, on September 30, 1955, that James Dean stopped for a meal (pie and milk) as he continued on his journey the day of his tragic crash. The original Tip's later became J's Coffee Shop – where four CHP officers were gunned down in 1970 – and, still later, a Marie Callender Family Restaurant. Today the building is gone.

Highway 99 North

(approximately one mile before the Maricopa/Taft exit at pole marker 166)
Near Bakersfield, California

Shortly before his fatal car crash on September 30, 1955, at about 3:30 P.M., James Dean was stopped here for speeding. He was issued a ticket by patrolman Otie V. Hunter, on which he signed his last "autograph." Dean was clocked at what would typically be considered a snail's pace for him – 70 mph. This had to be particularly embarrassing for the actor, as he had just finished a commercial for highway safety. Regardless of the ticket, Dean was speeding recklessly along Highway 446 (now renamed Hwy 46), hurtling toward a death that would occur less than three hours later. The telephone pole at the exact site where Dean was stopped is marked with the metal letters D-E-A-N.

Dean, James

Kuehl Funeral Home

1703 Spring Street
Paso Robles, California
805-238-4383

After being pronounced dead at the nearby War Memorial Hospital in Paso Robles, Dean's body was taken here. Several days later, his body was driven to Los Angeles in preparation for the trip home to Fairmont, Illinois. The hospital, which no longer exists, had been located at 1732 Spring Street in Paso Robles.

The Dionne Quintuplets

1375 Seymour Street
North Bay, Ontario
888-249-8998

On May 28, 1934, the world was amazed by the birth of the Dionne Quintuplets (all identical girls), who were born to Elzire and Oliva Dionne here in this small town in Ontario.

Incredibly, the Quint's combined weight at birth was only 13 lbs., 5 oz., and they had to be kept in incubators for the first month of their lives. Their lungs were so small that diluted doses of rum were required daily to help the Quints breathe properly.

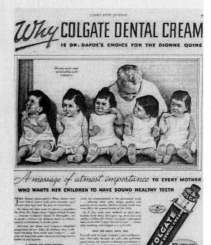

It was a one in 57 million chance of giving birth to identical quintuplets and even less chance of them surviving, but the Dionne Quints made it. This event attracted 3 million visitors to North Bay during the peak years of the Depression. Today, this museum (housed in the original Dionne Homestead) contains many artifacts from the Quint's early days and their growing years.

Einstein, Albert

Princeton Inn (now Forbes College)
99 Alexander Street
Princeton, New Jersey

The famous picture of physicist Albert Einstein sticking out his tongue was shot in front of the beautiful Princeton Inn, at one time an expansive, rambling hotel. The legendary thinker was leaving the Inn after celebrating his 72nd birthday on March 14, 1951 (part of the day's celebration also included the first Einstein Awards presentations), and he was asked by photographers to smile for them. Perhaps weary, bemused, or both, he got a bit frisky and thus created one of the most unexpected, most famous images ever captured. The building that once housed the Princeton Inn still stands and is now part of Forbes College. Note: Einstein lived nearby at 112 Mercer Street.

E-Mail (First)

BBN Technologies
10 Moulton Street
Cambridge, Massachusetts
617-873-8000

It is generally believed that the first network "e-mail" was sent by a man named Ray Tomlinson, a principal scientist at BBN, in 1971. At the time, Mr. Tomlinson was working for Boston-based Bolt, Beranek and Newman, which was helping to develop Arpanet, the forerunner of the modern internet.

Tomlinson sent the first message between two machines that were side-by-side in his lab here in Cambridge, then kept sending messages back and forth from one machine to the other until he was comfortable with how the process worked. The first e-mail message he sent outside of the lab was to the rest of his work team. A message announced the existence of network e-mail and explained how to use it, including the use of the @ sign to separate the user's name from the host computer name.

Food

Chasen's

9039 Beverly Boulevard (corner of Beverly & Doheny)
Beverly Hills, California

One of the most legendary restaurants (and celebrity hangouts) in Hollywood history, Chasen's closed its doors on April 1, 1995. It had stood for 59 years, and throughout its history, played host to many stars. Frank Sinatra, Greta Garbo, Jack Benny, and Eleanor Roosevelt were all huge fans of Chasen's chili, which was first served here in 1936 when the restaurant was known as vaudevillian Dave Chasen's "Chasen's Southern Pit." (The name became "Chasen's" in 1940.)

Elizabeth Taylor made it even more famous while filming *Cleopatra* in 1962, when she had the chili flown to Rome packed in dry ice. Though the restaurant is closed, the original building still stands, albeit in the form of an upscale market. And today, you can still order up Chasen's famous chili in the market's café, and enjoy it in one of the original Chasen's booths located there. Note: The booth where Ronald Reagan proposed to Nancy is gone, but it was located where the cheese section stands today.

Food

"Cheezeborger, Cheezeborger!"

Billy Goat Tavern
430 North Michigan Avenue at Lower Level
Chicago, Illinois
312-222-1525

Famously portrayed on *Saturday Night Live* in the mid-'70s as a burger diner where John Belushi barked in the orders in broken-Greek ("Cheezeborger, no fries – chips!), this place has long been a local legend, since original owner William Sianis was forbidden by the Chicago Cubs to bring his goat into Wrigley Field during a 1945 World Series game. Sianis' curse that the Cubs would never again win a championship has seemingly held true. A popular newspaper writer hangout, the walls here are plastered with blown-up bylines and numerous articles, and old-time SNL fans still arrive to hear the famous food orders.

Cobb Salad

The Brown Derby
1620-28 North Vine Street
Hollywood, California

One night in 1937, Bob Cobb, then owner of The Brown Derby, prowled hungrily in his restaurant's kitchen for a snack. Opening the huge refrigerator, he pulled out a head of lettuce, an avocado, some romaine, watercress, tomatoes, some cold breast of chicken, a hard-boiled egg, chives, cheese, some old-fashioned French dressing – in short, a little of everything. He started chopping, added some bacon, and bingo – the Cobb salad was born.

It was so good, Sid Grauman (of Grauman's Chinese Theatre), who was with Cobb that midnight, asked the next day for a "Cobb Salad." It was then put on the menu and Cobb's midnight invention became an overnight sensation with Derby customers like movie mogul Jack Warner, who regularly dispatched his chauffeur to pick up a carton of the mouth-watering salad.

The Vine Street landmark restaurant was demolished in 1994, but the famous huge Derby Hat that housed the Wilshire Boulevard location lives on atop a downtown strip mall, across the street from the Ambassador Hotel at 9500 Wilshire Boulevard.

Food

Egg McMuffin

3940 State Street
Santa Barbara, California
805-687-6164

Perhaps the biggest innovation in McDonald's history was a product that ushered in the era of fast-food breakfasts. It happened like this: In 1971, a McDonald's restaurant owner/operator named Herb Peterson heard that some other McDonald's proprietors had started serving pancakes and doughnuts during breakfast. Peterson liked the idea of serving breakfast, but thought it needed to be something unique – and something that could be eaten by hand, like all other McDonald's products.

Experimenting with a newfangled version of an "Eggs Benedict Sandwich," Peterson discovered that when he added a piece of cheese the sandwich took on the exact consistency he was looking for. It was food history in the making. Peterson invited the legendary Ray Kroc to try the product and Kroc gave it the thumbs up. So why did the Egg McMuffin take nearly four years to roll out? Because McDonald's wanted to first perfect pancakes and sausage and add scrambled eggs as a third option so as to have an entire breakfast menu as opposed to just one item. A plaque here at this McDonald's identifies it as the home of the Egg McMuffin.

Hot Fudge Sundae

C.C. Brown's Ice Cream Shop
7007 Hollywood Boulevard
Hollywood, California

Legend has it that it was here that the hot fudge sundae was invented in 1906 by Clarence Clifton (C.C.) Brown. For many years, the most celebrated names in the entertainment business frequented this sweet shop; in fact, many years ago, on days of big movie premiers, fans used to line up outside Brown's for hours while mega-stars like Joan Crawford signed autographs. The location closed in 1996.

Food

Ice Cream Cone

Forest Park
St. Louis, Missouri

Forest Park, officially opened to the public on June 24, 1876, is one of the largest urban parks in the United States. At 1,370 acres, it is approximately 500 acres larger than Central Park in New York. In 1904, it was the site of The St. Louis World's Fair and drew more than 20 million visitors from around the world.

It was here during the fair that Charles Menches, an unlucky ice cream vendor, ran out of dishes in which to put his ice cream. In the stall next to Menches was Ernest Hamwi, who was selling Syrian pastry. Hamwi offered to help and rolled up some of the pastry so that the vendor could put his ice cream inside, thus creating the ice cream cone.

Potato Chips

Moon's Lakehouse
700 Crescent Avenue
Saratoga Lake
Saratoga, New York

In the summer of 1853, George Crum was employed as a chef at Moon's Lake Lodge, an elegant resort in Saratoga Springs along Saratoga Lake. On the restaurant menu were French-fried potatoes, prepared by Crum in the standard, thick-cut French style that was made popular in France in the 1700s. One guest found chef Crum's French fries too thick and asked if Crum could cut and fry a thinner batch. However, the customer rejected these, too.

Frustrated, Crum decided to deliberately annoy the guest by producing French fries that were extra, extra thin and crisp, and salted to excess. But the plan backfired. The guest loved the crispy, paper-thin potatoes, and other guests began to request Crum's potato chips, which subsequently appeared on the menu as "Saratoga Chips." The potato chip had been born. Moon's Lakehouse located at this upstate New York lake is long gone, and the approximate site where it once sat is now occupied with a lakeside house, owned by a technology company.

Food

Toll House Cookies

The Toll House Inn
Corner of Route 18 and Route 14
Whitman, Massachusetts

The original Toll House for whom the famous cookies are named was built in 1709 on the old Boston to New Bedford road, now called Route 18. Back then, travelers paid tolls at the house for the use of the road, but could also rest there and enjoy a meal while their horses were changed.

In 1930, a couple named Kenneth and Ruth Graves Wakefield purchased the property and opened the Toll House Inn. Ruth, a 1924 graduate of the Framingham State Normal School Department of Household Arts, was in charge of the Inn's kitchen. One day, Ruth wanted to make chocolate cookies but was out of baker's chocolate. Instead, she substituted broken pieces of semi-sweet chocolate made by Andrew Nestlé. Instead of melting into the dough like she thought they would, the morsels remained clumps of melted chocolate, and thus the toll house cookie (also known as the chocolate chip cookie) was born.

Ruth licensed the recipe to chocolate maker Nestlé, who, in 1939, began marketing Toll House Morsels designed for her cookie recipe. The Wakefield's place of business grew into a major restaurant, but Kenneth and Ruth sold the Inn in 1966. It became a night-club, then a restaurant again, but the building burned down on New Years Eve in 1984. (Ruth Graves Wakefield passed away in 1977.) Today, a Wendy's sits on the original site, but a classic sign from the old Inn still stands nearby.

Foster, Stephen

Corner building at Bloomfield and 6th Streets
Hoboken, New Jersey

Legendary American composer Stephen Foster was born in Pennsylvania in 1826 and spent most of his life there and in Ohio. But Foster, who wrote and published hundreds of songs, including staples like "Camptown Races," "Oh! Susanna," and "Beautiful Dreamer," lived here in Hoboken in 1854. While residing in this building, Foster penned the classic "Jeannie with the Light Brown Hair." Sadly (and due largely to the poor pro-visions for music copyright and composer royalties at the time), Foster died penniless in 1864 at Bellevue Hospital in New York. He was just 38.

Gage, Phineas

Cavendish, Vermont
Directions: About 3/4 mile south of the town, along the track of the old Rutland and Burlington Rail Road — now the Green Mountain Rail Road. Local tradition has it that the accident occurred in the second of two cuttings or cuts along the track.

On September 13, 1848, while in the process of setting an explosive powder charge on a railroad track cutting in Cavendish, Vermont, the charge prematurely went off and sent a 13½ pound, 3-foot-7-inch-long "tamping iron" (referred to historically as a "crowbar") up through the lower left jaw and out through the top of the skull of 25-year-old Phineas P. Gage. Incredibly, Phineas remained conscious and communicated with his friends as they rushed him to a tavern in town. He was treated and survived the freak accident and went on to live just short of 12 more years, becoming a national folk hero in the process.

After the accident, Phineas did undergo a dramatic change in personality (not for the better) which is why he became a classically studied case in the textbooks of neurology. The part of the brain which he had lost was forever associated to the mental and emotional functions which he no longer had control over. One scientist wrote, "The equilibrium between his intellectual faculties and animal propensities seems to have been destroyed."

In 1998, the town of Cavendish, Vermont hosted a celebration of the 150th anniversary of this event, which attracted scholars from around the globe (the commemorative memorial was unveiled at this time). To this day, doctors are amazed at the fact that Phineas Gage was able to survive such an accident.

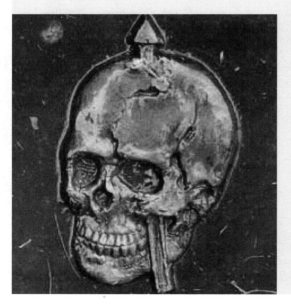

Gatorade

Giants Stadium
50 Route 120
East Rutherford, New Jersey

It was on October 20, 1985 that New York Giants defensive tackle Jim Burt and line-backer Harry Carson crept up behind Giants coach Bill Parcells in the final moments of a 17-3 win over Washington and drenched him with a cooler of Gatorade. Little did they know that they'd started the famous tradition of "Gatorade dunking."

Ironically, the dunk had more to do with vengeance than celebration – evidently Parcells had been on Burt's back all week, egging him on to not get beat by Redskin center Jeff Bostic. Burt had a great game that day and wanted to get back at his coach so he recruited Carson (maybe because Carson was a favorite of Parcells and thus might buffer some of the anger that might have arisen). Though it wasn't the first time anyone had doused a coach in celebration, it did spawn a whole new kind of copycat dunkings at all levels of football, and became an iconic moment for the Gatorade brand.

Hope, Bob

March Field
Located just off the I-215 freeway at the Van Buren exit
Riverside, California
909-697-6602

Entertainer Bob Hope had tried to enlist in the armed forces, but after being told he could be of more use as an entertainer, he had a new mission. And so on May 6, 1941 at California's March Field, seven months before Pearl Harbor, Bob Hope performed his very first USO show. He continued entertaining troops for the rest of World War II, the Korean War, the Vietnam War, and all the way until the 1990-1991 Persian Gulf War.

He took the matter to heart when entertaining and was almost always seen in army duds, just like his audience, as a sign of support for the troops for whom he performed. Hope's USO career spanned six decades, during which he headlined approximately 60 tours. Today, the March Air Force base is an incredible air museum that is open to the public.

Hottest Day (United States)

Death Valley, California

On July 10, 1913, the hottest day in the history of both the United States and North America was recorded here. It actually reached 134 degrees at the bottom of the valley.

Houdini, Harry

Princess Theater
480 Ste-Catherine Street (west corner at City Councillors Avenue)
Montreal, Canada

On October 22, 1926, famed escape artist Harry Houdini was in Montreal, Canada performing at the Princess Theater. (While in town, Houdini had also given a lecture exposing spiritualism at nearby McGill University.) While relaxing in his dressing room at the theater, a young athlete from McGill University approached the legend and asked if could actually withstand punches to the stomach as he had heard. Before Houdini could prepare himself by tightening his stomach muscles, the student punched him in the mid-section. Houdini did not know it, but his appendix had become ruptured.

Despite the injury, Houdini did several more shows in Montreal and then headed for Detroit. Houdini did one performance there at the Garrick Theater (formerly located at Griswold Street and Michigan Avenue) and then collapsed and was rushed to Grace hospital (formerly located on the corner of Willis Avenue and John R Street) where he died almost a week later on October 31, 1926, of peritonitis (an inflammation of the peritoneum, the lining of the abdominal cavity). The Princess Theater was gutted in the 1980s to make room for a movie theater multiplex.

Hughes, Howard

The Westin Bayshore Resort & Marina
1601 Bayshore Drive
Vancouver, British Columbia, Canada
604-682-3377

Billionaire Howard Hughes' elegant suite in the Westin Bayshore Resort and Marina, Vancouver, may cost up to $2,500 a night, but it's still in demand. Hughes first arrived at the Bayshore on March 14, 1972. He had not been seen in public for many years, and it is believed he was on the run from U.S. tax authorities. The eccentric, 66-year-old Hughes had called from his private plane demanding the top four floors. After the manager told him they were full, Hughes threatened to buy the hotel if his demand wasn't met. (This was no idle threat. When the Desert Inn tried to evict him, Hughes bought the Las Vegas landmark.)

So when Hughes and his entourage arrived, everything was ready. After secretly entering via the housekeeping elevator, his handlers closed off all the elevators to the top four floors and installed security cameras. Photographers tried in vain to get shots of Hughes, but the recluse remained all but invisible. He apparently lived alone in the three-room penthouse, rooms 2089–2091, for six months. Only his maid, chef and security detail were allowed in the suite during that time. From Vancouver, Hughes traveled to Mexico, taking over the penthouse of the Acapulco Princess. This was Hughes's last residence, and he died en route from Acapulco to his native Houston on April 5, 1976.

Indian Gaming

Seminole Indian Bingo and Casino
4150 North State Road 7 (at Stirling Road)
Hollywood, Florida
954-961-3220

It was here that today's multibillion-dollar Indian gambling industry first got its start. Back in 1979, Seminole Howard Tommie had an idea, inspired by the fact that he oversaw a tribal budget of just $400 a member. Bingo already was legal in Florida, but state law permitted a maximum jackpot of just $100. So Tommie figured the Seminoles could offer much bigger cash winnings via "High Stakes Bingo." And since the status of Indian tribes ("sovereign nations") means there is little interference by federal and state government, the profits would be astronomical.

So the Seminoles became the first tribe in the nation to offer high-stakes gambling and three years later, the tribe expanded their operations to Tampa, by now adding poker and video slot machines. Other Indian tribes around the nation soon followed the drumbeat and today, 184 tribes in 28 states have gambling operations.

Joplin, Scott

2658 Delmar Boulevard
St. Louis, Missouri

Ragtime composer Scott Joplin (1868–1917) resided here from 1885 to 1894, and again from 1900 to 1906. He composed the "lost" opera *A Guest of Honor,* and the rag "The Entertainer" at this home, which was opened to the public as a Missouri State Historic site in 1991. The home's turn-of-the-century appearance has been restored. It includes a room for musical performances, displays centering on Joplin's life and music, and a gallery for displays related to African-American history and culture.

The Kecksburg Incident

Kecksburg, Pennsylvania
Kecksburg is located approximately 40 miles from Pittsburgh in a rural area of Western Pennsylvania.

On December 9, 1965, an object landed here in the woods of the tiny town of Kecksburg. It was observed as a fireball in the sky, and seen across several U.S. states and Canada. Eventually, dozens of witnesses would describe a heavy military presence at the crash site, the cordoning off of the area, and the retrieval of an object transported by an army truck. (Many of these witnesses have provided signed affidavits attesting to these facts.)

Some of the witnesses claim they came upon a large, metallic, acorn-shaped object partially buried in the ground. They said that the device was large enough for a man to stand inside, was a bronze-gold color, and appeared to be one solid piece of metal, displaying no rivets or seams. The craft was also said to have unusual markings, similar to ancient Egyptian hieroglyphics. To date, the event remains unsolved.

Kelly, Alvin "Shipwreck"

The Steel Pier
Across from the Taj Majal on the boardwalk at Virginia Avenue
Atlantic City, New Jersey
866-386-6659

Alvin Kelly was the acknowledged master of flagpole-sitting, a wacky public fad of the 1920s. He would clamber to the top of a specially prepared flagpole and remain there for days, usually as a paid publicity stunt. It was here at Atlantic City's famous Steel Pier that Kelly set a world's record of 49 days for sitting on top of a flag pole in 1930. (Kelly was an ex-sailor who claimed to have been shipwrecked several times, thus earning him the nickname "Shipwreck.")

Lee, Bruce

4145 Broadway, between 41st and 42nd Streets
(part of the Downtown Auto Center – Downtown Toyota to be exact)
Oakland, California

In 1964, legendary martial artist Bruce Lee founded his second school here in Oakland (the first, the Jun Fan Gung Fu Institute was located in Seattle at 4750 University Way). The notable event that took place here in Oakland is the stuff of Kung Fu legend. Upset that Lee was teaching martial arts to Caucasians, venerable master Wong Jack Man challenged Lee to a fight. According to witnesses, Lee overwhelmed Wong Jack Man in a matter of minutes, but still, Lee was unhappy with his performance. This dissatisfaction pushed him to develop his own style of fighting, which of course made him world famous. Incidentally, Bruce Lee was born nearby at: Chinese Hospital, 845 Jackson Street (between Stockton and Powell Streets), San Francisco, California, 415-982-2400. A plaque in the lobby identifies the hospital as Bruce Lee's birthplace.

Lloyd, Earl

Rochester Edgerton Park Sports Arena (now Edgerton Park)
Dewey Avenue and Emerson Street
Rochester, New York

On Halloween night in 1950, Washington Capitols' basketball player Earl Lloyd became the NBA's first black player in a 78-70 loss to the Rochester Royals. Lloyd ended up playing in over 560 games in nine seasons, and the 6-foot-5, 225-pound forward averaged 8.4 points and 6.4 rebounds per game. Today, at Edgerton Park, the arena is gone; it sat where the athletic fields are now located.

The Lucky Corner

116th Street and Lexington Avenue
East Harlem, New York City

In the early 1930s, Congressman Fiorello LaGuardia began holding election-eve rallies at this intersection on East Harlem's "Main Street." It became known as his "Lucky Corner." His political protégé, Vito Marcantonio, continued the tradition during his 15 years as a Congressman on the American Labor Party ticket.

By the 1940s, the neighborhood mood had grown a bit tense as it was now shared by both Puerto Ricans and Italians. However, the often taut relations between these two groups were defused with great aplomb by the savvy Marcantonio, who was equally adored by both groups. Marcantonio's biannual gatherings at the "Lucky Corner" typically attracted tens of thousands of supporters and remain the stuff of New York City legend.

The McDonald's Coffee Spill

5001 Gibson Boulevard S.E.
Albuquerque, New Mexico

In February 1992, 79-year-old Stella Liebeck was in the passenger seat of her grandson's car here when she received a cup of coffee that was served in a Styrofoam cup at the drive-through window. Her grandson pulled the car forward and stopped so Stella could add cream and sugar. Placing the cup between her knees while trying to remove the lid, the hot coffee spilled into her lap. (Her sweatpants absorbed the scalding coffee and then stuck to her skin.)

A vascular surgeon determined that Liebeck suffered "third-degree burns over 6% of her body, including her inner thighs, perineum, buttocks, and genital and groin areas." After eight days in the hospital and undergoing skin grafting, she sought a settlement from McDonald's of $20,000. McDonald's refused though, and so it was off to court they went, where a jury eventually awarded Liebeck $200,000 in compensatory damages (reduced to $160,000 because the jury found Liebeck 20% at fault).

In addition, the jury also awarded Liebeck $2.7 million in punitive damages, equaling approximately two days of McDonald's total coffee sales. (The court later reduced the punitive award to $480,000.) In the end, a "secret" settlement was reached, so the final amount may never be known. However, this event changed the way hot beverages (and lawsuits) are served and gave late-night TV gag writers a wealth of material.

McPherson, Aimee Semple

1100 Glendale Boulevard
Los Angeles, California

Built in 1923, the beautiful 5,500 seat Angelus Temple was the center of evangelist Aimee Semple McPherson's revival, healing and benevolent ministries. Having experienced a profound religious conversion at age 17, McPherson began preaching across the United States and, later, the world.

In 1918, she established her base in Los Angeles, California, where in 1923, the Angelus Temple was dedicated and became the center of her ministry. She was the first woman to receive a FCC radio license and was a pioneer religious broadcaster. From Angelus Temple she provided hot meals for more than 1.5 million people during the Great Depression.

But there was controversy: She claimed to have been kidnapped when she reappeared after disappearing in May 1926. At first Aimee Semple McPherson was presumed drowned. After her return, many questioned the kidnapping story; gossip had her off on a romantic tryst, though a court case was dropped for lack of evidence. Aimee Semple McPherson died in 1944, while conducting a crusade in Oakland, California.

Monroe, Marilyn

Los Angeles General Hospital

1200 State Street
Los Angeles, California

Marilyn Monroe (Norma Jeane Baker) was delivered here at 9:30 A.M. on June 1, 1926, to Gladys Baker (it is believed that her father was not present). This hospital is now called the L.A. County USC Medical Center.

Foursquare Gospel Church

4503 West Broadway
Hawthorne, California

Norma Jeane was baptized here, in July 1926, at this church founded by the controversial evangelist Aimee Semple McPherson (who, it is believed, may actually have performed the baptism).

Los Angeles Orphans Home

815 North El Centro Avenue
Los Angeles, California

Norma Jeane Baker was brought here on September 13, 1935, at the age of nine. It was to be her home for about two years. The original building has since been torn down.

First Apartment

11348 Nebraska Avenue
Los Angeles, California

This was the first apartment Norma Jeane ever rented on her own. She lived here from 1938-1940, and again in 1942 for a short time.

First Marriage

432 South Bentley Avenue
West Los Angeles, California

Norma Jeane Baker married Jim Dougherty here at the home of the Howells on June 19, 1942. The Howells were close friends of the Bakers — they had had even thought of adopting Marilyn when she was a young girl. The bride was given away by Ana Lower, and the couple was married by Reverend Benjamin Lingen-Felder. Norma Jean had met her husband the year before, while she was a student at Van Nuys High School.

Monroe, Marilyn

Honeymoon

4524 Vista Del Monte Street
Sherman Oaks, California

Norma Jeane Baker and Jim Dougherty spent their first night as husband and wife here, at this one-room bungalow, where they had taken a six-month lease. The bungalow was so small that, as soon as the lease was up, they moved into the old Dougherty house at 14747 Archwood Street in Van Nuys, California. They lived there for a year, and then moved into another house in Van Nuys for a short while, and in 1944 ended up living in Hollywood at 5254 Hermitage Avenue. At his point, Jim had shipped out with the Marines, leaving Marilyn on her own.

Radio Plane Corporation

2627 North Hollywood Way
Burbank, California

It was here, at the Radio Plane Company (a munitions outfit), that Norma Jeane Baker was discovered on June 26, 1945, by U.S. Army photographer David Conover. Marilyn was working here (her first job), when Conover spotted her and took photographs of her for an army training magazine. Conover had received the assignment to snap various women on the base from his commanding officer, Ronald Reagan. The photos, featuring the beauty, led everyone who saw them to take notice and, of course, the rest is history. Today this is the site of Bob Hope (formerly Burbank) Airport.

Marilyn Monroe Dyed Here

Frank and Joseph's Salon
6513 Hollywood Boulevard
Hollywood, California

Norma Jeane Baker was offered a modeling job in the winter of 1945. The photographer

wanted the brunette to become a blonde, and Norma Jeane's agent, Emmeline Snively, agreed. And so it was here, at Frank and Joseph's Salon, that Norma Jeane Baker, soon to be Marilyn Monroe, first became a blonde – thus dramatically changing the course of her career and her life. The peroxiding was done by stylist Sylvia Barnhart, who went on to do Marilyn's hair for several more years. Today, there is a toy store at this location.

Monroe, Marilyn

Roosevelt Hotel

**7000 Hollywood Boulevard
Los Angeles, California
800-950-7667**

It was here, on the diving board of the famous Roosevelt swimming pool, that a young Marilyn Monroe posed for her first ad (it was for suntan lotion).

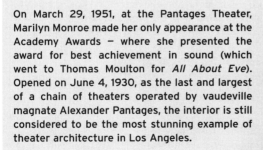

Mira Loma Hotel

**1420 North Indian Canyon Drive
Palm Springs, California
760-320-1178**

Today you can stay in the very room that Marilyn loved to stay in from the late 1940s on. Each room here is cleverly (and elaborately) themed after celebrities, movies, etc., and room 103 (the "Pretty in Pink" suite) was Marilyn's special hideaway in the desert. The poolside room is tricked out with Marilyn images and even has its own 1,000-piece Marilyn Monroe jigsaw puzzle. The hotel is now called Ballentines hotel.

The Pantages Theater

**6233 Hollywood Boulevard
Hollywood, California**

On March 29, 1951, at the Pantages Theater, Marilyn Monroe made her only appearance at the Academy Awards – where she presented the award for best achievement in sound (which went to Thomas Moulton for *All About Eve*). Opened on June 4, 1930, as the last and largest of a chain of theaters operated by vaudeville magnate Alexander Pantages, the interior is still considered to be the most stunning example of theater architecture in Los Angeles.

Monroe, Marilyn

Marilyn Meets Joe

Villa Nova
9015 Sunset Boulevard
Hollywood, California

It was here (at table 14), in March 1952, that Marilyn Monroe had a blind date with Joe DiMaggio. She arrived two hours late and, though the meal itself was reported to be a bit stiff and awkward, the couple drove around Hollywood that night after dinner and eventually began opening up to each other. They later married in January 1954. The club is now called The Rainbow Bar and Grill.

Brock Plaza Hotel

5685 Falls Avenue
Niagara Falls, Ontario, Canada

Marilyn stayed here in June of 1952, while she was on location in Niagara Falls filming the movie *Niagara* with co-star Joseph Cotten.

Hotel Bel-Air

701 Stone Canyon Road (at Bellagio Road)
Bel Air, California
800-648-4097

The posh, mission-style Hotel Bel Air is located on 11 acres of beautifully groomed grounds, situated high above Beverly Hills. To enter the secluded grounds, you drive through tropical gardens, across a stone bridge, and past a swan-filled lake. Marilyn lived here (in room 133) in 1952. On the evening of her 26th birthday, she celebrated alone in her suite with a steak dinner and a good bottle of champagne. She returned here for several more stays, most notably during the filming of *Some Like It Hot* (staying again in room 133), and in June 1962, when photographer Bert Stern photographed "The Last Sitting" session. The nearly 2,700 photos were taken in room 261 and bungalow 96.

Fairmont Banff Springs Hotel

405 Spray Avenue
Banff, Alberta, Canada
800-828-7447

Cradled in the Canadian Rocky Mountains in Banff National Park, the Banff Springs Hotel lies just 80 miles west of Calgary. Designed and built in 1888 with a style reminiscent of a stately 19th-century Scottish baronial castle, it was here that Marilyn stayed in 1953 while filming River of No Return with Robert Mitchum. (She stayed in room 816.) Joe DiMaggio joined Marilyn here after she sprained her ankle during a rafting scene.

Monroe, Marilyn

Beverly Hills Hotel

9641 Sunset Boulevard
Beverly Hills, California

This is where Marilyn lived for various periods of her life, and where she received her Photoplay Award for Fastest Rising Star in 1953. She stayed in bungalow 21A during the filming of *Let's Make Love* in 1960.

Doheny Apartments

882 North Doheny Drive
Hollywood, California

Marilyn moved into apartment #3 in 1953, and stayed here until she married Joe DiMaggio in January 1954. At the end of 1961, after returning to Los Angeles, she moved back into the same apartment.

Marriage to DiMaggio

San Francisco City Hall
1 Dr. Carlton B. Goode Place
San Francisco, California

Marilyn Monroe and Joe Di-Maggio were married here in a third-floor office on January 14, 1954. There was a slight delay in the ceremony while the clerk located a typewriter for the marriage license, and reporters all but swarmed the building before the couple could escape in Joe's blue Cadillac.

Monroe, Marilyn

Monroe-DiMaggio Honeymoon

Clifton Motel
125 Spring Street
Paso Robles, California

After getting married in San Francisco, Marilyn and Joe DiMaggio spent their first night as husband and wife here, in room 15. They were driving down the coast en

route to Palm Springs when they arrived in Paso Robles, about 200 miles south of San Francisco (and not far from where James Dean would be killed in little over a year). For years, while this was still a hotel, a plaque outside room 15 read, "Joe and Marilyn Slept Here." It is now the Clifton Apartments.

Monroe-DiMaggio Home

508 North Palm Drive
Beverly Hills, California

This is the house Marilyn and DiMaggio lived in after their wedding in 1954. They rented the house for $700 per month. Together for less than one year (a tumultuous year punctuated with many arguments – and two film shoots for Marilyn), the couple announced their plans for divorce on October 5, 1954. The residence was swarmed with more reporters than ever, and on October 6th Marilyn, dressed all in black, made a dramatic appearance in front of the house to answer several reporter's questions. (Marilyn would soon move to a duplex at the Brandon Hall Apartments at 8336 DeLongpre Avenue in Hollywood.)

Monroe, Marilyn

The Seven Year Itch

164 East 61st Street
New York City, New York

This is the apartment building that was used for the famous scene in *The Seven Year Itch* in which Marilyn dangles actor Tom Ewell's shoes out of the window. The movie also featured the now-legendary scene where Marilyn's white dress billows up over the subway grating (see *James Dean Died Here*).

Marilyn Monroe Was Here

155 West 23rd Street
New York City, New York

The words "Marilyn Monroe Was Here" were written in the wet cement in front of the hotel in which Marilyn was staying. Her longtime fan and friend, Jimmy Haspiel, scrawled the message in 1954 after meeting up with her, and it can still be seen here today.

Wrong Door Raid

8122 Waring Avenue
Hollywood, California

The infamous "Wrong Door Raid" took place here on November 5, 1954. During this time, ex-baseball star Joe DiMaggio was having Monroe tailed by a private detective, Barney Ruditsky. On this infamous night, Joe arrived here with Frank Sinatra, Ruditsky,

and another detective, Phil Irwin, hoping to catch Marilyn with another man. Mistakenly, they busted into the wrong house – one where a lady named Florenz Kotz lived. (It is believed that Kotz went on to sue the group, and that they eventually settled out of court for $7,500.) Marilyn, who had been staying a door or two away, was alerted by the commotion and slipped away.

Monroe, Marilyn

Connecticut Home

Fanton Hill Road
Weston, Connecticut

Marilyn left Hollywood in late 1954 to break away and start a new life on the East Coast. Throughout 1955, she lived a quiet life in the country at this idyllic, rural home belonging to her friends Amy and Milton Greene. She recovered from her divorce, collected herself and prepared to move ahead with the formation of her own production company. On April 8, 1955, CBS TV's program *Person to Person* with Edward R. Murrow was broadcast from here.

Bement Visit

101 East Wing Street
Bement, Illinois

In the summer of 1955, Marilyn paid a brief visit to the small village of Bement as part of their centennial celebration. She spent the day and hosted part of a function called "Art for the People." Accompanying Monroe was photographer Eve Arnold, who shot one of her famous sessions with Monroe during the trip. The town still recalls the visit fondly. This is the house that Monroe used as her home-base while in Bement.

Sahara Motor Hotel

401 North First Street
Phoenix, Arizona

Marilyn stayed at this hotel in March 1956, while on location in Phoenix to shoot scenes for the film *Bus Stop.* It is now called the Phoenix Plaza.

Grauman's Chinese Theatre

6925 Hollywood Boulevard
Hollywood, California

On June 26, 1956, Marilyn and Jane Russell were invited to put their handprints in the wet cement here, in front of Grauman's Chinese Theatre (now Mann's Chinese Theatre).

Monroe, Marilyn

The Walk of Fame

6774 Hollywood Boulevard
Hollywood, California

Marilyn's star is just down the street from Grauman's Chinese Theater, on the Hollywood "Walk of Fame" along Hollywood Boulevard. It sits on the sidewalk just outside the front door of a McDonald's restaurant. The star was placed here on February 9, 1960.

Greene Home

595 North Beverly Glen Boulevard
West Los Angeles, California

In 1956, Marilyn returned to California for the filming of the movie *Bus Stop*. She rented this house with her friends Milton and Amy Greene, but ended up staying at an unidentified apartment on Sunset Boulevard because of the late-night parties hosted by the Greenes.

Marriage to Arthur Miller

Westchester County Court House
111 Grove Street
White Plains, New York

Marilyn married playwright Arthur Miller here on June 29, 1956 (they divorced January 20, 1961). The day was marred by a tragic event when, earlier that day, a journalist for the French magazine *Paris-Match*, sent to cover the event, was killed in an auto accident.

White House Restaurant

17307 Gulf Boulevard
St. Petersburg, Florida

Following Marilyn's discharge from two New York City psychiatric hospitals in March 1961, she and former husband Joe DiMaggio traveled to North Redington Beach. Amid rumors of reconciliation and remarriage, they visited the Tides Resort & Bath Club. Built in 1936, the hotel hosted many celebrities. Marilyn and Joe registered in separate guest rooms in the main building. The couple dined nearby at the elegant White House Restaurant, now called The Wine Cellar. The historic Tides was demolished in 1995, and its 1,500 feet of prime beachfront property was developed into The Tides Luxury Condominiums (located at 16450 Gulf Boulevard, North Redington Beach, Florida).

Monroe, Marilyn

Affair with JFK

Carlysle Hotel
35 East 76th Street
New York City, New York
212-744-1600

It has been claimed, with some authority, that this elegant hotel played host to the alleged affair between Marilyn Monroe and John F. Kennedy in the early 1960s. In addition to possibly meeting here, it has been fairly well-documented that the couple did indeed spend a weekend together in Palm Springs on March 25, 1962, at Bing Crosby's estate.

Originally, President Kennedy planned on staying at the residence of Frank Sinatra from March 24-26, but as the weekend approached, Bobby Kennedy (the president's brother and attorney general) became concerned about Sinatra's extensive links to organized crime. He persuaded his brother to cancel the stay with Sinatra and opt for Crosby's place instead. Sinatra was supposedly livid after being informed by Peter Lawford, a Kennedy relative by marriage.

Washoe County Courthouse

5 Virginia Street
Reno, Nevada

Marilyn gets a divorce here (as many others did in real life) in the 1961 film *The Misfits.* The film was directed by John Huston and co-starred Clark Gable and Montgomery Clift.

Monroe, Marilyn

George Barris Photo Sessions

625 Pacific Coast Highway
Santa Monica, California

On June 1st, 1962, renowned photographer and journalist George Barris arrived at the set where Marilyn Monroe was making her last film, *Something's Got To Give*. It was Marilyn's 36th birthday, and Barris was assigned by a national magazine to photograph and interview her. For the next six weeks, he photographed Marilyn on the beach at Santa Monica and in a house in the Hollywood Hills (at 1506 Blue Jay Way). They remain some of the most beautiful, emotional images ever captured of Monroe.

Parisian Florist

7528 Sunset Boulevard
Hollywood, California

It was well known that after Marilyn died, Joe DiMaggio had fresh flowers sent to her tomb twice a week from this florist shop (he did this regularly until 1982, then stopped). Marilyn herself used this florist, and many fans stop here today to buy flowers before visiting Marilyn's tomb in Westwood, so they can help continue the tradition.

Westwood Cemetery

1218 Glendon Avenue
Westwood, California

Marilyn Monroe rests here at this small cemetery at the corner of Wilshire Boulevard and Glendon Avenue. The chapel is near the southwest corner, and Marilyn's crypt is near the northeast corner. People from all over the world come to visit this site every day, as evidenced by the many lipstick traces at the crypt.

National Anthem

Sure, Jimi Hendrix's version of our National Anthem at Woodstock remains an unconventional musical moment, but what of the other famous (and infamous) versions?

Feliciano, Jose

Tiger Stadium
At the corner of Michigan Avenue and Trumbull Avenue
Detroit, Michigan

On October 7, 1968, Puerto Rican blind singer/guitarist Jose Feliciano wowed the crowd at Tiger Stadium in Detroit when he strummed a slow, bluesy rendition of the national anthem before game five of the 1968 World Series between Detroit and St. Louis.

The 23-year-old's unique performance was the first non-traditional version experienced by the masses, and the response was strong and not exactly positive – evidently, given that we were in the middle of the Vietnam War, many were not ready for something so unconventional when mega-patriotism was in such high demand. Regardless, this performance set the stage for many other offbeat interpretations of the "Star-Spangled Banner." (Tiger Stadium has since closed but remains standing.)

Gaye, Marvin

Los Angeles Forum
3900 West Manchester Boulevard
Inglewood, California

On February 13, 1983, Marvin Gaye soulfully performed the national anthem before the 1983 NBA All-Star Game at The Forum in Inglewood. Accompanied by a syncopated drum machine, Gaye's stirring, emotional interpretation added elements of soul, funk and spontaneity to the national anthem, which was met with mixed reviews by the crowd (though Julius Irving, who would be voted MVP of the game, said he loved it). Coincidentally, Marvin Gaye also sang the anthem during the same World Series as Jose Feliciano in 1968, to much less fanfare.

National Anthem

Houston, Whitney

Houlihan's Stadium
4201 North Dale Mabry Highway
Tampa, Florida

Performed at Super Bowl XXV during the Gulf War, Houston's classic rendition of the National Anthem was released after the September 11th terrorist attacks and once again quickly became a hot-selling single. The soaring, spine-tingling version was first released in 1991, and had been re-released in 2000 on Houston's greatest hits collection.

Star Spangled Manglers – forget about "special renditions" and "artistic interpretations," these are folks who just plain blew it. "Oh say, can you wince?"

Aerosmith

Indianapolis Motor Speedway
4790 West 16th Street
Indianapolis, Indiana

On May 27, 2001 (Memorial Day), Boston rockers Aerosmith got the nod to perform the anthem before the start of the Indianapolis 500. However, lead singer, Steven Tyler, angered many veterans by tweaking the last line of the song. Instead of singing "home of the brave," Tyler sang "home of the Indianapolis 500." Tyler apologized profusely the next day, releasing the following statement: "I got in trouble my whole life for having a big mouth. I'm very proud to be an American and live in the home of the brave."

Barr, Roseanne

QualComm Stadium
9449 Friars Road
San Diego, California
619-641-3100

On July 25, 1990, Roseanne Barr added her own ribald brand of humor to the singing of the National Anthem before a baseball game in San Diego. After screeching through a brutally off-key version of the song, she added some bawdy, clichéd baseball humor by spitting and grabbing her crotch. The popular sitcom comedian immediately became public enemy number one. After hearing a tape of Barr, President George Bush called it "disgusting" and "a disgrace."

National Anthem

Goulet, Robert

St. Dominick's Arena (now the Central Maine Civic Center)
190 Birch Street
Lewiston, Maine
207-783-2009

On May 25, 1965, singer Robert Goulet performed the anthem publicly for the first time in his career before the much-anticipated rematch of boxing heavyweight champion Muhammad Ali and Sonny Liston. Goulet began, "Oh say, can you see, by the dawn's early night . . ." Although he's done the song without incident hundreds of times since then, Goulet says he is always asked about his infamous flub, one of the great gaffes in the history of the National Anthem.

Lewis, Carl

Continental Arena
50 State RT 120
East Rutherford, New Jersey

He can run but he can't hide. On January 21, 1993, nine-time Olympic track-and-field gold medallist Carl Lewis, before a sold-out Chicago Bulls–New Jersey Nets basketball game, "dropped the baton" during his turn at the National Anthem. Hoarse, screechy and faltering on some of the lyrics, Lewis later blamed his performance on being worn out after participating in inaugural events at the White House the day before.

Oswald, Lee Harvey

2 Canal Street
New Orleans, Louisiana

On August 16, 1963, Lee Harvey Oswald was distributing "Fair Play for Cuba" literature outside of the International Trade Mart in New Orleans. Johann Rush, a cameraman for New Orleans' WSDU-TV, captured images of Oswald which were soon to become very famous. The grainy, black-and-white footage remains compelling today – a glimpse into the daily habits of a leaflet-pushing radical who would soon change the world from the sixth floor of the Texas School Book Depository.

Place, Martha

Auburn Correctional Facility
135 State Street
Auburn, New York
315-253-8401

In 1899, Martha Place became the first woman to die in the electric chair. Place was sentenced to death for the murder of her stepdaughter, Ida, at this prison. She was escorted to the chamber – carrying a Bible – where the execution was completed with 1,760 volts of electricity. The electric chair was actually introduced here at Auburn Prison; among others executed was Leon Czolgosz, assassin of President William McKinley. Opened in 1817, the Auburn Correctional Facility is the oldest prison facility in the United States.

Playboy Magazine

**6052 South Harper Street
Chicago, Illinois**

It was in the kitchen of his first floor apartment here on the south side of Chicago in 1953 that a 27-year-old named Hugh Hefner laid out and pasted up the very first issue of *Playboy* magazine. Originally, it was to be called *Stag Party*, however

there was already a magazine called *Stag*, which led him to re-name his as *Playboy*. The first issue broke in December 1953, but interestingly, no date was on the cover because Hefner was not positive there would ever be a second issue (given the controversial nature of the magazine). The cover featured Marilyn Monroe.

Presley, Elvis

Birthplace

**306 Elvis Presley Drive
Tupelo, Mississippi
662-841-1245**

Elvis Presley was born here in this modest two-story house on January 8, 1935. Now designated a Mississippi historic landmark, the Elvis Presley birthplace has been restored to the period when Elvis lived there. It is located in Elvis Presley Park, which also includes the Elvis Presley Museum, Memorial Chapel, Gift Shop and a life-size stat-

ue of "Elvis at 13." (The Park offers complete recreation facili-ties for picnics and community events.)

Presley, Elvis

Lauderdale Courts

Market Mall
185 Winchester Road
Memphis, Tennessee

From 1949 to 1953, Elvis and his family lived in a public housing project in downtown Memphis called Lauderdale Courts (unit number 328). He would practice in the basement laundry room and on the grassy Market Mall, and he would perform at parties in the Recreation Hall. After he became famous, he would drive his friends and visitors past Lauderdale Courts to show them where he had come from.

The two-bedroom apartment here cost the Presleys $35 a month, and in February 1952 they signed a new lease with the rent raised to $43 a month. However, by November 17, 1952, they were evicted because they were making too much money to live in assisted housing. When the Memphis Housing Authority voted to demolish the building, Elvis fans banded together and, thanks in large part to their efforts, Lauderdale Courts underwent a $35 million restoration project and can still be seen today.

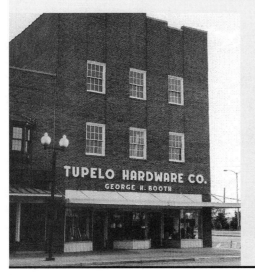

First Guitar

Tupelo Hardware Store
114 West Main Street
Tupelo, Mississippi

Elvis fans often consider Tupelo Hardware the second most important Presley site in Tupelo, after his birthplace. It was here that Gladys Presley bought her son his very first guitar. The business was founded by George H. Booth in 1926, and is still owned and managed by the family's third generation under the leadership of George H. Booth II.

Presley, Elvis

Humes High School

659 North Mannassas Street
Memphis, Tennessee

Elvis attended Humes High School from grades 7 to 12, transferring from Milam Junior High in Tupelo. By his senior year, the once shy Elvis had broken out of his shell – wearing his hair long and donning flashy, colorful clothes. Many students took issue with his radical appearance, but teachers allowed him to be different because Elvis was so polite and never started any trouble. Today, Humes is a Middle School, grades 6 to 8, and the auditorium has been renamed for Elvis. (It is open for tours at various times throughout the year.)

Loew's State Theater

152 South Main Street
Memphis, Tennessee

Elvis worked here as an usher when he was 15, until he was fired for fighting with another usher. Seven years later, when *Jailhouse Rock* premiered here, Elvis came back and posed for pictures while holding his old usher's uniform. The Loew's State Theater had opened in 1925, and closed in 1964. It was demolished in 1971.

Ellis Auditorium

Main Street and Poplar Avenue
Memphis, Tennessee

This was Memphis' most important concert hall during Elvis' teenage years. Here, the Blackwood Brothers Gospel Quartet organized Saturday night gospel music shows or "sings" that Elvis would often attend. Elvis pals and bandmates James Blackwood and J. D. Sumner remember Elvis being allowed to enter for free, because he could not always afford the 50-cent admission.

First Album

Fort Homer W. Hesterly Armory
510 North Howard Avenue
Tampa, Florida

The cover of the very first Elvis album was shot here during a concert on May 8, 1955, by William S. Randolph. Interestingly, its art direction would later inspire the cover of the Clash album, *London Calling.*

Presley, Elvis

The Haircut

Fort Chaffee
Highway 22
Several miles east of Fort Smith, Arkansas
479-452-4554

In 1958, Elvis Presley was inducted into the U.S. army. He began his basic training at Fort Chaffee, and this is where he received, on March 25th, what may be the most famous haircut in history – referred to as "The haircut that shook the world." In a mere few minutes, the famous, slicked-back coif had given way to a standard-issue Army buzz cut.

Built in 1941, this 72,000-acre military base was the training site for thousands of troops heading overseas during World War II. Today, several memorial plaques honor World War II units formed here. (No longer a working base, the area of the camp that includes the barracks facilities is now part of the 7,000 acres being developed for commercial, residential and industrial purposes known as Chaffee Crossing.)

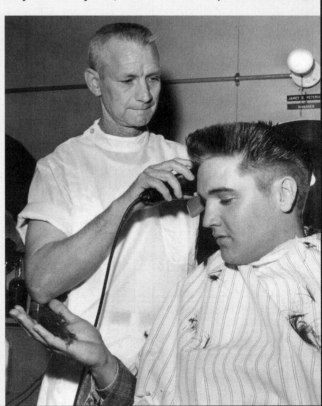

The building where he got the haircut (where the barbershop was located), still stands. It is building #803. Just a stone's throw away is building #823, which was the barracks where Elvis stayed. It is still possible to view the buildings close up, but you should call for an appointment. Fort Chaffee was also used in the movies *Biloxi Blues* and *A Soldier's Story*.

Presley, Elvis

Radio Recorders

7000 Santa Monica Boulevard
Hollywood, California

Founded in 1933 as a studio called Radio Recorders (now Explosive Records), it was here in the 1950s that Elvis recorded "Jailhouse Rock," "All Shook Up," "Loving You" and "Teddy Bear" (among others.) Among the hundreds of other hits recorded here over the years were Sam Cooke's "You Send Me" and Bobby Darin's "Mac the Knife."

Elvis Meets the Beatles

565 Perugia Way
Beverly Hills, California

The original house is gone, but this was the site where, on August 27, 1965, Elvis Presley first met the Beatles. The Fab Four were in town to play the Hollywood Bowl, and it has been reported that the meeting was uncomfortable — the Beatles were in awe and fawned a bit; Elvis didn't care for their music.

Marriage to Priscilla

Aladdin Hotel
3667 South Las Vegas Boulevard
Las Vegas, Nevada
800-851-1703

On May 1, 1967, Elvis Presley (then 32) married Priscilla Anne Beaulieu (then 21) at Milton Prell's Aladdin Hotel. The couple was wed in a quiet ceremony (attended by a few

relatives and close friends) in Prell's suite at the Aladdin at 9:00 A.M. Following the ceremony, an elaborate banquet was held just below the hotel's casino. An estimated 100 people attended the reception, including Mr. and Mrs. Milton Prell and State Supreme Court Justice David Zenoff, who had performed the eight-minute ceremony. Guests dined on ham, eggs, Southern fried chicken, oysters Rockefeller, roast suckling pig, poached and candied salmon, lobster, eggs minnette, and champagne.

Presley, Elvis

Best Western Trade Winds Courtyard Inn

2128 Gary Boulevard
Clinton, Oklahoma
580-323-2610

Elvis stayed at this hotel four times back in the 1960s, and today his room (number 215) is maintained as a mini-shrine with memorabilia and time-period furnishings. Elvis and his entourage liked it here because it was a convenient stopover when driving from Memphis to Las Vegas.

Quayle, Dan

Munoz Rivera School
400 North Montgomery Street
Trenton, New Jersey
609-989-2670

This was Dan Quayle's iconic moment of embarrassment; the granddaddy of them all. In a classroom here on June 15, 1992, William Figueroa, 12, spelled "potato." It was then that the vice president incorrectly insisted on adding an "e" to the end. In his 1994 memoir, Quayle devoted an entire chapter to this event, and the impact it had on his career.

Seabiscuit

Ridgewood Ranch
U.S. 101
Willits, California (about 140 miles north of San Francisco)

It's here that the beloved racehorse Seabiscuit spent the last years of his life, from 1939 until 1947, when he died of a heart attack. The inspirational little horse, stocky and short for a racing thoroughbred, captivated a nation during the 1930s and early '40s, and a biography by Laura Hillenbrand was recently a long-running best-seller (and was the basis for a popular film).

Though he was bred in Kentucky and bought in Detroit, Seabiscuit's owner was a rich San Franciscan, Charles Howard. So after the horse's great career, "the Biscuit" retired here to Howard's ranch near Fort Bragg. Seabiscuit is buried under a California oak on the ranch site and the current ranch owner allows walking tours on certain weekend days throughout the summer and fall.

Note: Seabiscuit first entered the public eye in 1936 at nearby Bay Meadows Racetrack, where he set a track record in the Bay Bridge Handicap that year. Bay Meadows Racetrack is located at: 2600 South Delaware Street, San Mateo, California, 650-574-RACE.

Sinatra, Frank

Birthplace

415 Monroe Street
Hoboken, New Jersey

Frank Sinatra was born here on December 12, 1915. The original wooden building burned down in 1967, and a small archway is the only original thing that remains here today. In the sidewalk, near the site, a star-shaped plaque marks the spot. While there are no formal Sinatra memorials in

town, other pertinent addresses are 841 Garden Street, where the Sinatra family lived in 1939, and 600 Hudson Street, former site of the Union Club, where Sinatra got his first singing job in 1935.

Sinatra, Frank

Villa Maggio

Carrizo Road
12 miles south of Palm Desert, up Route 74 to Pinyon Crest
Pinyon Crest, California

Frank Sinatra built this secret mountain hideaway compound from 1968 to 1969 in order to have a very private place to share with his family and friends. For a while it was Frank's full-time residence. Select Sinatra V.I.P.s were flown into Palm Springs on his private jet, then brought up to the compound by helicopter. Situated on five acres in Pinyon Crest, Villa Maggio (named for his Oscar-winning *From Here to Eternity* character, Maggio) features panoramic views of the entire Coachella Valley.

Cal Neva Lodge

2 Stateline Road
Crystal Bay, Nevada
800-CAL-NEVA

When Frank Sinatra owned this resort in the 1960s, it became the playground of the stars. Hollywood followers were enamored with Sinatra and the "Rat Pack," an unforgettable fraternity that linked itself with the White House through Peter Lawford, brother-in-law of then president-elect John F. Kennedy. Dean Martin, Sammy Davis Jr., Juliet Prowse, and Marilyn Monroe, among others, "sang for their suppers" in the Celebrity Showroom and the Indian Room, while politicians and Hollywood stars played at the tables and relaxed in the private cottages overlooking Lake Tahoe. Back then, the Cal Neva consisted of 57 chalets, spread around the main lodge-casino complex.

Marilyn Monroe was a frequent guest of the Cal Neva Lodge, and scandal generally surrounded her because of her "alleged" secret rendezvous with John F. Kennedy. Monroe occupied a chalet that had the best view of the lake (Sinatra reserved it for Marilyn to use at any time). Her chalet, near Sinatra's, is still available for guest use.

Sinatra had a tunnel installed leading from his private chalet into the main building. This brick-lined tunnel allowed him to avoid the crowds before and after his performances. The tunnel exists to this day, including a staircase covered by the original patterned casino carpet. Sinatra's chalet, containing the now-sealed tunnel entrance, is still available for guest use. Today, the resort is a popular wedding location, and is renowned for its European Health Spa.

Sinatra, Frank

Holmby Hills Rat Pack

232 South Mapleton Drive
Los Angeles, California

This, the former home of Humphrey Bogart and Lauren Bacall, is where Sinatra hung out with the original and infamous Holmby Hills "Rat Pack," back in the 1940s. The group was comprised of Frank Sinatra, Humphrey Bogart, Lauren Bacall, Judy Garland, David Niven, and John Huston.

Mob Photo

Westchester Premier Theater
555 White Plains Road
Tarrytown, New York

An infamous (and much-publicized) photo of Sinatra and some gangster pals was taken backstage at the Westchester Premier Theater in Tarrytown, New York, on April 11, 1976. According to sources, it was Carlo Gambino's idea to go backstage and pay a visit to the singer after his performance. Also in the shot were Gambino's brother-in-law Paul Castellano (who would later succeed Gambino as head of the family only to be gunned down in a palace coup orchestrated by *his* successor, John Gotti), and west coast boss Jimmy "the Weasel" Fratianno (who would later turn state's witness against his Mafia pals).

When the Nevada Gaming Control Board asked Sinatra about the picture in 1981, he called the photo the work of "this fink, the Weasel" and explained that the men were not invited backstage. The theater, believed to have had mob connections over the years, was torn down in the mid-1980s.

Sinatra, Frank

Palm Springs Airport

3400 East Tahquitz Canyon Way
Palm Springs, California
760-318-3800

On January 6, 1977, Sinatra's mother, Dolly, took off in light rain on a Lear jet headed for Las Vegas, Nevada, from this airport. The plane climbed to 9,000 feet, but never changed its runway heading and flew directly into a nearby mountain range at an altitude of 9,700 feet. The 82-year-old Natalie "Dolly" Sinatra and her traveling companion were killed, and crew error was determined as the cause. After the crash, Phyllis McGuire and Johnny Carson were asked to finish Sinatra's Caesars Palace engagement.

Sinead O'Connor

PNC Bank Arts Center
At Exit 166 off the Garden State Parkway
Holmdel, New Jersey

This is where, in the early 1990s, singer Sinead O'Connor refused to perform if "The Star Spangled Banner" was played prior to her appearance (as was the arena's custom). The controversial move brought stinging public criticism, and when Sinatra played this same venue soon after, it was here that he famously declared that he was ready to "kick her ass."

Mugging

Near 915 Foothill Road
Beverly Hills, California

Here, on June 23, 1998, just a few weeks after Sinatra's death, Frank's widow, Barbara Sinatra; her son, Robert Marx; and *Laugh-In* producer George Schlatter and his wife were mugged by three young males. They had just finished dinner and were walking from Schlatter's home on Doheny Road to the Sinatra home on Foothill. After all four victims complied with the robbers, a fight broke out, and the robbers ended up fleeing with the ladies' purses.

The Tailhook Scandal

Las Vegas Hilton Hotel
3000 Paradise Road
Las Vegas, Nevada
888-732-7117

At the 35th Annual Tailhook Symposium, held September 5-7, 1991, 83 women and 7 men were allegedly assaulted during the three-day aviators' convention, according to a report by the Inspector General of the Department of Defense (DOD). The scandal resulted in 119 Navy and 21 Marine Corps officers being referred by Pentagon investigators for possible disciplinary actions.

They were cited for incidents of indecent assault, indecent exposure, conduct unbecoming an officer, or failure to act in a proper leadership capacity while at Tailhook '91. Fifty-one individuals were found to have made false statements during the investigation. However, none of these 140 cases ever went to trial – and approximately half were dropped for lack of evidence.

Test Tube Twins

North Shore University Hospital
300 Community Drive
Manhasset, New York

On March 24, 1983, Heather Jean and Todd McDonald Tilton II, America's first "test tube" twins, were born here on Long Island. The babies were delivered by cesarean section to parents Nancy and Todd Tilton, who lived in nearby Sea Cliff.

"Three Blind Mice" Organist

Jack Russell Stadium
800 Phillies Drive
Clearwater, Florida

On June 26, 1985, organist Wilbur Snapp played "Three Blind Mice" following what he felt was a bad call by umpire Keith O'Connor. The umpire was not amused, and saw to it that Mr. Snapp was ejected from the game. The ejection made Snapp momentarily famous and led to a number of interviews and articles, including coverage on the *Today* show and on Paul Harvey's radio show. Whenever he was asked for his autograph, he signed it, "Wilbur Snapp, Three Blind Mice organist." Snapp, a World War II veteran of the Army Air Forces, died on September 6, 2003 at the age of 83.

Three Stooges

The Three Stooges remain one of the most popular American comedy acts of the 20th century. Commonly known by their names Larry, Moe, and Curly (and, later, Shemp Howard, Joe Besser, and finally, Curly Joe DeRita) the original Three Stooges starred in nearly two hundred theatrical short films in the '30s, '40s and '50s – the longest such series in film history. These short features showcased their extreme brand of slapstick comedy.

Fine, Larry

Knickerbocker Hotel
1714 Ivar Avenue
Hollywood, California
323-962-8898

Larry Fine, the popular, nasally Stooge who had performed with Moe Howard since the mid-1920s, lived here in the Knickerbocker Hotel in Hollywood until 1970, when he moved into the Motion Picture Country Home. He died there on Friday January 24, 1975. He was 72 years old.

Howard, Curly

4524 Fulton Avenue
Van Nuys, California

Curly Howard, born in 1903, was arguably the most popular member of the Three Stooges comedy troupe. His classic catch-phrases of "N'yuk-n'yuk-n'yuk!" and "Wooo-wooo-wooo!" live on today. This was Curly's last home, before his brother Moe moved him into the North Hollywood Hospital and Sanatorium in 1952. But the surly Curly was kicked out of the hospital for being unruly, and so Moe moved him to Baldy View Sanitarium (8101 East Hill Drive, Rosemead, California) where he died 11 days later on January 18, 1952. Curly was just 48 years old. (Today, Baldy View is called the Green Acres Lodge.)

Howard, Moe

9061 Thrasher Avenue
Los Angeles, California

This was Moe's last official residence. It was just after completing his memoirs, on Sunday, May 4, 1975, that the 77-year-old Howard, the bully with the bowl haircut, succumbed to lung cancer at the Hollywood Presbyterian Hospital at 1300 North Vermont Avenue in Los Angeles.

Three Stooges

Howard, Shemp

10522 Riverside Drive
North Hollywood, California

Shemp Howard (Moe and Curly's brother) lived here with his wife, Gertrude, until he had a heart attack on November 22, 1955. He suffered the heart attack on his way home from the fights, and died on the way to St. Joseph's Medical Center in Burbank. Shemp had performed with the Stooges until leaving to pursue a separate film career.

Trees

Hangman's Tree Tavern

305 Main Street
Placerville, California

The history of Placerville began with the "rush for gold" in the 1840s. The highly publicized discovery of gold at Sutter's Mill in Coloma (only 10 miles from Placerville) in 1848 resulted in the migration of thousands of fortune-seekers to Northern California in the mid-1800s.

The town of Placerville was named after the placer deposits found in the riverbed between Spanish Ravine and the town plaza. During the gold rush, Placerville became an important supply center for the surrounding mining camps. Placerville was also known as "Hangtown" in its early days, because of a gambler named Lopez who gained a lot of attention for his big winnings one night at a local saloon. After he retired for the evening, several men tried to overpower him. Lopez fought back, and with the help of others, the robbers were captured.

During their "flogging," three of the robbers were also accused of being wanted for a murder and robbery that occurred at a gold camp on the Stanislaus River. With no more evidence than that, a short, stilted, 30-minute trial took place and a unanimous "guilty" verdict was given. The crowd demanded that the men be sentenced to "death by hanging" and so here they hung. The famous hanging tree once stood in Elstner's Hay Yard, next to the Jackass Inn. Today, the original stump from the old tree remains in the cellar of "The Hangman's Tree" tavern on Historic Main Street.

Trees

The Hare Krishna Elm Tree

Tompkins Square Park
From 7th to 10th Streets between Avenues A and B
New York City, New York

An old elm in the plaza near the center of this historic park in lower Manhattan is considered sacred to the Hare Krishna religion, as it is the site of the movement's first outdoor chanting ceremony outside of India. The ceremony was performed in 1966 by Krishna Consciousness guru Bhaktivedanta Swami Srila Prabhupada; one of the participants was the famous poet, Allen Ginsberg.

Kissing Oak

Near the intersection of C.M. Allen Parkway and University Drive
San Marcos, Texas

Senator Sam Houston made a campaign address beneath this tree during his unsuccessful gubernatorial effort in 1857. In honor of his visit, several young ladies created a Texas flag to present to the former president of the Republic of Texas. While thanking the crowd after his speech, Houston kissed each of the women to show his appreciation, and thus provided the inspiration for the tree's name.

Kyle Hanging Tree

About 10 miles south of Kyle on Old Post Road (CR 136) on your left
Austin, Texas

The story goes like this: In the 1840s, cowboys searching for stray cattle came upon a man hanging from this tree. The identity of the man, who hung him, and for what reason has never been determined. The man was buried on the spot and eventually a Kyle family friend was also buried there. Colonel Kyle (Captain Kyle's father) donated 15 acres of land to serve as a community cemetery, and today the tree is near the cemetery's entrance.

Trees

The Oak of Peace

2211 Bonita Drive
Glendale, California

Glendale's oldest building, an adobe home at this address, was most likely built for Teodoro Verdugo, grandson of Don Jose Maria Verdugo. The Oak of Peace, located here, is said to have been the site where Jesus Pico and other "Californio" leaders of Mexican California decided to surrender to the American forces of John Fremont on January 11, 1847.

Situated at the rear of a spacious garden, the adobe is not visible from the street. It is listed on the National Register of Historic Places, and the grounds are open daily from dawn until dusk. The home is closed but can be viewed from the outside.

The Tree of Hope

132nd Street and Adam Clayton Powell Boulevard
Harlem, New York City

The original tree was located here in front of Lafayette Theater, and it was believed that black performers who hung out near the tree got lucky and won jobs. Also, it was considered good luck for performers to kiss the tree before entering the Lafayette. About the time that the Apollo Theater first opened in 1934, the area around Seventh Avenue was widened and many of the trees that had once lined the block had to be removed, including the Tree of Hope, which was cut up as firewood (pieces were also sold as good-luck souvenirs). But it still lives on today: the stump now resides at Harlem's famous Apollo Theater on 125th Street, where performers still touch it for luck before going onstage.

The Washington Elm

John F. Kennedy Drive (just west of the Conservatory of Flowers)
Cambridge, Massachusetts

It was here, under the parent of this tree, on what is now the Harvard campus, that George Washington took control of the Revolutionary army and first drew his sword on July 3, 1775. (The original tree died in 1924.) The tree went on to inspire the Oliver Wendell Holmes' poem, *Under the Washington Elm*. Note: There is a plaque at the site.

Trees

The White Sox Redwood

Low Park
Near the corner of Arlington and Magnolia
Riverside, California

On Arbor Day, 1914, members of the Chicago White Sox planted a tree in this park, a tree

that has thrived ever since. "The White Sox Redwood," as it is known, was placed by first baseman Hal Chase and third baseman Harry Lord during a ceremony before the Sox played an exhibition game at Evans Park, located just a couple of blocks away. Near the base of the tree is a plaque commemorating the event (it was placed there the same day the tree was planted). Also, a mere baseball toss from the tree, behind a gate, stands the very first orange tree planted in California.

Turner, Lana

The Top Hat Malt Shop
1500 North Highland Avenue
Hollywood, California

The mythmakers always had it that Lana Turner was famously discovered at Schwab's Drugstore in Hollywood, but they always had it wrong. Though Schwab's was indeed the archetypal Hollywood haunt, it was at a place called the Top Hat Malt Shop where the soon-to-be-famous actress was discovered at the counter. She had recently moved to California from Idaho (in the mid-1930s), and one day after school, the 15-year-old Turner (who was still going by her given name, Julia Jean Mildred Frances Turner) stopped here for a soda. That's when the publisher of the *Hollywood Reporter,* W.R. Wilkerson, saw her and was taken aback by her beauty.

He gave the teen his card and suggested she call Zeppo Marx (the straight man in the Marx Bros. comedy troupe) who had recently become an agent after leaving his brothers' act. Wilkerson also personally helped put her in touch with director Mervyn LeRoy who was instrumental in having her name changed to the more alluring "Lana Turner." The Top Hat is long gone, replaced today by a mini-mall.

Wedding Chapels of the Stars

It started with Elvis, and today Las Vegas has become the celebrity wedding capitol of the world. Though many big names get married in many exotic corners of the globe, at the end of the day there's no place with a higher ratio of celebrity weddings per block than Sin City. Here is just a sampling:

Candlelight Wedding Chapel

2855 Las Vegas Boulevard
Las Vegas, Nevada
800-962-1818

Celebrities married here include Whoopie Goldberg, Patty Duke, Bette Midler, Bob Seger, Michael Cain, and Barry White.

The Chapel of the Bells

2233 Las Vegas Boulevard South
Las Vegas, Nevada
800-233-2391

Popular as a movie location, this church has been seen in the movies *Vegas Vacation, Honeymoon in Vegas, Indecent Proposal* and *Mars Attacks.* Celebrities who have wed here include Jenny Jones, Jerry Weintraub, Al Hirt, Leslie Nielson, and Bobby Unser.

The Little Church of the West

4617 Las Vegas Boulevard South
Las Vegas, Nevada
800-821-2452

Greg Allman, David Cassidy, and Richard Gere and Cindy Crawford were married here.

The Little White Chapel

1301 Las Vegas Boulevard South
Las Vegas, Nevada
800-545-8111

Some of the celebrities who have been married at the Little White Chapel in Las Vegas include Joan Collins, Judy Garland, Michael Jordan, Demi Moore and Bruce Willis, Mickey Rooney, Patty Duke, Frank Sinatra, and most recently (for what turned out to be less than 55 hours), Britney Spears.

Wyeth, Andrew

Olson House at the Farnsworth Art Museum
384 Hathorn Point Road
Cushing, Maine
207-596-6457

The famous 1948 painting called "Christina's World," artist Andrew Wyeth's signature work of art, was based on an image that was modeled here, at the famous Olson House. Wyeth's depiction of the crippled Christina Olson crawling through a field toward the house she shared with her brother, Alvaro, has become one of only a handful of iconic American paintings, and every year from Memorial Day weekend to October 15th about 8,000 art-loving visitors come here to pay tribute (and some, as seen below, even act as Christina near the house, replicating her pose from the painting). "Christina's World" is now owned by the Museum of Modern Art in New York. Note: The Olson House is located 14.5 miles from the Farnsworth Museum. Admission can be purchased in combination with general museum admission or can be purchased on-site separately.

History and Tragedy

Air Show

18450 Wilmington Avenue
Carson, California

The very first air show ever held in the United States took place right here in 1910, seven years after the Wright Brothers made the first-ever flight near Kitty Hawk (and just two years after Henry Ford introduced the Model-T automobile). The show was held from January 10-20 near the present site of California State University at Dominguez Hills. Called "The Great Air Meet," it was a huge success that attracted over 175,000 people. (At that time, that number represented more than half of the entire population of Los Angeles.)

Early aircraft from all over the planet engaged in air races and exhibitions. As we know today, the greater Los Angeles area was to become one of the central spots in the aerospace industry with Boeing, Douglas, Lockheed and Northrop located here, as well as one of the busiest international airports in the world. Today, a bronze marker sits about a half mile northwest of the location where the air show was held.

Amana Colonies National Historic Landmark

39 38th Avenue
Amana, Iowa
800-579-2294

Incorporated in 1859, the Amana Society was by far the most successful of the utopian communities founded in America during the 19th century. An outgrowth of the pietist movement begun in Germany in 1714, this religious community originally settled in upstate New York and Canada during the 1840s and called itself the Ebenezer Society. In the 1850s, the Ebenezer Society relocated to Iowa, establishing seven villages on 26,000 acres purchased here.

Under the original organization, land and industries were owned in common and were managed by the elders of the church; in 1932, by vote of all members, secular and religious matters were separated. Today, seven quaint villages comprise the Amana Colonies – a 26,000-acre National Historic Landmark just 20 miles west of Coralville. The once religious communal system still bears the heritage of the German settlers in the form of outstanding restaurants, wineries, historic sites and specialty shops.

The Archeodome

3200 Indian Village Road
Mitchell, South Dakota
605-996-5473

The Archeodome and archeological dig site (Mitchell's Prehistoric Indian Village) date back to the 10th century. The Archeodome covers portions of the prehistoric village, allowing for year-round excavation and interpretation at the site. It is set up for archeologists as well as students, educators and the general public. With three earth lodges

and an active laboratory, a visit here reveals the importance of studying the past and uncovering the beginnings of South Dakota horticulture. The Archeodome is the only facility of its kind in the country.

Arnold, Benedict

Fort Griswold Battlefield
Groton, Connecticut
860-424-3200
Directions: Take I-91S to Exit 22. Take Route 9S to the end.
Take I-95N to Groton and then take the second exit after the Gold Star Bridge
(over the Thames River) onto the Clarence B. Sharp Highway.
Follow signs to Fort Griswold.

This is the historic site where, on September 6, 1781, the British Forces, commanded by the infamous Benedict Arnold, captured the Fort and massacred the soldiers of the Continental Army stationed here. The Ebenezer Avery House, which sheltered the wounded after the battle, has been restored on the grounds, and a Revolutionary War museum depicts the era. A granite monument was dedicated in 1830 to the men who had defended Fort Griswold.

Bentsen, Lloyd/Quayle, Dan

Omaha Civic Auditorium
1804 Capitol Street
Omaha, Nebraska
402-444-5070

On October 5, 1988, in Omaha, Nebraska, Dan Quayle, the Republican candidate for the vice presidency, met Lloyd Bentsen, the Democratic candidate, in a nationally televised debate. It was here that this now-famous exchange took place:

Quayle: "I have as much experience in the Congress as Jack Kennedy did when he sought the presidency."

Bentsen: "Senator, I served with Jack Kennedy. I knew Jack Kennedy. Jack Kennedy was a friend of mine. Senator, you're no Jack Kennedy."

Birch Coulee Battlefield

Located three miles north of Morton, at the junction of Renville County
Highways 2 and 18, one mile east of U.S. Highway 71.
Morton, Minnesota

This was the site of the Indian siege during the Dakota
Conflict of 1862, one of the hardest fought battles of the
U.S.-Dakota War. The Dakota kept U.S. soldiers under siege
for 36 hours before a relief detachment arrived from Fort
Ridgely. Today, you can walk a self-guided trail through a
re-created prairie and read about the battle from the per-
spectives of Joseph Anderson, a captain in the U.S. Army,
and Wamditanka (Big Eagle), a Mdewakanton soldier.

Sketches from soldier Albert Colgrave provide vivid battle
details. Guideposts pinpoint the locations where the U.S.
soldiers were camped and the positions the Dakota took
while surrounding the U.S. soldiers. Visitors can learn more
about the U.S.-Dakota War at the nearby Fort Ridgely
Historic Site, and get more information on the Dakota people and the causes of the war at the Lower Sioux Agency
Historic Site.

Bush, George

Orange County Convention Center
9800 International Drive
Orlando, Florida

In February 1992, then-president George Bush paid a visit to this exhibition hall during
the National Grocers Association convention. While here, the president spent some time
near a mock-up of a supermarket checkout lane. During the visit, he signed his name on
an electronic pad used to detect check forgeries and asked, "If some guy came in and
spelled George Bush differently, could you catch it?" Upon being told they could, he
shook his head, seemingly in wonder. Then he electronically scanned several objects
(including a quart of milk and a light bulb), ran them over an electronic scanner and
asked, "This is for checking out?"

"I just took a tour through the exhibits here," he expressed to the grocers later. "Amazed
by some of the technology." This moment, while innocent enough to those in attendance,
was mocked in a front-page *New York Times* headline which read: "Bush Encounters the
Supermarket, Amazed." The pointed article helped sink the president, who was then
viewed as being out of touch with the everyday lives of Americans.

Camp David

**Park Central Road
Thurmont, Maryland**

This legendary presidential hideaway in the Catoctin Mountains, established by F.D.R. as "Shangi-La" and then renamed after David Eisenhower, has been the site of many major political events, most notably the first brokered Middle East Peace Accord. (Muhammad Anwar al-Sadat, president of the Arab Republic of Egypt, and Menachem Begin, prime minister of Israel, met here at this secluded camp with Jimmy Carter from September 5 to September 17, 1978, eventually agreeing on a framework for peace in the Middle East.) Over its history, a majority of the presidents have used Camp David to host visiting foreign leaders; the first such visitor was Prime Minister Winston Churchill of Great Britain in May 1943.

Carter, Jimmy

Jimmy Carter National Historic Site
300 North Bond Street
Plains, Georgia

It was on a lake here on April 20, 1979, that the strange "rabbit incident" occurred. Carter was taking a few days off in Plains, Georgia. He was fishing from a canoe in a pond when he spotted an angry rabbit swimming toward him. According to press accounts, "It was hissing menacingly, its teeth flashing and nostrils flared and making straight for the president."

Initially it was reported that he had hit the rabbit with his paddle, but Carter later backed off to say he had merely splashed water at the wild creature, which then swam off toward shore. The entire episode became a symbol of Carter's floundering presidency.
This site includes President Carter's residence, boyhood farm, school, and the railroad depot, which served as his campaign headquarters during the 1976 election. The area surrounding the residence is under the protection of the Secret Service and the home is not open to the public.

Cherry Coal Mine Disaster

Village Park
IL 89
Cherry, Illinois

Just north of town are remnants of the Cherry Coal Mine, where 259 miners lost their lives in one of the worst mine disasters in United States history. The St. Paul Coal Company began mining coal at Cherry in 1905, and by 1909 was mining 300,000 tons annually. The owner and sole customer was the Chicago, Milwaukee and St. Paul Railroad.

On Saturday, November 13, 1909, the mine caught fire. A load of hay, intended for the mule stables at the bottom of the mine, was apparently ignited by burning oil dripping from a kerosene torch. The fire spread rapidly. Several miners reached safety; others were trapped in the mine. The dead included 12 rescuers. The disaster prompted the state legislature to establish stricter regulations for mine safety and to pass a Workmen's Compensation Act, making an employer liable even when there is contributory negligence.

Civil Rights

Bates, Daisy

1207 West 28th Street
Little Rock, Arkansas

The Daisy Bates House, a National Historic Landmark, was the command post for the Central High School desegregation crisis in Little Rock, Arkansas. Mrs. Daisy Lee Gaston Bates and her husband Lucius Christopher (L.C.) Bates, lived here during the crisis in 1957-1958. The house served as a haven for the nine African-American students who desegregated the school, and as a place where they could plan the best way to achieve their goals.

The Bates' home became the official pick-up and drop-off site for the Little Rock Nine's trips to and from Central High School each school day, and consequently, a gathering spot for the Nine and members of the press. As such, the house became a frequent target of violence and damage at the hands of segregation's supporters. It is private property and is not open to the public.

Brown, John

1900 4th Corso
Nebraska City, Nebraska
402-873-3115

Abolitionist John Brown hid runaway slaves in the cellar of an old log cabin here on 19th Street in the 1850s. Known as John Brown's Cave, the cellar had a tunnel that led to Table Creek. Brown was later executed for leading the raid on a government armory in Harper's Ferry, West Virginia on October 16, 1859. Today it's part of the Mayhew Cabin & Historical Village Non-Profit Foundation, which is dedicated to educating the nation's youth in regard to the Underground Railroad. It's open all year for tourists, schools, etc.

Civil Rights

Central High School

2125 Daisy L. Gatson Bates Drive
Little Rock, Arkansas
501-374-1957

In 1957, nine students enrolled here at Central High School. However, when they showed up for classes, they found that the Arkansas National Guard had been sent to prevent them from attending the school. The reason they were singled out was because they were black students who wanted to attend an all-white school. On that morning of September 23, 1957, these nine African-American high school students faced

an angry mob of over 1,000 whites in front of the school protesting integration. As the students were escorted inside by the Little Rock police, violence escalated and they were removed from the school.

The next day, President Dwight D. Eisenhower ordered 1,200 members of the U.S. Army's 101st Airborne Division from Fort Campbell to escort the nine students into the school. This event, watched by the nation and world, was the site of the first important test for the implementation of the U.S. Supreme Court's historic Brown v. Board of Education of Topeka decision of 1954. Today, this National Historic Site is open to the public as an important museum and Civil Rights landmark.

Coffin, Levi

113 US 27 North
Fountain City, Indiana
317-847-2432

This was the home of Levi and Catharine Coffin, North Carolina Quakers who opposed slavery. During the 20 years they lived here, the Coffins helped more than two thousand slaves reach safety. Levi Coffin was called the "President of the Underground Railroad," and to the thousands of escaped slaves, this eight-room Federal style brick home was a safe haven on their journey to Canada. The home is open for tours.

Civil Rights

Craft, Juanita

Wheatley Place Historic District
2618 Warren Avenue
Dallas, Texas

Juanita Craft lived in this house for 50 years, and both Lyndon Johnson and Martin Luther King, Jr., visited her here to discuss the future of the civil rights movement. Craft played a crucial role in integrating two universities and the 1954 Texas State Fair, as well as Dallas theaters, restaurants and lunch counters.

Craft joined demonstrations against the segregated University of Texas Law School and North Texas State University, each resulting in successful lawsuits in 1950 and 1955. Afterwards, she opened a dropout preparation program in Dallas. Craft also served as a delegate to the White House Conference on Children and Youth, and as a member of the Governor's Human Relations Committee. In 1975, at the age of 73, she was elected to the Dallas City Council, where she spent the next two years working to improve the status of Hispanic and Native Americans. The house is open to the public Monday to Friday, 9:00 A.M. to 5:30 P.M.

Edmund Pettus Bridge

Highway 80 at the intersection of Broad Street and Water Avenue
Selma, Alabama
Directions: To get there, take I-65 South toward Mobile and take exit 167 to US 80 West, toward Selma. Follow US 80 West for a little more than 40 miles.

On March 7, 1965, six hundred civil rights marchers were attacked by state troopers on the Edmund Pettus Bridge, on what became known as "Bloody Sunday." Two weeks later, there was another march. But by that time, the movement had grown. The six hundred people had swelled to more than three thousand who began the now-famous four-day march to Montgomery under the leadership of the Reverend Martin Luther King and other black leaders, and under the protection of Army troops. By the time the group reached Montgomery, the marchers numbered more than twenty-five thousand. As they progressed, so did the voting rights bill. Powered by public opinion that had been galvanized by "Bloody Sunday," the bill was signed into law on August 6, 1965.

Civil Rights

Greyhound Bus Station

210 South Court Street
Montgomery, Alabama

This bus station was the site of a mob riot that greeted Freedom Riders hoping to end discrimination in interstate transportation. It is now a historic landmark.

Liuzzo, Viola

A.M.E. Zion Church
U.S. Highway 80 between Lowndesboro and White Hall, near Wright Chapel
Selma, Alabama

The marker placed on this spot identifies where Mrs. Liuozzo, a Detroit housewife, was shot and killed by four Klansmen when she was driving back to Selma after the successful Selma-to-Montgomery March. Liuzzo, a white woman, was driving with a black man named Leroy Moton. Indicative of how unfair the times were, three of the members of the Ku Klux Klan were acquitted of murder by an Alabama jury, despite the testimony of the fourth man in the car.

However, President Lyndon Johnson instructed his officials to arrange for the men to be charged under an 1870 federal law of conspiring to deprive Viola Liuzzo of her civil rights. And so the men – Collie Wilkins, William Eaton and Eugene Thomas – were found guilty and sentenced to 10 years in prison.

Civil Rights

Malcolm X Home

3448 Pinkney Street
Omaha, Nebraska

On May 19, 1925, Malcolm X (born Malcolm Little) was born in a now-demolished house on this site. As a civil rights leader, he advocated racial separatism over integration and the legitimacy of violence in self-defense. He also championed the beauty and worth of blackness and black Americans' African past. On February 14, 1965, unidentified attackers firebombed Malcolm X's New York house while he and his family were asleep inside. One week later, on February 21st, Malcolm X was assassinated by Black Muslim extremists at a rally in New York City's Audubon Ballroom. The home was torn down prior to 1970.

Clinton Characters

Foster, Vince

Ft. Marcy Park
McLean, Virginia

On July 20, 1993, six months to the day after Bill Clinton took office as President of the United States, the White House Deputy Council, Vincent Foster, told his secretary Deborah Gorham, "I'll be right back." He then walked out of his office, after offering his co-worker Linda Tripp the leftover M&Ms from his lunch tray. That was the last time Foster was seen alive.

Foster was later found dead in Fort Marcy Park, with a revolver in his hand and a bullet hole in his head. It has been speculated that Foster either killed himself because of his involvement with many of Clinton's scandals (including Whitewater), or was murdered. Many witnesses claim that this was a murder, and that the body was originally found in a car in the White House parking lot.

Clinton Characters

Lewinsky, Monica

Watergate
26550 Virginia Avenue
Washington, D.C.

Monica Lewinsky lived here during her affair with President Bill Clinton. (The Nixon Watergate burglary of the Democratic Headquarters occurred here in rooms 214 and 314 in 1972.)

Monica Lewinsky was taped by Linda Tripp at the nearby Ritz Carlton Hotel, which is also where sports announcer Marv Alpert was charged with biting a woman's back.

Morris, Dick

Jefferson Hotel
16th and M streets NW
Washington, D.C.
202-347-2200

Former Clinton advisor Dick Morris entertained his prostitute pal Sherry Rowlands here (room 205) during the time he was consulting the president. Morris stayed here on a regular basis during his visits to Washington, and so trusted Rowlands that he gave her a key to the room. Rowland's diaries were eventually printed by the *Star* tabloid and Morris was secretly photographed with Rowlands on a balcony at the hotel.

Colonial National Historical Park

Yorktown, Virginia
757-898-3400
Colonial National Historical Park is located a short distance from Interstate 64.

Colonial National Historical Park administers two of the most historically significant English sites in North America-Jamestown and Yorktown. Jamestown, the first permanent English settlement in North America (established in 1607), and the Yorktown battlefield, site of the final major battle of the American Revolutionary War in 1781, represent the beginning and end of English colonial America.

Situated on the Virginia Peninsula, these two sites are connected by the scenic 23-mile Colonial Parkway. Colonial National Historical Park also includes Green Spring, the 17th-century plantation home of Virginia's colonial governor, Sir William Berkeley, and the Cape Henry Memorial, which marks the approximate site of the first landing of the Jamestown colonists in April of 1607.

Columbus, Christopher

Salt River Bay National Park
St. Croix
340-773-3663

Salt River Bay National Park is one of St. Croix's designated national park areas. Immediately to the west of the bay's opening into the Caribbean Sea is the site thought to be where Christopher Columbus' second landing at the "New World" occurred in 1493.

Columbus had spotted a settlement on the shores of Salt River and sent a group to explore and look for potable water. The group came into conflict with the Indians onshore, thus resulting in the first documented violent conflict between Europeans and Indians on (what is today) United States soil.

Coolidge, Calvin

Route 100-A, Plymouth Notch
Plymouth, Vermont
802-672-3773
Directions: Plymouth Notch is 6 miles south of US 4 on VT 100A, about midway across the state. Nearby is the Coolidge State Forest.

It was here at his boyhood home that vacationing Vice President Calvin Coolidge received a message from Washington, D.C. informing him of the death of President Warren Harding. Coolidge was immediately sworn in as the 30th president of the United States by his father, a notary public. The event occurred by the light of a kerosene lamp in the old family homestead on August 3, 1923 at 2:47 A.M.

The historic district — called Plymouth Notch — was the birthplace, boyhood home and also the "Summer White House" of Calvin Coolidge. The rural Vermont village has remained basically the same since that time. The homes of Coolidge's family, the community church, cheese factory, one-room schoolhouse and general store have been carefully preserved, as have many of their original furnishings. Coolidge himself is buried in the town cemetery.

Custer, General George A.

Washita Battlefield National Historic Site
Cheyenne, Oklahoma
Directions: From I-40 take exit 20 (Sayre) and travel north on US 283 to Cheyenne. Park Headquarters and The Black Kettle Museum are located near the intersection of US 283 and SH-47. The site is 2 miles west of Cheyenne on SH-47A (follow the National Historic Site signs).

Just before dawn on November 27, 1868, the legendary Lt. Col. George A. Custer led his soldiers on a surprise attack of the Washita Indian village here while the Indians slept. In all, more than one hundred Indians were killed, including women and children, and the village was burned down. The controversial strike was hailed 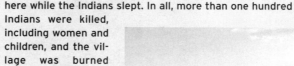  at the time by the military and many civilians as a significant victory aimed at reducing Indian raids on frontier settlements, but is today labelled a massacre by many Indians and whites.

DeSoto National Site

Bradenton, Florida
941-792-0458
Directions: From Bradenton, go west on SR 64 for 5 miles and turn north on
West 75th Street. Travel 2.5 miles to the park entrance.

In May of 1539, Hernando de Soto and an army of over six hundred soldiers came ashore here in the Tampa Bay area. They arrived in nine sailing ships loaded with supplies: 220 horses, a herd of pigs, a pack of vicious war dogs, cannon, matchlock muskets, armor, tools and rations. It was everything they would need to execute the order of King Charles V — to sail to La Florida and "conquer, populate and pacify" the land.

However, this expedition would never yield the gold and treasure these men so desperately sought. Instead, they marched from one village to the next, taking food and enslaving the native peoples to use as guides and porters. Hopes were dashed, fortunes squandered, and hundreds of lives lost on this calamitous journey. The De Soto expedition would change the face of the American Southeast forever, and cause Spain to drastically re-evaluate her role in the New World.

Dinosaur Discovery

Hadrosaurus Park
Maple Avenue
Haddonfield, New Jersey
Directions: Haddonfield is located in Camden County, in southern New Jersey,
about 10 miles east across the Delaware River from Philadelphia, Pennsylvania.
Hadrosaurus Park is located at the end of Maple Avenue off Grove Street
in Haddonfield.

In the summer of 1858, Victorian gentleman and fossil hobbyist William Parker Foulke was vacationing here in Haddonfield when he heard that, 20 years earlier, workers had found huge animal bones in a local pit. Foulke spent the next few months directing a crew of hired diggers, and eventually he found the bones of a creature larger than an elephant with the structural features of both a lizard and a bird.

Yes, Foulke had discovered the first nearly-complete skeleton of a dinosaur — an event that would rock the scientific world and forever change our view of natural history. Today, the historic site is marked with a modest commemorative stone and a tiny landscaped park.

Donner Memorial State Park

Old Hwy 40 (Donner Pass Rd) at I-80 and Truckee exit
Truckee, California

In 1846, a great westward movement began. A small part of the movement, the Donner Party (a loose-knit band of Midwestern farmers and adventurers), left Independence, Missouri, in April 1846. Traveling west through the Great Plains, they crossed the Rocky Mountain crest at South Pass, in Wyoming territory, and then headed southwest through a relatively new and unexplored shortcut, or "cutoff." Bad move, as this cutoff added precious weeks to their travel time.

The party reached present-day Truckee in late October 1846, but the trip had taken its toll. Starving and weak, and unable to climb out of the Truckee basin, the emigrants stayed there to wait out the brutal winter. In January 1847, a few broke through westward, over the 7,088 foot pass (now called Donner Pass), and summoned relief parties. By April 1847, only 48 of the 89 original members of the Donner Party were still alive. The others, 41 in all, had died of starvation or cold in the long Sierra winter. Tragically, those who survived subsisted on their few meager provisions, the ox hides and, finally, the bodies of their dead friends and relatives.

Donner Memorial State Park is now located where many of the emigrants spent their last days, and the site of one of the emigrant cabins is today marked by a looming monument to the western pioneers. Symbolically, its base is 22-feet high, the height of the snow in that terrible winter of 1846–47.

Dukakis, Mike

General Dynamics Land Systems
38500 Mound Road
Sterling Heights, Michigan

On September 13, 1988, presidential candidate, Mike Dukakis, wearing an army tanker's helmet, was videotaped as he peered out with a goofy expression from behind the loader's weapon of an MIAI Abrams Main Battle Tank during a demonstration ride at the headquarters of General Dynamics Land Systems Division where the tank was manufactured. The footage made Dukakis, a candidate already perceived as "soft," look even mushier, and all but ended his chances for election against Republican George Bush.

Earhart, Amelia

The Harbour Grace Airstrip
Newfoundland, Canada

On May 20, 1932, five years to the day after Charles Lindbergh set off on his legendary flight across the Atlantic, Amelia Earhart took off from the Harbor Grace Airstrip in Newfoundland at 12 minutes after 7:00 P.M. Despite some major technical snafus with her aircraft, she landed at Springfield, six miles from Londonderry, Ireland, on May 21, at 2:30 P.M., becoming the first woman to cross the Atlantic alone. For this epic flight, she was awarded the National Geographic Society Medal by President Herbert Hoover on June 21, 1932.

The Harbour Grace Airstrip was originally built in 1927 to be used for the journey of William Brock and Edward Schlee, who were attempting an around-the-world flight. From 1927–1936, more than 20 flights, some of them piloted by such famous aviators as Amelia Earhart and Captain Eddie Rickenbacker, took off from Harbour Grace to fly the Atlantic. In 1935, Earhart became the first woman to fly the Pacific Ocean, crossing from Hawaii to California, and later the same year she set a speed record by flying non-stop from Mexico City to New York City in 14 hours, 19 minutes.

But on June 1, 1937, she began a flight around the world, traveling eastward from the Miami Municipal Airport, Florida. Tragically, her plane disappeared on July 2nd near Howland Island in the middle of the Pacific Ocean. An extensive search by planes and ships failed to uncover any trace of Earhart, her navigator Fred Noonan or her Lockheed 10E Electra plane, and her fate remains a mystery.

Note: Another interesting Earhart-related landmark is the Amelia Earhart Birthplace Museum: 223 North Terrace Street, Atchison, Kansas. 913-367-4217.

El Morro National Monument

Located near Ramah, New Mexico
(56 miles Southeast of Gallup via Highways 602 and 53).
505-783-4226

Looming two hundred feet above the valley floor, this massive sandstone bluff was at one time a welcome landmark for weary travelers. The reason it became such a popular campsite over the years? A reliable waterhole hidden at its base. Starting in the late 1500s, El Morro (or Inscription Rock, as it is also called), was visited by many Spanish, and later, Americans.

While they rested in its shade and drank from the refreshing pool, many of these ancient travelers carved their signatures, dates, and messages into the rock. Before the Spanish, petroglyphs were inscribed by Ancestral Puebloans living on top of the bluff over seven hundred years ago. Today, El Morro National Monument protects over two thousand inscriptions and petroglyphs, as well as Ancestral Puebloan ruins.

Ephrata Cloister

632 West Main Street
Ephrata, Pennsylvania
717-733-6600
Directions: I-76 West to Exit 21. Rt. 222 South to Ephrata to Rt. 322 (Main Street) West. About 2 miles to Cloister. The ride is about 90-120 minutes north-west of Philadelphia.

Founded in 1732 by Conrad Beissel, the Ephrata Cloister was one of America's earliest communal societies. Here, Beissel and his followers lived quiet lives of prayer and char-ity. The community consisted of three orders, a brotherhood and a sisterhood, both of which practiced celibacy, and a married order of householders who supported Cloister activities. While the householders were farmers or craftsmen who lived nearby, the brothers and sisters lived at the Cloister in log, stone, and half-timbered buildings rem-iniscent of their Rhenish homeland.

Today, the site contains all of the main original buildings and a graveyard where many of the earliest members are buried. Visitors can enjoy a guided tour of the main buildings (smaller building tours are self-guided).

Fires

Beverly Hills Supper Club Fire

Located along US 27 south, just south of
Moock Road., on the hillside along US 27.
(Office buildings and parking lots are in
front of the club's old driveway.)
Southgate, Kentucky

On the night of May 28, 1977, a devastating fire
swept through the Beverly Hills Supper Club in
Southgate, killing 165 people. The club had been
built in 1937 atop a hill in Northern Kentucky, just across the Ohio River from Cincinnati,
and over the years it hosted some of entertainment's biggest stars. But on this
Memorial Day weekend in 1977, with 2,500 people inside, things took a tragic turn.

The first sign that anything was amiss may have come as early as 8:15 P.M., when some
complained of unusual heat in one of the reception rooms. It wasn't until 8:50 P.M. that
the first smell of smoke appeared and the raging fire was discovered in the reception
room. Singer John Davidson was the main act that evening and was just waiting for the
comedy act before him in the Cabaret Room to finish up, when Walter Bailey, a young
busboy, grabbed the mike and announced there was a "small fire."

At 9:02 P.M., the ferocity of the fire swept down toward the Crystal Room. The fire was
so strong at this point that smoke was already pouring out through the ducts, causing
intense panic; twelve hundred people began scrambling out through three small exits.
In the darkness, many encountered locked doors. The official investigations into what
caused the fire at the Beverly Hills Supper Club were inconclusive, but the factor most
often cited is aluminum wiring. Today, the site is still vacant.

Fires

The Iroquois Theater Fire

24 West Randolph Street
Chicago, Illinois

On December 30, 1903, a fire broke out in this popular theater during a show by famed comedian Eddie Foy. The tragic fire, believed to have been started by faulty wiring, killed 572 people — another 30 died from injuries. The passageway behind the theater is still referred to as "Death Alley" after the hundreds of bodies placed there during the recovery. It remains the most deadly fire in American theater history. Today the Ford Theater is located here (and the alley still exists behind the building).

The Station Nightclub Fire

2-11 Cowesett Avenue
West Warwick, Rhode Island

The Station Nightclub fire on February 20, 2003, was the fourth-deadliest nightclub fire in U.S. history, killing 100 people and injuring nearly 200. Ninety-six perished on the night of the fire, and four died later from their injuries at local hospitals. It was the deadliest fire in the United States since the 1977 Southgate, Kentucky Beverly Hills Supper Club fire that claimed 165 lives.

The Station was a nightclub in West Warwick, Kent County, Rhode Island. The fire started when pyrotechnics set off by Great White, the rock band playing that night, lit flammable soundproofing foam behind the stage. The flames were first thought to be part of the act; only as the fire reached the ceiling and smoke began to billow did people realize it was uncontrolled. The ensuing stampede in the inferno led to the numerous deaths among the patrons, who numbered somewhat more than 300, the official capacity.

Today, the site at 2-11 Cowesett Avenue has been stripped of the club's debris. The foundation has been filled and the fence surrounding the site has been taken down. A ring of wooden crosses now circle what was the club's perimeter. Balloons, pictures, poems and candles sit at the bases of the crosses.

Fires

Sunshine Mine Fire

Four miles east of Kellogg at Big Creek (Exit 54)
Near Kellogg, Idaho

The 1972 Sunshine Mine fire was the worst mining disaster in recent history, killing 91 miners. This monument near the site, a 12-foot-tall sculpture of a miner with his drill raised, is surrounded by plaques listing the names of the dead. A quirky local landmark nearby is the Miner's Hat. This building, constructed in the shape of a miner's hat, was at one time a tavern. Today, it is the Miner's Hat Realty.

Triangle Shirtwaist Fire

23-29 Washington Place
New York City, New York

The is the site of the worst factory fire in the history of New York City. It occurred on March 25, 1911, in the Asch building at the northwest corner of Washington and Greene Streets, where the Triangle Shirtwaist Company occupied the top three of ten floors. Five hundred women were employed there, mostly Jewish immigrants between the ages of 13 and 23. To keep the women at their sewing machines, the proprietors had locked the doors leading to the exits.

The fire began shortly after 4:30 P.M. in the cutting room on the eighth floor, and fed by thousands of pounds of fabric it spread rapidly. Panicked workers rushed to the stairs, the freight elevator, and the fire escape. Most on the eighth and tenth floors escaped; dozens on the ninth floor died, unable to force open the locked door to the exit. The rear fire escape collapsed, killing many and eliminating an escape route for others still trapped. Some tried to slide down elevator cables but lost their grip; many more, their dresses on fire, jumped to their death from open windows.

Pump Engine Company 20 and Ladder Company 20 arrived quickly, but were hindered by the bodies of victims who had jumped. The ladders of the fire department extended only to the sixth floor, and life nets broke when workers jumped in groups of three and four. Additional companies were summoned by four more alarms transmitted in rapid succession. The Triangle Shirtwaist Factory Building, a National Historic Landmark is now used as classrooms and offices by New York University and is not open to the public

Fires

Winecoff Hotel Fire

Corner of Peachtree and Ellis Streets
Atlanta, Georgia

The Winecoff Hotel fire, a fire that killed 119 of the 280 people who were staying in the hotel at the time, is still listed as the deadliest hotel fire in North America. The fire occurred at approximately 3:00 A.M. on December 7, 1946.

At 15 stories, the Winecoff was Atlanta's tallest hotel. It was advertised as a "fireproof" hotel, and was constructed of brick with a central spiral staircase and an elevator that was under the control of an operator. The remains of the Winecoff Hotel are located on the corner of Peachtree Street and Ellis Street in the heart of downtown Atlanta. A marker stands as a reminder of the devastating fire.

Forts

Fort Astoria

Intersection of 15th and Exchange Streets
Astoria, Oregon

Erected in 1811 by fur trader John Jacob Astor (1763–1848) in an effort to break the British monopoly in the Pacific Northwest, the establishment of Fort Astoria represented an important American claim to the Oregon Territory. In 1813, Astor sold the site to his competitor, the British Northwest Company. A small park with a partial replica of the fort is located here on the site of the original structure. A mural re-creates the vista from the fort in 1813 as a backdrop to the re-created stockade building on the Fort Astoria Park property.

Forts

Fort Bowie

Willcox, Arizona

Directions: From Willcox, Arizona drive southeast for 20 miles on Arizona Highway 186 to the Fort Bowie turn off, then drive another 8 miles on the unpaved road to the Fort Bowie Trailhead. The walk to the ruins is three miles round-trip.

Fort Bowie commemorates the site of the bitter conflict between the Chiricahua Apaches and the United States military. For more than 30 years, Fort Bowie and Apache Pass were the focal point of military operations, eventually culminating in the surrender of Geronimo in 1886 and the banishment of the Chiricahuas to Florida and Alabama. It was also the site of the Bascom Affair, a wagon train massacre, and the legendary battle of Apache Pass, where a large force of Chiricahua Apaches under the leadership of Mangus Colorados and Cochise fought the California Volunteers.

Fort Christina

Fort Christina State Park
East 7th Street and the Christina River
Wilmington, Delaware
302-652-5629

This is the site of the first permanent settlement in Delaware Valley, where the Swedes landed in 1638, in one of the oddest episodes in American colonial history. It happened when the Swedish ships *Kalmar Nyckel* and *Fogel Grip* sailed up the South River to a spot on the Minquas Kill tributary, and made anchor before a rocky outcropping that formed a natural dock. There, its captain, the famed Peter Minuit (who as leader of the Dutch province of New Netherland had bought the island of Manhattan from the local Indians in 1626), declared the river and the area around it the colony of New Sweden.

Since the Dutch had claimed this land going back to Henry Hudson's voyage in 1609, the new claim meant in effect that New Sweden would be a province within a province. Minuit chose the locale for his base, called "Fort Christina" after the queen of Sweden, carefully. It was located at the point where Indians bearing furs from the interior would arrive in their canoes.

The spot where Minuit came ashore is today memorialized by a monument. The waterfront in Wilmington is also the home port of the reconstructed *Kalmar Nyckel*, Minuit's flag ship, which regularly plies East Coast waterways.

Forts

Fort Clatsop

92343 Fort Clatsop Road
Astoria, Oregon
503-861-2471

This site commemorates the harsh 1805–1806 winter encampment of the 33-member Lewis and Clark Expedition. The focus of the park is a 1955 community-built replica of the explorers' 50-by-50 foot fort – Fort Clatsop. The fort, historic canoe landing and spring are nestled in the coastal forests and wetlands of the Coast

Range as it merges with the Columbia River Estuary. The Salt Works unit commemorates the expedition's salt-making activities. Salt obtained from seawater was essential to the explorers' winter survival at Fort Clatsop.

Fort Necessity

Located in southwestern Pennsylvania about 11 miles east of Uniontown
Uniontown, Pennsylvania
724-329-5805

Colonial troops commanded by 22-year-old Colonel George Washington were defeated here in this small stockade at the "Great Meadow." This opening battle of the French and Indian War began a seven-year struggle between Great Britain and France for control of North America. Great Britain's success in this war helped pave the way for the American Revolution.

The park comprises approximately 900 acres in three separate sites. The main unit contains the visitor center, the battlefield with the reconstructed Fort Necessity, and the Mount Washington Tavern. The Braddock Grave unit is approximately 1.5 miles west of the main unit and the Jumonville Glen unit is approximately seven miles northwest of the main unit.

Forts

Fort Raleigh

1401 National Park Drive (3 miles north of Manteo)
Manteo, North Carolina

The first English attempts at colonization in the New World (1585-1587) are commemorated here. These efforts, sponsored by the famed Sir Walter Raleigh, ended tragically with the disappearance of 116 men, women and children (including two that were born in the New World). The fate of this "lost colony" remains a compelling mystery to this day.

The park was established in 1941, and enlarged in 1990 by Public Law 1001-603 to include the preservation of Native American culture, The American Civil War, the Freedman's Colony and the activities of radio pioneer Reginald Fessenden. The park is also home to the outdoor symphonic drama *Lost Colony,* performed during the summer at the Waterside Theatre since 1937.

Fort Robinson

3200 Highway 20
Crawford, Nebraska
308-665-2900

Fort Robinson, Nebraska's largest and most historic state park, was an active military post from 1874 to 1948. Crazy Horse, Walter Reed, Red Cloud, Arthur MacArthur, Dull Knife, General Crook and Doc Middleton are but a few of the colorful characters who played significant roles in carving Fort Robinson's place in western lore. In fact, Indian Chief Crazy Horse was killed here during a struggle on September 5, 1877 – wounded by a soldier's bayonet while an Indian held his arms.

Today, this state park offers train and stagecoach rides, two museums and a buffalo herd; the fort site includes the 1905 post headquarters (now the museum) and more than a dozen other sites on base such as the blacksmith shop, veterinary hospital and guardhouse.

Frank, Leo

Corner of Frey's Gin and Roswell Road
Marietta, Georgia

On April 26, 1913, Mary Phagan, a teenage employee of the National Pencil Factory in Atlanta, was murdered sometime after picking up her wages from the factory. The brutal murder was sensationalized across the United States, and Leo Frank, her Jewish manager, was found guilty and sentenced to be hanged. He was convicted primarily on the testimony of Jim Conley, a janitor who was initially suspected of the crime and who changed his story several times.

Governor John Slaton commuted Frank's sentence to life imprisonment, but on August 16, 1915, 25 armed men took Frank out of jail and hanged him here at this site. The incident is one of many that led to the rebirth of the Ku Klux Klan. For years, the Anti-Defamation League of B'nai B'rith, founded in New York largely because of the Leo Frank case and its aftermath, fought to obtain a pardon for Frank.

In 1982, 69 years after the murder, a man who had been a 13-year-old factory employee at the time of the murder came forward and stated that he had seen Conley carrying Phagan's body down the stairs, and that Conley had threatened him into silence. In 1986, the Georgia Board of Pardons and Paroles finally issued a posthumous pardon to Leo Frank, based on the state's failure to protect him while he was in custody.

The Galveston Hurricane

Galveston, Texas

The Great Galveston Hurricane made landfall on the city of Galveston, Texas on September 8, 1900, with estimated winds of 135 miles per hour, making it a category-four storm with similar magnitude to hurricane Andrew in 1992. Significant to this storm was the loss of life, which is estimated by some sources as 6,000 and by others as 12,000.

On the night of September 7, 1900, winds arose that heralded the arrival of the hurricane, which struck the island early in the morning of September 8th and lasted through September 9th. Wind speed was estimated to have reached up to 155 MPH, although no one knows for sure because the anometer blew off of the National Weather Service building.

Because of the storm, the Galveston Seawall was built, the entire grade of Galveston was raised and the Houston Ship Channel was constructed. Today, a plaque and statue commemorating the event can be found by the seawall where the hurricane first touched ground.

The Garfield Campaign

8095 Mentor Avenue
Mentor, Ohio

FARMER GARFIELD
Cutting a Swath to the White House.

President James Garfield acquired this home in 1876 to accommodate his large family. Named "Lawnfield" by reporters, it was the site of the first successful "front porch campaign" in 1880. (Front porch campaigns allowed candidates to stay at home, entertaining and visiting with groups of voters on their front porches, thus getting media attention with each visit.)

James A. Garfield was president from March 4, 1881 until his assassination on September 19, 1881. Four years after his death, the Memorial Library wing was added here by Mrs. Garfield and her family, thus setting the precedence for presidential libraries. Today, the home is operated by the National Park Service and the Western Reserve Historical Society and is open for visi-

Goodyear Blimp Disaster

231 South LaSalle Street
Chicago, Illinois

Many people remember the Hindenberg disaster, but on July 21, 1919, the Goodyear dirigible "Wing Foot" crashed into this building, then the Illinois Trust and Savings Building. The blimp, powered by 95,000 cubic feet of flammable hydrogen, then fell to the earth.

The ship ripped into the iron supports that held the glass skylight

of the building in place, and the two engines and gasoline tanks crashed to the bank's floor. The rotunda was instantly aflame, trapping tellers and stenographers. Twelve people died and many more were injured. The accident was said to be caused by static electricity and a rush of air from the propellers. The historic building remains today.

The Green

Dover, Delaware
302-739-4266

This famous town square was laid out in 1717 in accordance with William Penn's orders of 1683, and has changed little since then. One of the nation's most historic sites, it was here that Delaware voted to ratify the U.S. Constitution, making it the first state to do so. The Green was the site of early fairs and markets when Dover was the county seat and then state capital. It now hosts political rallies and public events such as Old Dover Days in May, when many private homes and buildings are open to the public.

Harrison, Benjamin

North Delaware Street
Indianapolis, Indiana
317-631-1898

This, the former residence of President Benjamin Harrison, is now a museum dedicated to his life. Operated by The Benjamin Harrison Foundation, the 16-room house was home to the president from 1875 until his death in 1901, and it is here that he held his famous "front porch" campaign in 1888.

Haymarket Riot

Randolph and Desplaines Streets, several blocks west of the Loop.
(The marker sits in the sidewalk on the eastside of Desplaines just a few steps north of Randolph.)
Chicago, Illinois

It was during the nationwide strike for the 8-hour workday that a mass meeting was held in the Chicago haymarket to protest a police action of the previous day in which workers were killed. When police ordered the protest meeting to disperse (even though it was a peaceful gathering), a bomb was anonymously set off, killing several officers.

The bronze marker here reads: "A decade of strife between labor and industry culminated here in a confrontation that resulted in the tragic death of both workers and policemen. On May 4, 1886, spectators at a labor rally had gathered around the mouth of Crane's Alley. A contingent of police approaching on DesPlaines Street were met by a bomb thrown from just south of the alley. The resultant trial of eight activists gained worldwide attention for the labor movement, and initiated the tradition of 'May Day' labor rallies in many cities."

Hoover, Herbert

Stanford University
Palo Alto, California

Designed by Lou Henry Hoover, wife of Herbert Hoover (31st president of the United States), this pretty house was built from 1919 to 1920, and it was the couple's first and only permanent residence. It was here that Hoover awaited the presidential election returns in 1928, when he won against Alfred E. Smith, and again in 1932, when he lost the election to Franklin Delano Roosevelt. After Lou's death in 1944, her husband deeded the house to Stanford University to serve as a home for university professors. The Lou Henry and Herbert Hoover House is located on the Stanford University Campus and is not open to the public.

Indiana Coliseum Explosion

Pepsi Coliseum
1202 East 38th Street
Indianapolis, Indiana

On October 31, 1963, an explosion ripped through the Indiana State Fairgrounds Coliseum, claiming the lives of 74 people and injuring nearly 400. It was one of the worst tragedies in Indiana history. It was the opening night for the Holiday on Ice show, and more than 4,000 spectators were in attendance.

Propane, used to keep pre-popped popcorn warm, was leaking from a faulty valve. At 11:04 P.M. an explosion sent bodies flying nearly 60 feet. A second blast took place a few minutes later, caused by heat rising and air rushing into the vacuumized area. The victims were either severely burned or crushed to death. The Coliseum was restored and is still used today for many events. It was renamed the Pepsi Coliseum in 1991.

Ishi Discovery Site

2547 Oroville Quincy Highway, intersection of Oak Avenue (two miles east of downtown)
Oroville, California

Ishi, a Yahi Yana Indian, was literally the last of his native people. At one time, the Yana population numbered approximately 3,000, but in 1865 Ishi and his family were the victims of the Three Knolls Massacre, from which only about 30 Yahi survived. The remaining Yahi escaped but were forced into hiding after cattlemen killed about half of the survivors.

Eventually, all of Ishi's companions died, and he was discovered by a group of butchers in their corral here at Oroville on August 29, 1911. Two anthropologists from Berkeley, Alfred L. Kroeber and T. T. Waterman, brought Ishi to San Francisco where he helped them reconstruct the entire Yahi culture. Ishi identified material items and showed how they were made, filling in the blanks with incredibly sharp firsthand knowledge.

Ishi contracted tuberculosis and died on March 25, 1916, but he left behind a legacy of invaluable information about his people and helped bridge the divide between two worlds. Today, a small monument made of fieldstone rocks gathered from the Deer Creek Canyon area is located where the noble Indian was discovered. It bears a California Registered Historic Landmark plaque.

Jackson, Andrew

U.S. Capitol Building
Washington, D.C.

 President Andrew Jackson was well into his second term when he was attacked here on January 30, 1835. Richard Lawrence, a deranged house painter, approached Jackson outside the U.S. Capitol building with two Derringer pistols. He took aim with the first at less than 15 feet, but the pistol misfired. The enraged Jackson raised his cane to thwart his attacker, who fired again. Amazingly, the second weapon also misfired and the  67-year-old president escaped unharmed.

Evidently, the crazed Richard Lawrence believed that Jackson had conspired to keep him poor and out of work. However, Jackson was convinced that Lawrence was hired by his political enemies, the Whigs, to stop his plan to destroy the Bank of the United States. Lawrence spent the rest of his life in jails and asylums.

Johnson, Lyndon B.

White House Lawn
Pennsylvania Boulevard
Washington, D.C.

Him and Her, the most well-known of President Lyndon Johnson's dogs, were registered Beagles born on June 27, 1963. The president frequently played with the dogs and was often photographed with them. In 1964, President Johnson raised the ire of many when he infamously lifted Him by his ears while greeting a group on the White House lawn. The photos of the event became a sore point for the president for years to come.

The Kennedy Family

Crownlands

Pondfield Road
Bronxville, New York

This estate was purchased in 1929 by Joseph Kennedy for $250,000. A great red-brick Georgian house with tall white columns, set on more than five acres of meticulously landscaped grounds, it was the Kennedy Compound throughout the 1930s and 1940s. The grand manor had 20 bedrooms, more than enough for all the children, maids, nurses, and any guests that Joe might invite. Joe Jr., Jack, and Kathleen had sovereignty over the third floor, which also contained an enormous playroom and the governess' bedroom. The other children resided on the second floor.

The Kennedy Family

Kennedy, Robert F.

Hickory Hill
Chain Bridge Road
McLean, Virginia

When word of the assassination of J.F.K. made its way to Bobby Kennedy, he was here at Hickory Hill, his house in suburban Virginia, having a casual lunch with, among others, Robert Morgenthau, the U.S. attorney for the Southern District of New York. This famous house is where Robert and Ethel Kennedy raised their sprawling family and hosted a broad array of political, social and human rights personalities over the years.

The 18-room house has 13 bedrooms, 13 bathrooms, 12 fireplaces, two pools, paddocks, a small movie theater and lighted tennis courts. Bobby Kennedy bought the house in 1957 from his brother, John F. Kennedy, who was then a U.S. senator. (John and Jacqueline Kennedy had bought Hickory Hill in 1953, the year they married.) The house is no longer owned by the Kennedy family.

Good Samaritan Hospital

1225 Wilshire Boulevard
Los Angeles, California
213-977-4141

Senator Robert Francis Kennedy, brother of the late President John F. Kennedy, attorney general in the latter's administration and a candidate for the Democratic nomination in the 1968 Presidential election, died at 1:44 A.M. on June 6th here at the Good Samaritan Hospital in Los Angeles. He had been shot 26 hours earlier by a Jordanian Arab, Sirhan Bishara Sirhan.

The assassination of 42-year-old Senator Kennedy came 4½ years after the assassination of his brother in Dallas on November 22, 1968, and only two months after the killing of Dr. Martin Luther King, the civil rights leader, in Memphis. The shooting occurred shortly before midnight on June 4th at the Ambassador Hotel in Los Angeles, which was packed with Kennedy supporters celebrating Senator Kennedy's victory in the California presidential primary election held the same day.

The Kennedy Family

Kennedy, David

**Brazilian Court Hotel
301 Australian Avenue
Palm Beach, Florida
888-254-0637**

On, April 25, 1984, David Kennedy, the son of Robert and Ethyl Kennedy, died here of a drug overdose. David, who was just 13 years old when he witnessed his father's assassination while watching TV in his hotel room, was found in his room with lethal doses of cocaine and Demerol in his system. Built in 1926, the famed historic hotel has played host to several stars including Judy Garland, Cary Grant, Errol Flynn and many others.

Smith, William Kennedy

**La Guerida (Kennedy compound)
1095 North Ocean Boulevard
Palm Beach, Florida**

This is the famed former Kennedy compound in Palm Beach, where everyone from Joseph Kennedy to John F. Kennedy would come to escape the rigors and distractions of political life. Called "La Guerida," it was here that William Kennedy Smith, son of Jean Kennedy Smith, was accused of raping a woman. He was eventually tried and acquitted. The estate went on the market in 1993 and sold in 1995 for $4.9 million to New York banker John K. Castle, who has preserved the "Florida White House."

Kennedy, John F.

Birthplace

**33 Beals Street
Brookline, Massachusetts
617-566-7937**

This is where John F. Kennedy was born in 1917. Today, this National Historic Site preserves the birthplace and boyhood home of the 35th president of the United States. The modest frame house in suburban Boston was also the first home shared by the president's father and mother, Joseph P. and Rose Fitzgerald Kennedy, and represents the social and political beginnings of one of the world's most prominent families.

Kennedy, John F.

Omni Parker House

60 School Street
Boston, Massachusetts

It was in this hotel that J.F.K. announced his 1946 candidacy for a U.S. House seat, thus effectively starting his political career. (One of his bachelor dinners was held here as well.)

Union Oyster House

41 Union Street
Boston, Massachusetts
617-227-2750

Established in 1826, the historic Union Oyster House is officially America's oldest restaurant. Located on the Freedom Trail near Faneuil Hall, it was also a favorite spot of J.F.K.'s when he was a bachelor living on nearby Bowdin Street. In fact, he sat, ate and strategized so much at table number eight that today a plaque there honors the former President.

J.F.K. Residence

3260 N Street
Washington, D.C.

This is one of a series of residences in the Georgetown area of Washington D.C. that J.F.K. occupied briefly in the early 1950s. A magnolia tree that he planted in the backyard remains today.

J.F.K. and Jackie's First Residence

3321 Dent Place
Washington, D.C.

This rented home was the first residence of J.F.K. and his new bride, Jackie; they lived here from 1953-1957. The home is near Georgetown University, where Jackie was taking a course in American government, and Wisconsin Avenue, where Jackie browsed for home furnishings.

Kennedy, John F.

Profiles in Courage

Merrywood
Chain Bridge Road
McLean, Virginia

Merrywood, the former home of Jacqueline Kennedy Onassis, is where John Kennedy wrote the book *Profiles in Courage.* He had recently had back surgery after he and Jackie were married, and thus was bed-ridden for eight months. During this period, needing to occupy his time, he wrote the book that became a best-seller and won him a Pulitzer Prize.

Honeymoon

San Ysidro Ranch
900 San Ysidro Lane
Santa Barbara, California
800-368-6788

This beautiful ranch, built in 1893, is nestled among orange trees and its charming bungalows look out over the rolling Santa Ynez hills. Vivien Leigh and Laurence Olivier were married at San Ysidro, and this is also where John and Jackie Kennedy spent their honeymoon in 1953.

In memory of the romantic and historic honeymoon stay of Jacqueline and J.F.K., the ranch offers the "Kennedy Classic" – a two-night stay in the Kennedy Cottage, J.F.K.'s favorite dessert delivered to the room, continental breakfast for two, two one-hour Swedish massages in-cottage and a $100 gift certificate for the legendary Stonehouse Restaurant located here.

The Rossmore House

522 North Rossmore Avenue
Los Angeles, California

During the Democratic National Convention in 1960, John F. Kennedy used what is now apartment 301 in this building as his private residence when things got too crazy at the downtown Biltmore Hotel. Back then it was a hotel, The Rossmore House, but today it's an apartment building.

Kennedy, John F.

Texas Hotel

815 Main Street
Fort Worth, Texas
817-870-2100

On Thursday, November 21, 1963, J.F.K. and his wife, Jacqueline, arrived at this hotel (now the Radisson Hotel) where they spent the night on the seventh floor. The next morning, Kennedy gave a brief speech in front of the hotel, then spoke at a breakfast held in his honor inside the hotel, before heading to the airport where Air Force One was waiting to take him to Dallas.

These were the last public speeches Kennedy gave, as he would be assassinated later that day while en route to a banquet being held at the Dallas Trade Mart. The suite in which he and Jackie Kennedy stayed that November became known as the "Kennedy Suite."

Air Force Museum

1100 Spaatz Street
Wright-Patterson Air Force Base
Fairborn, Ohio
937-255-3286

The plane that transported J.F.K. that fateful last day, and served as the swearing-in location for Lyndon B. Johnson at Love Field in Dallas soon after Kennedy's death, is located here. You can walk the length of the plane and see exactly where the swearing in took place and also where J.F.K.'s coffin rode back to Washington.

Interestingly, the Air Force Museum is on the Huffman Prairie where the Wright Brothers

did many of their post-Kitty Hawk aviation experiments. As well, some UFO experts say the air force complex is the resting place of the captured Roswell aliens (or at least the controversial debris) recovered in New Mexico in the 1940s.

King, Jr., Martin Luther

Ebenezer Baptist Church

407 Auburn Avenue, NE
Atlanta, Georgia
404-688-7263

In, 1931, Martin Luther King, Sr., took over as pastor at this church and served until he retired in 1975. Five-year-old Martin Jr. and his sister, Christine, formally joined the church in 1934 at a revival led by a visiting evangelist. In fact, the young King preached his first sermon here at age 17 and joined his father as co-pastor from 1960 to 1968.

Ebenezer was also the scene of tragic events. Crowds gathered here in April 1968 to view Martin Luther King, Jr.'s, body as it lay in state. Six years later, in 1974, Dr. King's mother was fatally shot by an assassin as she was playing the church organ. Today, the church is part of The Martin Luther King, Jr., National Historic Site.

Dexter Avenue Baptist Church

454 Dexter Avenue
Montgomery, Alabama
334-263-3970

While serving his first pastoral assignment, Dr. Martin Luther King, Jr., began his Civil Rights leadership at this Montgomery, Alabama church. A mural depicts Dr. King's journey from Montgomery to Memphis. This church was also the backbone of the 1955-1956 Montgomery bus boycott – the first locally initiated mass protest against racial discrimination and a model for other grass-roots demonstrations.

The boycott proved how members of a black community could unite in resistance to segregation, and it heralded a new era of "direct action." The event also propelled Martin Luther King, Jr., into the national spotlight. Today, the church is a National Historic Landmark and individual tours of the church are available Monday through Thursday.

King, Jr., Martin Luther

Blumstein's Department Store

230 West 125th Street
Harlem, New York

In 1958, Martin Luther King, Jr., was still basking in the success of his 13-month Montgomery bus boycott. His first book was about to be released and the decision was made to bring King to New York for a book tour. During a book signing here at this former department store in Harlem, King was stabbed by a deranged black woman named Izola Ware Curry. He was rushed to Harlem Hospital where a team of doctors successfully removed a seven-inch letter opener from his chest. The building that once held this popular department store still exists.

Joseph T. Smitherman Historic Building

109 Union Street
Selma, Alabama
334-874-2174

On January 18, 1965, Martin Luther King successfully registered to vote at the Hotel Albert in Selma and was assaulted by James George Robinson of Birmingham. Today, the hotel is gone but columns from it remain here in a park alongside the Joseph T. Smitherman Historic Building. This small structure, with four paintings by Selma native Kirk Miller which depict the history of the city, is a popular museum dedicated to Alabama heritage.

Selma City Hall

1300 Alabama Avenue
Selma, Alabama

This building was at one time used as the city and county jail, and it is where Dr. King and other protesters were imprisoned in 1965. It is now the Cecil C. Jackson, Jr., Public Safety Building.

King, Jr., Martin Luther

Mason Temple

938 Mason Street
Memphis, Tennessee
901-578-3800

Martin Luther King, Jr., delivered his prophetic "Mountaintop" speech in this church in Memphis, Tennessee, on the eve of his assassination – April 3, 1968. Mason Temple served as a focal point of civil rights activities in Memphis during the 1950s and 1960s. Mason Temple was built between 1940 and 1945 as the administrative and spiritual center of the Church of God in Christ, the second-largest black denomination.

The temple is the centerpiece of a group of six buildings that form the church's world headquarters. A vast concrete building designed with simplified Art Moderne styling and detail and capable of seating 7,500 people on two levels, the temple was constructed for regular services as well as to house the annual national convention of church representatives.

Kings Mountain National Military Park

2625 Park Road
Blacksburg, South Carolina
864-936-7921

Kings Mountain National Military Park commemorates a pivotal and significant victory by American Patriots over American Loyalists during the southern campaign of the Revolutionary War. The battle, fought on October 7, 1780, destroyed the left wing of Cornwallis' army and effectively ended Loyalist ascendance in the Carolinas. The victory halted the British advance into North Carolina, forced Lord Cornwallis to retreat from Charlotte into South Carolina, and gave General Nathanael Greene the opportunity to reorganize the American Army.

Klondike Gold Rush National Historical Park

Second Avenue and Broadway
Skagway, Alaska
(Skagway is reached by the South Klondike Highway and is 110 miles south of
Whitehorse, Yukon Territory.)
907-983-2921

This park celebrates the Klondike Gold Rush of
1897-98 through 15 restored buildings within the
Skagway Historic District. The park also administers
the Chilkoot Trail and a small portion of the White Pass
Trail. Included in the park is a segment of the Dyea
Townsite at the foot of the Chilkoot Trail. Back during
the peak of the boom, in 1898, Dyea had an estimated
population of 8,000, with 48 hotels, 47 restaurants,
39 saloons and 19 freighting companies.

Lincoln, Abraham

House Divided Speech

Old State Capitol State Historic Site
Sixth and Adams Streets
Springfield, Illinois

This beautiful building served as the Illinois statehouse from 1839-1876 and was the
scene of many furious political battles between Abraham Lincoln and his main rival,
Stephen A. Douglas. Additionally, on June 16, 1858, Lincoln kicked off his bid for the

U.S. Senate here during the Illinois
Republican convention with what
would become known as the famed
"House Divided" speech. This is also
where Lincoln laid in state on May 3
and 4, 1865, after being assassinated.
An estimated 70,000 people paid
their final respects to him on those
two days.

Lincoln, Abraham

Other Lincoln/Springfield Sites

Some other nearby Lincoln sites in Springfield:

Across the street from the courthouse at Sixth and Adams Streets are the Lincoln-Herndon Law Offices. This State Historic Site marks the only surviving building where Lincoln had law offices (he was here from 1843–52). Illinois' first federal court was also located here. The restored offices and court feature period furnishings. Guided tours are offered.

Close by at 10th and Monroe Streets is the Lincoln Depot, the railway station from which president-elect Lincoln left for Washington, D.C., on February 11, 1861. Lincoln's impromptu farewell to Springfield ranks among his greatest speeches. Open April through August, the depot has restored waiting rooms, exhibits and an audio-visual presentation.

Lincoln-Douglas Debates of 1858

The debates between Stephen A. Douglas and Abraham Lincoln were held during the 1858 campaign for the U.S. Senate seat from Illinois. The debates were held at seven sites throughout Illinois, one in each of the seven congressional districts. Douglas, a Democrat, was the incumbent senator, having been elected in 1847. Lincoln was a relative unknown at the beginning of the debates. The Lincoln-Douglas debates drew the attention of the entire nation and, although Lincoln would lose the senate race in 1858, he would beat Douglas out in the 1860 race for the U.S. presidency.

These are the seven Lincoln-Douglas debate sites, all of which are marked with historical plaques.

1. Washington Square, Ottawa, Illinois

The very first Lincoln-Douglas senatorial debate was held in historic Washington Square on August 21, 1858. Approximately 40,000 spectators witnessed the famous debate, and today at the exact site of the platform where they spoke is a commemorative plaque (at the east end of public square).

Lincoln, Abraham

2. Freeport, Illinois

On August 27, 1858, over 15,000 people attended the debate in Freeport, then a town of 5,000. The Freeport Doctrine, which was famously invoked by Douglas at this debate, stated that people of a United States territory had the right to choose whether or not to exclude slavery from its limits prior to the formation of a state constitution.

3. Union County Fairgrounds, Jonesboro, Illinois

Union County Fairgrounds is today part of Shawnee National Forest's Lincoln Park. Union County is south of the Mason-Dixon Line. The September 15, 1858 debate split families into Confederate and Union factions. Over 50 cemeteries throughout Union County tell of those who lost their lives in the Civil War.

4. Coles County Fairgrounds, Charleston, Illinois

This debate was held on September 18, 1858. This area was very familiar to Lincoln – many friends and relatives, including his father and stepmother, lived and died here, and Lincoln had a thriving law practice in the community. A majority of the townspeople had moved here from Kentucky and Tennessee, coming north to avoid competition with slave labor.

5. Old Main, Knox College, Galesburg, Illinois

Located on the east side on East South Street, between Cedar and South Cherry Streets, this was the site of the fifth debate on October 17, 1858. Today, this is the only remaining structure from any of the seven debates.

6. Washington Park, Quincy, Illinois

On October 13, 1858, the sixth Lincoln-Douglas debate was held here in Quincy, just a few blocks from the Mississippi River. Today, a sculpture in the park commemorates the event.

7. Broadway and Market Streets, Alton, Illinois

On October 15, 1858, the City of Alton hosted the seventh and final Lincoln-Douglas debate. Over 6,000 people gathered for the 3½ hour event, which took place in front of City Hall. Today, full-size bronze replicas of Abraham Lincoln and Stephen Douglas can be found at the site.

Lincoln, Abraham

The Summer White House

Anderson Cottage
3700 North Capitol Street NW
Washington, D.C.
800-422-9988
Directions: From I-95, north of D.C., take I-495
("The Beltway") westbound. Take exit 31 for Silver Spring.
Stay on Georgia Avenue through Silver Spring. Turn left on Upshur Street.
Cross Rock Creek Church Road into the AFRH-W "Eagle Gate"
at Upshur Avenue.

One of the most significant sites associated with President Abraham Lincoln is located in Washington, D.C.. The President Lincoln and Soldiers' Home National Monument, formerly known as Anderson Cottage, is located on the grounds of the Armed Forces Retirement Home – Washington. President Lincoln spent one-quarter of his presidency at the Soldiers' Home, where he lived in a Gothic Revival-style cottage. Lincoln commuted daily from this cottage to the White House by horseback or carriage between June and November of 1862–1864.

While residing at the Soldiers' Home, Lincoln worked on drafts of the Emancipation Proclamation, met privately with the politicians of his day, monitored troop movements from an adjacent tower, and pondered the right course of leadership during the Civil War. Lincoln last visited the cottage the day before John Wilkes Booth shot him.

Interestingly, there was an earlier assassination attempt made on Lincoln at this house. In August of 1864, as Lincoln rode here on horseback from the Capitol, a shot rang out as he neared the entrance. He raced his horse until he reached the gate of the grounds, where soldiers let him in. Later, when searchers went to the area where Lincoln was fired upon, they found his hat on the ground with a bullet hole through the "stovepipe."

In 1999, the Armed Forces Retirement Home (AFRH) formally asked the National Trust for Historic Preservation to steward the site's restoration and, as of this writing, work is well under way. By 2006, the site should be ready for public visitations. Note: The cottage also served as a summer retreat for three other Presidents – Buchanan, Hayes, and Arthur.

Lincoln, Abraham

Lincoln's Last Public Address

The White House
1600 Pennsylvania Avenue
Washington, D.C.

On April 11, 1865, two days after Lee surrendered to Grant, a big, jubilant crowd gathered at the White House, calling for President Lincoln. According to reporter Noah Brooks, "Outside was a vast sea of faces, illuminated by the lights that burned in the festal array of the White House, and stretching far out into the misty darkness. It was a silent, intent, and perhaps surprised, multitude. Within stood the tall, gaunt figure

of the president, deeply thoughtful, intent upon the elucidation of the generous policy that should be pursued toward the South. That this was not the sort of speech which the multitude had expected is tolerably certain."

When Lincoln emerged to address the crowd, Brooks actually held a light so Lincoln could read it. (This, while young Tad Lincoln grabbed at the pages of the speech as they fell near his feet.) The speech dealt with the tough topic of reconstruction, particularly as it related to the state of Louisiana. For the first time, Lincoln publicly expressed his support for black suffrage. This comment enraged one John Wilkes Booth, a member of the audience. A white supremacist and Confederate activist, Booth shot Lincoln three days later.

Manassas, First Battle of

Route 29, west of Route 234
Manassas, Virginia
703-361-1339

Manassas National Battlefield Park was established in 1940 to preserve the scene of two major Civil War battles. Located just a few miles north of the prized railroad junction of Manassas, the tranquil Virginia countryside saw clashes between the armies of the North and South in 1861 and 1862. Today, the park provides the opportunity for visitors to explore the historic terrain where men boldly fought and died – easily one of America's most historic battlefields and a must-see when conducting a Civil War battlefield tour.

The Mormons

Hill Cumorah

On New York Route 21
About 4 miles south of Palmyra, New York

Hill Cumorah figures prominently in events that led to the organization of The Church of Jesus Christ of Latter-day Saints. According to the Church, in 421 A.D., Moroni, the last survivor of a great civilization that had inhabited the Americas since about 600 B.C., buried in this hill a set of gold plates on which was recorded the history of his people. In 1827, Moroni returned as an angel and delivered the plates to Joseph Smith, supposedly here at this site, who then translated them and published them as the *Book of Mormon: Another Testament of Jesus Christ.*

Through paintings, exhibits, and video presentations, the significance of the hill is explained in the visitor center located there. Free guided tours are conducted daily and each summer the Hill Cumorah is the site of a spectacular outdoors religious pageant. The free production, "America's Witness for Christ," features a cast of over six hundred and attracts audiences of up to one hundred thousand each year.

The Mormons

Haun's Mill Massacre Site

North of Kingston, Missouri
Directions: Haun's Mill is located less than 15 miles east of Far West.
Traveling on US 36, turn south onto Highway 13. Turn left on U Street heading
east. Continue east on U Street for about 12 miles until the road becomes a
less-traveled gravel road. (When the road bends left to K Street, continue
straight on gravel to U Street.) Stay on this gravel road (still U Street) as it
curves to the south. Signs have been put up to help you find your way,
but unfortunately some have been vandalized. Continue south for about 1 mile
before coming to a bridge. Don't cross the bridge. Turn right just before the
bridge and follow the winding road for 1/2 mile to its end. You are now in the
general area of Haun's Mill.

On October 30, 1838, the Missouri militia attacked a settlement of Latter-day Saints
here at Jacob Haun's mill, which is located on Shoal Creek in eastern Caldwell County,
Missouri. Because the attack was unprovoked in a time of truce, had no specific author-
ization, and was made by a vastly superior force with unusual brutality, it has come to
be known as "The Haun's Mill Massacre." It was one incident in the conflict between the
Missourians and the Latter-day Saints that resulted in the Latter-day Saints' expulsion
from the state in 1839.

Smith, Joseph

307 Walnut Street
Carthage, Illinois
217-357-2989

The old jail in the town of Carthage, Illinois was the
site of the killing of Mormon founder Joseph Smith
and his brother Hyrum Smith by a mob of approximately 150 men. The two brothers had been arrested
for instigating a riot; to bring calm, Illinois Governor
Thomas Ford assured their protection if they would turn themselves in for trial.

The men complied, but on June 27, 1844, the Smiths, who were being held on the jail's
second floor along with John Taylor and Dr. Willard Richards, saw a large group of threat-
ening, armed men rush toward the jail. The anti-Mormon mob broke in and shot and killed
Hyrum first. Joseph leaped from the window and was shot twice in the back and twice in
the chest as he fell from the second story. John Taylor was shot four times but survived,
and Willard Richards escaped unharmed. The jail, which was constructed from 1839–40,
became a private home until 1903 when The Church of Jesus Christ of Latter-day Saints
bought it. They restored the building in 1938 and today it is open for tours.

The Mormons

Mountain Meadows Massacre

Mountain Meadows, Utah
(Located in the southwest corner of Utah, about 35 miles southwest of Cedar City via the old pioneer road, 54 miles via the current paved highway and 32 miles northwest of St. George, Utah)

On September 11, 1857, a wagon train laden with gold was attacked while passing through Utah. Approximately 140 people were slaughtered; only 17 children under the age of eight were spared. This incident, which took place in an open field called Mountain Meadows, has ever since been the focus of an important historical debate – were official Mormon dignitaries responsible for the massacre?

The Mountain Meadows Massacre was first blamed on American Indians, but many historians now believe early settlers of the Church of Jesus Christ of Latter-day Saints carried out the murders. (One of them, John D. Lee, was executed 20 years later for the event.) A monument to the victims is located on Dan Sill Hill, overlooking the valley where the tragedy took place.

MOVE Fire

6221 Osage Avenue
Philadelphia, Pennsylvania

On the morning of May 13, 1985, Philadelphia police officers arrived here in west Philly at the home of the radical group, MOVE, to serve arrest warrants on four MOVE members. They were met with gunfire, and police fired back, touching off a 90-minute gun battle; a bomb dropped by the police subsequently started a devastating fire.

Eleven years later, a jury ordered the city of Philadelphia and two former city officials to pay $1.5 million to a survivor and relatives of two MOVE members of the group who died in the fire. (The jury found that excessive force had been used and thus violated the MOVE members' constitutional protections against unreasonable search and seizure.) Ironically, a police station stands at this address today.

Mulholland/St. Francis Dam Break

San Francisquito Canyon Road
(Approximately 7.2 miles from the intersection of Copper Hill Road
and San Francisquito Canyon Road)
Santa Clarita, California

The St. Francis Dam, designed and built by William Mulholland in 1926 near Saugus in the San Francisquito Canyon, was 180 feet high and 600 feet long. In one of the greatest tragedies ever to hit California, the dam gave way on March 12, 1928, three minutes before midnight. Its waters swept through the Santa Clara Valley toward the Pacific Ocean, about 54 miles away. Sixty-five miles of valley were devastated before the water finally made its way into the ocean between Oxnard and Ventura.

At its peak, the wall of water was said to be 78 feet high; by the time it hit Santa Paula, 42 miles south of the dam, the water was estimated to be 25 feet deep. Almost everything in its path was destroyed: structures, railways, bridges, livestock and orchards. Over 500 people were killed and damage estimates topped $20 million. After the June 2002 "Copper Fire," this section of the Angeles National Forest was closed, but you can still drive along San Francisquito Canyon Road and see the ruins left by the devastating damn break.

Muskie, Edmund

The Union Leader
100 William Loeb Drive
Manchester, New Hampshire

On a snowy day in 1972, Edmund Muskie's presidential campaign went south after he supposedly started crying while defending his wife, Jane, against an attack from this local paper. *The Union Leader,* a conservative paper, wrote that Jane Muskie smoked cigarettes and wanted to tell dirty jokes on the campaign bus. In a moment which many say cost Muskie the Democratic nomination, he stood outside the paper's offices and denounced the newspaper, then broke into tears.

The Union Leader regularly plays a pivotal role in Primary politics; even J.F.K. was known to have stood in the parking lot in 1960 to publicly decry the paper's accusation that he was soft on communism.

Naval Pier Explosion

Port Chicago
Concord, California

Just before 10:20 P.M. on July 17, 1944, the worst home-front disaster of World War II occurred at a naval pier in the San Francisco Bay Area. Five thousand tons of ammunition being loaded into two ships by sailors exploded – sending a blast more than 12,000 feet into the sky. The explosion destroyed the pier, a train, and both ships, instantly killing everyone aboard (some 320 men) and injuring another 390, some as far as 15 miles away. The depot, now the Concord Naval Weapons Station, is about 30 miles northeast of San Francisco. A simple marker there stands on the shore of Suisun Bay where the explosion occurred.

9/11

On September 11, 2001, 19 terrorists hijacked four airplanes as part of an attack on the Pentagon in Washington, D.C., and the World Trade Center Towers in New York City. Three of the planes were flown into the buildings, resulting in the deaths of over three thousand individuals, the complete destruction of the Trade Center Towers, and extensive damage to the Pentagon. The fourth plane crashed in Southwestern Pennsylvania, killing all 44 people on board.

The primary crash sites at the former site of the World Trade Center and the Pentagon are well known and a matter of distinct public record. However, there are other lesser-known, but still notable sites related to that terrible day.

9/11

Mohammed Atta and Abdul Aziz Al-Omari

Various Sites

Two of the terrorist hijackers, Mohammed Atta and Abdul Aziz Al-Omari, operated mysteriously in Maine on September 10 (the day before the attacks) and on the morning of September 11, 2001. The following is a detailed account of their movements:

Monday, September 10, 2001
At 5:43 P.M., terrorists Mohammed Atta and Abdul Aziz Al-Omari checked into the Comfort Inn, located at 90 Maine Mall Road, South Portland, Maine.

Sometime between 8:00 P.M. and 9:00 P.M., two Middle-Eastern males were seen at Pizza Hut, 415 Maine Mall Road, South Portland, Maine, for approximately 15 minutes. It is believed the two were Atta and Al-Omari.

At exactly 8:31 P.M., Atta and Al-Omari were both photographed by a Key Bank drive-up ATM located at 445 Gorham Road, South Portland, Maine. They were driving a 2001 blue Nissan Altima rental car bearing Massachusetts license plate 3335VI.

At 8:41 P.M., Atta and Al-Omari were photographed by a Fast Green ATM located in the parking lot of Uno's restaurant, 280 Maine Mall Road, South Portland, Maine.

At 9:15 P.M., Atta and Al-Omari were at Jetport Gas Station, 446 Western Avenue, South Portland, Maine.

At 9:22 P.M., Atta was seen at Wal-Mart, 451 Payne Road, Scarborough, Maine, for approximately 20 minutes.

Tuesday, September 11, 2001
At 5:33 A.M., Atta and Al-Omari checked out of the Comfort Inn.

At 5:40 A.M., the 2001 blue Nissan Altima rental car, bearing Massachusetts license plate 3335VI, entered Portland International Jetport Airport parking lot. It was parked on the first floor directly across from the airport entrance.

At 5:43 A.M., Atta and Al-Omari both checked in at the U.S. Airways counter.

At 5:45 A.M., Atta and Al-Omari passed through airport security.

At 6:00 A.M., Atta and Al-Omari departed on Colgan Air en route to Boston, Massachusetts, where the attacks would soon commence.

9/11

Flight 93 Crash Site

Directions: From Somerset Interchange #10/110, go straight ahead to the 3rd traffic signal. Turn left onto Route 281 North, 10 miles to Route 30 East. Turn right onto Route 30 East, 3 miles to Highland Tank Manufacturing. Turn right onto Lambertsville Road, 2¹/₂ miles to Skyline Drive. Turn left onto Skyline Drive, 1¹/₂ miles to the United Flight 93 Memorial.

A memorial here marks the site where the brave passengers and crew of United Flight 93 brought their plane down after it was taken over by hijackers on September 11, 2001, saving perhaps thousands of lives.

Huffman Aviation International

400 East Airport Avenue
Venice, Florida

Mohammed Atta and Marwan Alshehhi, two of the suicide hijackers, learned to fly the planes that they would ultimately crash into the Twin Towers at this flight school. It is no longer in business.

9/11

President Bush

Emma E. Booker Elementary School
Sarasota, Florida

According to most reliable reports, President George W. Bush was informed of the first plane's hit into the World Trade Center while in his motorcade, on Highway 301, just north of Main Street in Sarasota, Florida. He was en route to an appearance at a local school, where he was to spend some time reading with grade school kids. Within minutes of entering the school, Andrew Card, Bush's chief of staff, told President Bush that a second passenger plane had hit the South Tower of the World Trade center.

Bush left soon after making a statement about the tragedy-in-progress and was then flown on Air Force One to Barksdale Air Force base near Shreveport, Louisiana, where he landed at about 11:45 A.M. From there, President Bush was shuttled to Offutt Air Force Base in Nebraska, home of the Strategic Air Command. There, the president established a telephone link to key security advisers.

Osama bin Laden

Gramercy Towers
1177 California Street
San Francisco, California

According to the *San Francisco Examiner*, 9/11 terrorist mastermind Osama bin Laden lived here at the Gramercy Towers, 1177 California Street on Nob Hill, in the 1970s. Little is known about his stay in the Bay Area.

Nixon, Richard

Ambassador Hotel

3400 Wilshire Boulevard
Los Angeles, California

Two of the defining moments in Richard Nixon's political career occurred here, at the same place where Robert F. Kennedy was shot in 1968. The first, the famous "Checkers" speech, took place on September 23, 1952. Appearing on the then-new medium of television, Nixon defended himself against a sensational headline that declared, "Secret Rich Men's Trust Fund Keeps Nixon in Style Far Beyond His Salary." With his wife, Pat, nearby, the newly-named running mate of Eisenhower described her "respectable Republican cloth coat" and the tale of "A little dog named Checkers given as a present to his young daughters." The humbling plea became a brilliant political maneuver and he and Ike won by a landslide that year.

The second Nixon moment here was a speech given on November 7, 1962. It was a concession speech made after losing the 1962 gubernatorial race to Pat Brown. Nixon, who was angry with the press, declared infamously during his rambling allegations, "You won't have Dick Nixon to kick around any more." The Ambassador Hotel itself still stands, but it has been closed since 1988 and there are no immediate plans to re-open it.

Nixon, Richard

Six Crises

901 North Bundy Drive
Brentwood, California

Richard Nixon leased this house after losing the 1960 presidential election to John F. Kennedy, and it is here that he wrote the best-selling book *Six Crises*. The book, considered by many to be one of the best ever written by a politician, focused on what Nixon considered the six most monumental moments of his political career up to 1961.

The first "crisis" is the "Hiss Case" in 1948, which catapulted a then-unknown Nixon into national prominence for the first time. The second crisis occurred in 1952 during Nixon's first vice-presidential campaign, when the press accused him of being a bribe-taker. (Nixon saved himself with the aforementioned "Checkers" speech.)

The third crisis occurred in 1955 when President Eisenhower had a heart attack, forcing Nixon to function as the "acting president" for a few weeks. Crisis number four occurred in 1958, when Nixon and his wife Pat were nearly killed by pro-Communist mobs in Venezuela. Number five came a year later when Nixon debated Nikita Krushchev in Moscow. And the sixth crisis was the hard-fought 1960 presidential campaign between Nixon and Senator John F. Kennedy.

Western White House

4100 Calle Isabella
San Clemente, California

Located in a gated community called Cypress Shores, this is where the famed Nixon hideaway (which he called Casa Pacifica) was located. Many others called it the Western

White House, and Nixon would visit frequently while president, entertaining such world leaders here as Leonid Brezhnev.

This is also where Nixon retreated after resigning during the Watergate scandal (he could often be seen taking lonely walks on the beach, talking to himself). The road is private, but the red-and-white adobe house, perched on the bluff overlooking the ocean, can be seen from the beach (a popular surfing spot called Cotton's Point). Nixon moved out in 1980.

Pearl Harbor

USS Arizona
1 Arizona Memorial Place
Honolulu, Hawaii
808-422-0561

On a quiet Sunday morning, December 7, 1941, a Japanese surprise air attack left the Pacific Fleet in smoldering heaps of broken, twisted steel. Approximately 100 ships of the U.S. Navy were present that morning, including battleships, destroyers, cruisers and various support ships. In a mere few hours, 2,390 lives were lost. The surprise attack was conceived by Japanese Admiral Isoroku Yamamoto; the striking force of 353 Japanese aircraft was led by Commander Mitsuo Fuchida. There had been no formal declaration of war.

Today, the USS Arizona Memorial serves as a national shrine symbolizing American sacrifice and resolve. The USS Arizona Visitor Center is located on the Pearl Harbor Naval Base adjacent to the sunken remains of the USS Arizona. The center is operated and maintained by the National Park Service in a use agreement with the U.S. Navy. The center and USS Arizona Memorial are free of charge to the public and there are no reservations.

Pearl Harbor

USS Missouri
11 Arizona Memorial Drive
Honolulu, Hawaii

Next to the USS Arizona Memorial, which marks the beginning of World War II, sits the USS Missouri, which marks the end of the war. On the deck of the USS Missouri, on September 2, 1945, General Douglas MacArthur accepted Japan's surrender, thereby ending World War II. On the Surrender Deck of the USS Missouri, visitors can experience the unmistakable voice of General MacArthur and see the precise spot where the surrender occurred and the world's bloodiest war came to an end.

Pluto is Discovered

Lowell Observatory
1400 West Mars Hill Road
Flagstaff, Arizona
928-774-3358

Lowell Observatory was founded by a man named Percival Lowell. Lowell was obsessed with the idea of discovering what he called a "trans-Neptunian" planet, which he believed could be detected from the effect it would have on Neptune's orbit. (The planet Neptune had been discovered in 1846 when the irregularities in the orbit of Uranus had been properly examined).

Lowell founded this observatory in his name and eventually funded three separate searches for this mysterious "Planet X." For the third search, observatory director Dr. Vesto Slipher hired a young man from Kansas named Clyde Tombaugh, and his hiring hunch paid off. On February 18, 1930, here in Flagstaff, Arizona, Clyde Tombaugh became the only American to discover a planet – Pluto.

Over the years, Tombaugh went on to discover a comet, five open clusters, and a super-cluster of galaxies stretching from Andromeda to Perseus. Clyde Tombaugh died at the age of 90 on January 17, 1997. Today at the Lowell Observatory, you can see the actual telescope used to discover Pluto, making it one of the most significant astronomical landmarks in the country.

Point Pleasant, Battle of

Point Pleasant, West Virginia
304-675-0869
(Located in west-central West Virginia, Point Pleasant lies 1 mile north of junction US 35 and WV 2 or at the intersection of WV 62 and WV 2 in Mason County. The park itself is just west of this intersection at 1 Main Street.)

The Battle of Point Pleasant, fought between the Long Knives of Virginia and the Shawnee Indians and their allies on October 10, 1774, was the final battle of Lord Dunmore's War and is considered by many to be the first battle of the American Revolution. Today, an 84-foot granite obelisk in the park honors the Virginia militiamen who gave their lives during the battle, while the statue of a frontiersman stands at the base. Other smaller memorial tablets can be seen in the park, including an interesting marker on the exact spot where Pierre Joseph de Celoron de Blainville, a French explorer, buried a leaden plate in 1749, claiming the land for his country.

Reagan, Ronald/Carter, Jimmy

Convention Center Music Hall
500 Lakeside Avenue
Cleveland, Ohio

Held just one week before the election, the October 28, 1980, debate between Reagan and Carter received much attention. In response to Carter's attack that he would cut Medicare, Reagan quipped, "There you go again." And in his closing remarks, Reagan famously asked, "Are you better off than you were four years ago?" producing two of the most memorable lines in presidential debate history.

Reagan, Ronald/Mondale, Walter

Music Hall, Municipal Auditorium
301 West 13th Street
Kansas City, Kansas
800-821-7060

On October 21, 1984, incumbent President Ronald Reagan and challenger Walter Mondale squared off in their second (and final) debate. The issue of age had been dogging Reagan, and when the subject was posed by a moderator, "The Great Communicator" uttered one of the great (albeit scripted) lines in modern political history. This was the exchange:

Henry Trewhitt (Moderator): "Mr. President . . . You already are the oldest president in history, and some of your staff say you were tired after your most recent encounter with Mr. Mondale. I recall, yes, that President Kennedy, who had to go for days on end with very little sleep during the Cuba missile crisis [sic]. Is there any doubt in your mind that you would be able to function in such circumstances?"

Reagan: "Not at all, Mr. Trewhitt, and I want you to know that also I will not make age an issue of this campaign. I am not going to exploit for political purposes my opponent's youth and inexperience. If I still have time, I might add, Mr. Trewhitt, I might add that it was Seneca or it was Cicero, I don't know which, that said if it was not for the elders correcting the mistakes of the young, there would be no state."

Reagan had effectively dismissed the concern and thus helped garner a re-election.

Roosevelt, Franklin Delano

Assassination Attempt

Bayfront Park
Miami, Florida

On February 13, 1933, Franklin D. Roosevelt gave a speech in Bayfront Park in the city of Miami, Florida, not knowing an Italian immigrant named Giuseppe Zangara was waiting for him. The 33-year-old Zangara, who worked as a brick layer, was clutching a .32 caliber pistol; as Roosevelt approached, he started shooting. Being only five feet tall, Zangara was unable to see over the crowd and had to stand on a wobbly wooden chair to get a clear shot at his target.

A gun novice, Zangara missed F.D.R. with all six shots fired. However, one bullet managed to hit Anton Cermak, the mayor of Chicago, who was touring with F.D.R. (Four other members of the crowd were also wounded.) "I'm glad it was me instead of you," Cermak told Roosevelt. He also asked: "Where was that SOB of a bodyguard?"

Cermak died later that day of an abdominal wound, and was the only fatality from the shooting. Zangara, who supposedly attempted the murder because he thought the president-elect was somehow supernaturally causing his severe stomach pain, was executed in the electric chair at Florida State Penitentiary on March 20, 1933.

His last words, spoken to the judge present at his execution, were, "You give me electric chair. I no afraid of that chair! You one of capitalists. You is crook man too. Put me in electric chair. I no care!" (It has also been documented that a Miami housewife named Lillian Cross may have helped save F.D.R.'s life by pulling on Zangara's arm to misdirect the shot.)

Roosevelt, Franklin Delano

Fireside Chats

The White House
Washington, D.C.

The Diplomatic Reception Room at the White House today serves as an entrance from the South Grounds for the president's family, as well as a location for arriving ambassadors to present their credentials to the president. In the past, the area served as a boiler and furnace room, but most famously was the site of President Franklin D. Roosevelt's fireside chats over the radio.

The first of these broadcasts occurred on Sunday evening, March 12, 1933, as a worried nation sat down to listen to its president. The U.S.A. was in the midst of the Great Depression and between one-quarter and one-third of the work force was unemployed. Every bank in America had been closed for eight days – many of them since March 1st – and much of the public had been scraping by on a combination of scrip, barter, and credit.

With chaos imminent, F.D.R. sat down to provide some comfort over the airwaves. Speaking simply and clearly, he began by explaining how the banking system worked, and went on to announce that the banks would reopen the next day (and that those that chose to participate would have most of their deposits guaranteed by the federal government). It was not the end of the Depression, but it was a light at the end of the tunnel – the end of the downward spiral that had brought the economy to a standstill.

Roosevelt would go on to give 30 more fireside chats from this room, which currently is not part of the regular White House tour.

Roosevelt, Franklin Delano

The Little White House

401 Little White House Road
Warm Springs, Georgia
706-655-5870

This rustic six-room cottage is where Franklin D. Roosevelt died in 1945. Nestled in the beautiful and rustic Pine Mountains, F.D.R. came here regularly to retreat from the pressures of the presidency and to take hot thermal baths for his polio.

F.D.R. first came to Warm Springs in 1924, hoping to find a cure for the infantile paralysis (polio) which had struck him in 1921. He built the Little White House in 1932 while he was Governor of New York, prior to being inaugurated as president in 1933.

While sitting for a portrait on April 12, 1945, during his 41st visit to this rural community of five hundred, F.D.R. suffered a massive stroke and died. Today, the "Unfinished Portrait" is a focal point of the Little White House tour. The house and furnishings have been carefully preserved very much as Roosevelt left them in 1945. Included on the tour is a museum, guest house, servants' quarters, pools, movie and two of his vehicles.

Roosevelt, Theodore

Maltese Cross Cabin

Medora, North Dakota
Directions: The South Unit entrance and visitor center are just off Interstate 94, exits 23 and 27, and are 135 miles west of Bismarck, North Dakota.

"I never would have been president if it had not been for my experiences in North Dakota," Theodore Roosevelt once remarked. Roosevelt first came here to the rugged badlands in September 1883 on a hunting trip. While staying here he became interested in the cattle business and invested in the Maltese Cross Ranch. He returned the following year and established the Elkhorn Ranch. Whenever he managed to spend time in the badlands, he became more and more alarmed by the damage that was being done to the land and its wildlife, and thus conservation became one of Roosevelt's major concerns.

To that end, during his presidency, Roosevelt established the U.S. Forest Service and signed the 1906 Antiquities Act under which he proclaimed 18 national monuments. He also established 5 national parks, 51 wildlife refuges and 150 national forests. Here, in the North Dakota badlands, where many of his personal concerns first gave rise to his later environmental efforts, Roosevelt is remembered with a national park that bears his name and honors the memory of this great conservationist. The actual Maltese Cross cabin, which was Roosevelt's first ranch house in the badlands, is located near the visitor center.

Roosevelt, Theodore

The Teddy Bear

The Onward Store
Intersection of Highway 61 and Highway 1 in Sharkey County
Onward, Mississippi

The event which led to the creation of the Teddy Bear occurred here, near the small town of Onward, in 1902, when President Theodore Roosevelt, acting upon the suggestion of some friends, visited the state on a hunt for wild game. A member of the hunting party located a bear for the president. The bear was exhausted and possibly lame – some claim it was a mere cub. In any case, Roosevelt found it unsporting and refused to shoot the helpless animal.

News of the president's refusal to shoot the bear spread far and wide. Soon after, Morris Michtom, a New York merchant, made toy history when he created a stuffed toy bear and labeled it "Teddy's Bear." His success was so great that it led to the formation of the Ideal Toy Corporation in 1903. Today, a marker next to the general store in Onward (near where Roosevelt met the bear) tells about the bear hunt and ensuing events.

Assassination Attempt

Gilpatrick Hotel
333 West Kilbourn Avenue
Milwaukee, Wisconsin

On October 14, 1912, while greeting the public here in front of the Gilpatrick Hotel before a campaign speech, Progressive Party presidential candidate Theodore Roosevelt (who had lost the 1912 Republican nomination to Taft and thus decided to form a third party so he could make another run at the office) was shot at close range by saloon keeper William Schrank.

Schrank's .32-caliber bullet was aimed at Roosevelt's heart, but failed to kill Roosevelt due to the fact that its force was slowed by a glasses case and a thick bundle of manuscripts in the breast pocket of Roosevelt's heavy coat – a manuscript containing Roosevelt's evening speech. Schrank was immediately apprehended. Roosevelt suffered only a minor flesh wound from the attack and delivered his speech that night with the bullet still in his body. After a few words, the former "Rough Rider" pulled the blood-stained manuscript from his pocket and powerfully declared, "You see, it takes more than one bullet to kill a Bull Moose."

As for the shooter, Shrank was deemed insane and committed to a mental hospital where he died in 1943. The Gilpatrick Hotel was partially razed in 1942 and then fully demolished in 1970. There is no marker at the site where the Hyatt Regency Hotel now stands.

San Jacinto Battleground

3523 Battleground Road (Texas Highway 134)
LaPorte, Texas
281-479-2431

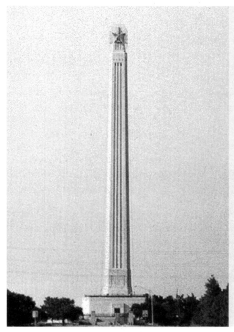

Located about 20 miles east of downtown Houston, The San Jacinto Battleground marks the exact spot where Texas won its independence from Mexico in 1836. Today, the 1,200-acre site commemorates the battle and preserves the battleground on which Texan troops, under General Sam Houston, achieved the independence of Texas by defeating a Mexican Army led by General Antonio Lopez de Santa Anna on April 21, 1836.

Visitors to the complex get to experience the towering San Jacinto Monument, the San Jacinto Museum of History and Battleship Texas. The battleship, commissioned in 1914, saw action in the Allied invasions of Normandy and Okinawa, and was presented to the people of Texas in 1948 as the first memorial ship. Admission is free.

Slater Mill

67 Roosevelt Avenue
Pawtucket, Rhode Island
401-725-8638

The old Slater Mill is sometimes referred to as the"Birthplace of American Industry." Built in 1793, it was the first factory in America to successfully produce cotton yarn with waterpowered machines. Today, the mill houses operating machinery used to illustrate the process of converting raw cotton to finished cloth.

Visitors to this "living history" museum can take part in the lives of the New England villagers, inventors, artisans and entrepreneurs who created the American Industrial Revolution. You can stroll the grounds and enter the authentic 18th- and 19th-century buildings, and meet costumed interpreters who will explain and demonstrate what life was like as America began moving from the farm to the factory back in the 1830s.

Thomas, Clarence

Russell Senate Office Building
Bounded by Constitution Avenue, First Street, Delaware Avenue, and C Street NE
Washington, D.C.

The Anita Hill-Clarence Thomas Hearings, conducted by the United States Senate Judiciary Committee to investigate Professor Anita Hill's allegations of prior sexual harassment by Supreme Court nominee Clarence Thomas, were televised nationally from October 11-13, 1991.

Although the hearings themselves had no legal significance, to many observers they symbolized a public referendum on sexual harassment and other gender inequities in

late 20th-century America. As riveting as live television could get, the hearings have been widely credited with increasing public awareness about gender discrimination and motivating female voters during the 1992 congressional elections. The hearings took place here in the Senate Caucus Room (room 325).

Truman, Harry S.

The Little White House
111 Front Street
Key West, Florida
305-294-9911

In 1946, President Harry S. Truman retreated to this house on Key West and ended up returning here to relax for 175 days during his presidency. Originally built as the first officer's quarters on the naval station, Quarters A became known as "the Winter White House." President Eisenhower used the home while recuperating from a heart attack in 1956, and in 1961, the Little White House played host to President John F. Kennedy and British Prime Minister Harold MacMillan during the Bay of Pigs incident.

Truman, Harry S.

Union Station
1820 Market Street, between 18th and 20th Streets
St. Louis, Missouri

The famous news photo of Harry Truman holding up a copy of the *Chicago Tribune* with a banner headline stating "DEWEY DEFEATS TRUMAN" on November 3, 1948, was taken here at this historic St. Louis train station.

On November 2, 1948, Truman and his family had voted in Independence, Missouri, and later went to Excelsior Springs where they spent the evening at the then-famous Elms Hotel waiting for election returns. Truman went to bed early, knowing that he was losing the election. When he woke up the next day, he learned that he had won, and began making his way to Washington, D.C. by train. While on a short stop in St. Louis, Truman was presented with one of the now-famous, prematurely printed "DEWEY DEFEATS TRUMAN" papers while on the back platform of the train. When asked to comment, Truman said, "This is for the books."

Note: The St. Louis Union Station has been restored and converted to a shopping mall. It's a beautiful facility worthy of a visit! A copy of the famous photo of Truman holding up the newspaper is displayed in the car.

The actual train that Truman stood on is located at the following museum: The Gold Coast Railroad, Inc., 12450 Southwest 152nd Street, Miami, Florida, 888-60-TRAIN. The Presidential Rail Car, U.S. Number 1, is a National Historic Landmark. When entering the car from the rear, one can see the platform used by the president for making speeches, especially when the car was used for "whistle stop" campaign trips.

Villa, Pancho

Pancho Villa State Park
Located 35 miles south of Deming via NM 11
Columbus, New Mexico
505-531-2711

On March 9, 1916, the soldiers of General Francisco "Pancho" Villa attacked the small border town and military camp at Columbus, New Mexico. Pancho Villa State Park contains extensive historical exhibits that depict this raid, which incidentally was the first armed invasion of the continental United States since the War of 1812 (and also the last). General "Black Jack" Pershing, who would later command the Allied forces of World War I, pursued Pancho Villa into Mexico. This 11-month pursuit led 10,000 American soldiers 400 miles into Mexico and ended without the capture of Pancho Villa.

Washington, George

Webb Deane Stevens Museum

211 Main Street
Wethersfield, Connecticut
860-529-0612

In 1752, merchant Joseph Webb built this large gambrel-roof house where George Washington met the Comte de Rochambeau to plan what would become the final campaign of the Revolutionary War at Yorktown. Tour the house today and you will see the original 18th-century flocked wallpaper hung in the chamber where Washington slept.

Washington's Headquarters

84 Liberty Street
Newburgh, New York
845-562-1195

The 1750-1770 home of Jonathan Hasbrouck became General George Washington's headquarters in 1782 and 1783. It was here in April of 1783 that Washington learned of the successful negotiation of the peace treaty with the British and announced to his troops the end of the American Revolution. Acquired and opened by the State of New York in 1850, this was the first publicly operated historic site in the United States. Today, the exhibits of artifacts recall the events of 1782-1783, when Washington's army stood ready for battle, and the house is furnished to appear as it did at the time the General, Mrs. Washington and their staff lived and worked in it.

Washington, George

Federal Hall Memorial

26 Wall Street
New York City, New York

This was the site of New York City's 18th-century City Hall, where George Washington was sworn in as president on April 30, 1789. Demolished in 1812, the current structure on the site was built as the Customs House in 1834–1842. In 1862, Customs moved to 55 Wall Street and the building became the U. S. Sub-Treasury. Millions of dollars of gold and silver were kept in the basement vaults until the Federal Reserve Bank replaced the Sub-Treasury system.

Water-to-Water Flight

Main Street (south end at ocean front)
Balboa, California

On May 10, 1912, Glenn L. Martin flew his own plane, built in Santa Ana, from the waters of the Pacific Ocean at Balboa to Catalina Island. This was the world's first water-to-water flight, and the longest and fastest over-water flight, to that date. On his return to the mainland, Martin carried the day's mail from Catalina – another first.

The Whitman Mission

Located in Southeast Washington, 7 miles west of Walla Walla, just off Highway 12
Near Walla Walla, Washington
509-529-2761

This historic site commemorates the role that Marcus and Narcissa Whitman played in establishing the Oregon Trail. The Whitmans were Christian missionaries who came west in covered wagons in 1836 and built their mission on this site in southeast Washington among the Cayuse Indians. The mission ended 10 years later when the Cayuse attacked and killed the Whitmans and 11 others and took more than 60 hostages. A hilltop monument has been erected at the site where the massacre took place. The deaths of the Whitmans sent a shock wave across the country and prompted Congress to make Oregon a U.S. territory.

The Women's Rights National Historical Park

136 Fall Street (U.S. 20)
Seneca Falls, New York
315-568-2991

As a 32-year-old mother of three, Elizabeth Cady Stanton felt like a "caged lioness," trapped and isolated in her home. After sharing her frustration with a group of Quaker abolitionists on July 9, 1848, the other women agreed wholeheartedly, and then demanded immediate action.

Ten days later, in the Wesleyan Chapel here in Seneca Falls, they held the First Women's Rights Convention in American history. Today, at the park, you can see the Elizabeth Cady Stanton House where she raised seven children and created a movement, the near-by the M'Clintock house, where the Declaration of Sentiments was written, and the actual preserved remains of the Wesleyan Chapel, site of The First Woman's Rights Convention.

The Yippies

30 St. Marks Place
New York City, New York

From 1967 to 1968, counter-culture spokesman Abbie Hoffman (along with Jerry Rubin) formed the radical group, the Yippies, in Hoffman's basement apartment where he lived with his wife, Anita. The Yippies (Youth International Party) went on to hold a Festival of Life at the 1968 Democratic National Convention, which led to violence and arrests.

These events led to the famous Chicago Seven trial (which started off as the Chicago Eight trial, but was reduced to seven when Bobby Seale of the Black Panthers was bound, gagged, and sent to prison for contempt of court). Going underground after some drug charges in the early 1970s, Hoffman emerged in 1980, served a brief prison sentence, and then re-entered the world of activism. He continued to fan the flames of campus revolution until his death by suicide in 1989. Today, there is a restaurant at this location.

The Yippies

Petrillo Band Shell in Grant Park
Near East Jackson and Columbus Drives
Chicago, Illinois

In 1968, this was the scene of the riot between the cops and the Yippies. Led by Abbie Hoffman and Jerry Rubin, the Yippies had organized a group 10,000-strong to protest during the 1968 Democratic National Convention. As the marchers approached the nearby Hilton Hotel, the police attacked in front of the world press, producing dramatic images that still resonate today.

Crime, Murder, and Assassination

Amedure, Scott

Chateau Orion Trailer Park
47 Bluebird Hill
Lake Orion, Michigan
248-373-0155

In March 1995, the *Jenny Jones Show* taped a segment about secret admirers and their fantasies, one of the more popular topics for daytime talk shows at the time. A man named Scott Amedure appeared on that segment and revealed that he had a secret, same-sex crush on another young man, Jonathan Schmitz. He also described a sexual fantasy involving Schmitz.

Three days later, on March 9, 1995, an angry and embarrassed Schmitz went to Amedure's home with a shotgun and fired two fatal blasts. Since Schmitz turned himself over to police and confessed an hour after the shooting, the trial that followed was never to determine guilt, but to decide the severity of the crime. In 1999, Schmitz was sentenced to prison for 25–50 years.

Barker, Ma

13250 East Highway C-25
Ocklawaha, Florida

On January 16, 1935, Ma Barker, leader of the Barker/Karpis gang, and her son, Fred, were shot and killed in a shootout here with the FBI. When the FBI agents knocked on the front door of this rental home near Lake Weir, 63-year-old Ma opened the door. Seconds later, 32-year-old Fred walked onto the porch and opened fire with a machine gun. For the next five hours, the two sides exchanged non-stop gunfire.

When the shooting from inside the house finally subsided, the agents entered and found Ma and Fred both dead. Ma was found in a second floor bedroom, where she had been shot three times. Her machine gun, still hot, was clutched across her breast. The house was riddled with nearly 3,500 bullets; the bodies of Ma and Fred were taken to Pyles Funeral home in Ocala.

Though the house, which sits on the property of a family estate, is not open for tours, the Lake Weir Chamber of Commerce still sponsors yearly re-enactments of the shootout. Call the Weir Chamber of Commerce (352-288-3751) for details

Bonnie and Clyde

James Dean Died Here included the location of the exact spot in Louisiana where Bonnie and Clyde were ambushed and killed by law enforcement officers. What follows here are other sites connected to the deadly duo who, although glamorized by Warren Beatty and Faye Dunaway in their 1967 cinematic paean, were in fact ruthless, cold-blooded killers. Note: Though unconfirmed, it is believed the pair spent their last night alive at the Old Grace Hotel on Oak Street in St. Joseph, Missouri (the building is no longer standing).

Bonnie and Clyde

Ambush

3111 North Winnetka
West Dallas, Texas

On January 6, 1933, Bonnie and Clyde were ambushed here in the home of Lillie McBride, the sister of Raymond Hamilton, a member of the notorious Clyde Barrow gang (the house is just around the corner from the Barrow Filling Station, where Clyde grew up).

Police had been staking out this house after investigating a bank robbery involving Odell Chambless, a friend of Clyde's. They were waiting for Chambless, who they thought might show up here, when at about midnight, a car pulled up to the residence and Clyde, not Chambless, got out of the vehicle.

Realizing he'd stepped into a trap, Clyde opened fire, killing deputy officer Malcolm Davis by the front porch. The car – which police believe carried either Chambless or Bonnie Parker – sped away and Barrow escaped on foot. (Davis died from his injuries before he reached the hospital.)

"The Devil's Back Porch"

On Singleton Boulevard heading toward Irving, as you approach the
West Fork Trinity River.
Near Irving, Texas

Back in the 1930s, this was a wide, desolate area known by locals as "The Devil's Back Porch." Today much of the expansive area has been developed into golf courses and homes, but in 1933 it was a desolate, dusty road in the middle of nowhere, perfect for Bonnie and Clyde's clandestine meetings. This was where they'd get back in touch, take photos and spend time together with loved ones before heading off to commit the next crime.

Bonnie and Clyde

Sowers Community Ambush Site

Intersection of Highway 183 (Airport Freeway) and Esters Road
Irving, Texas

Acting on an anonymous tip, sheriff's deputies ambushed Bonnie and Clyde here on November 22, 1933. The duo had met with family members here the day before so the cops had a good idea of where to wait. Still, they once again eluded the law. Although their car was shot up and they were both seriously wounded, Bonnie and Clyde managed to escape. (Two of the deputies, Ted Hinton and Bob Alcorn, would also be participants in the final ambush, which occurred a few months later near Gibsland, Louisiana.) Today, the area is much more developed than it was in 1933.

The Grapevine Murders

Intersection of Route 114 and Dove Road
Near Grapevine, Texas (just west of Dallas)

On Easter Sunday, April 1, 1934, Bonnie and Clyde and their partner, Henry Methvin, headed east on Highway 114 and turned north on Dove Lane, about six miles west of Grapevine. The team parked their 1934 Ford sedan along the side of the road and, while Methvin stood guard, Bonnie and Clyde caught up on some much-needed sleep. Roughly one-half hour later, two state troopers pulled up next to the car. Upon their approach, Methvin opened fire, killing one of the troopers instantly, and fatally wounding the other. Clyde put the pedal to the metal and they escaped down the highway. Today, a 6-foot monument sits at the exact spot where the troopers, E.B. Wheeler and H.D. Murphy, were killed.

Campbell, Cal

Main Street, just north of the police station
Commerce, Oklahoma

After the Grapevine murders, Bonnie and Clyde and their partner, Henry Methvin, drove to Oklahoma, where their truck got stuck in the mud. They flagged down a motorist to help push them out, but the alarmed driver alerted authorities instead after seeing the guns. Police Chief Percy Boyd and Constable Cal Campbell headed out to the location to investigate, and ended up exchanging gunfire with the criminals. Campbell was killed; his injured partner surrendered and was taken for a ride with the crew. They stopped at Ft. Scott near the Missouri border to buy a paper, enjoyed a picnic in the woods and then released Boyd nine miles south of Ft. Scott. Today, in the park off of Main Street just north of the police station, is a monument honoring Cal Campbell.

Bonnie and Clyde

Conger's Furniture Store and Funeral Parlor

North Railroad Street
Arcadia, Louisiana

After Bonnie and Clyde were killed on May 23, 1934, the motorcade towing the bullet-ridden car – with their bodies still inside – arrived here in Arcadia at Conger's Furniture Store and Funeral Parlor. The bodies were taken inside where an autopsy was performed, and the streets of Arcadia became flooded with curiosity-seekers straining for a peek at the slain criminals. The building has since been abandoned.

Booth, John Wilkes

Surratt House and Tavern
On Brandywine Road, just west of Route 5 and south of Route 223
(Woodyard Road)
Clinton, Maryland
301-868-1121

John Wilkes Booth and David Herold stopped here briefly on the night of the Lincoln assassination to retrieve guns and supplies they'd stashed earlier. The debate still goes on today as to the involvement of one Mary Surratt, who ran this boarding house at the time. (Eventually, she was hanged for her alleged role in the plot.) Today, guided tours are offered and the visitor center/gift shop is full of assassination materials and information related to the event.

Booth, John Wilkes

Dr. Samuel A. Mudd House
Dr. Samuel Mudd Road
Near Waldorf, Maryland
301-274-9358
Directions: Head south on State Route 5 and US 301 from Washington and
Baltimore. Turn left on State Route 5 South, marked "Lexington Park and
Leonardtown." Follow Route 5 (Mattawoman-Beantown Road) approximately
3 miles to Poplar Hill road (traffic light). Turn left. Follow Poplar Hill Road
approximately 3 miles to fork in road. Bear to your right on Dr. Samuel Mudd
Road. The Dr. Mudd House is one-quarter mile down on the right.
There is a sign at the entrance.

On April 14, 1865, John Wilkes Booth shot and killed President Abraham Lincoln. Booth
broke his left leg leaping to the stage at Ford's Theater and sought out Dr. Samuel Mudd
here at Mudd's house. Booth (and David Herold) arrived here at approximately 4:00 A.M.
on April 15, 1865. Mudd set, splinted, and bandaged Booth's broken leg. (Even though
Mudd had met Booth on at least two prior occasions, he claimed he did not recognize his
patient. He said the two used the names "Tyson" and "Henston.")

Booth and Herold stayed at the Mudd residence for roughly 12 hours. Mudd asked his
handyman, John Best, to make a pair of crutches for Booth, and Mudd was paid $25 for
his services. Several days later, Dr. Mudd was arrested by the United States Government
and charged with conspiracy and harboring Booth and Herold during their escape. He
was found guilty and sentenced to life imprisonment at Fort Jefferson in the Dry
Tortugas. However, in 1869, Mudd was pardoned by President Andrew Johnson, who
cited doubts about Mudd's guilt and noted his efforts during a yellow fever outbreak at
the prison.

The property today consists of the House Museum, Gift Shop, Kitchen, Exhibit Building
and some outbuildings located on 10 acres. The museum is open for public tours the first
weekend of April through late November. Museum hours are 11:00 A.M. to 4:00 P.M.
Saturday, Sunday and Wednesday.

Boston Strangler

Boston, Massachusetts

A brutal attack spree in Boston, Massachusetts — in which the attacker would first sexually molest his victims and then strangle them — began in the summer of 1962 and did not end until the winter of 1964. Ultimately, a man named Albert DeSalvo was arrested and convicted of the crimes, but there is still speculation as to whether or not he was the Boston Strangler. Although he had already confessed, DeSalvo later recanted and was killed in 1973, the night before he was to meet with a psychiatrist and reporter to "reveal" the "real killer" and why he had confessed to the crimes.

These are all of the known crime scenes of the Boston Strangler:

Anna A. Sleeser's House
77 Gainsborough Road
Boston, Massachusetts

Nina Nichols' House
1940 Commonwealth Avenue
Boston, Massachusetts

Ida Irga's House
7 Grove Avenue
Boston, Massachusetts

Jane Sullivan's House
435 Columbia Road
Boston, Massachusetts

Sophie Clark's House
315 Huntington Avenue
Boston, Massachusetts

Patricia Bissette's House
515 Park Avenue
Boston, Massachusetts

Mary Sullivan's House
44A Charles Street
Boston, Massachusetts

Boudin, Kathy

Nanuet Mall
Route 59 and Middletown Road
Nanuet, New York

On October 20, 1981, a gang of radical revolutionaries staged a daylight assault on a Brinks armored car at the Nanuet Mall, killing guard Peter Paige and severely wounding guard Joseph Trombino. The robbers then drove in a van from the mall and met up with a U-Haul truck in the parking lot of the former Korvettes department store, where Pathmark supermarket's parking lot is now, on Route 59 in Nanuet.

Waiting in the truck was wet-behind-the-ears radical Kathy Boudin, along with fellow 1960's revolutionary David Gilbert, who was acting as driver. After ditching the van, the gang left in the U-Haul truck but were stopped by a Nyack police roadblock at the entrance to the New York State Thruway.

When the gang was confronted, Boudin left the truck and approached the officers. She claims she was giving herself up. Police contend she distracted the officers into putting down their guns. Today, many believe this was an ambush – she had raised her hands and asked the officers to put away their guns. At that point, the six gunmen who'd committed the bank robbery jumped out of the rear of the truck with automatic weapons drawn.

In the ensuing gun battle between police and the revolutionaries, Officers Edward O'Grady and Wavery Brown were killed and another officer was wounded. In a move that stunned many, Boudin was recently released on parole after serving just 22 years in prison.

Brady, Al

Central Street (at the corner where Main and State Streets meet Central Street)
Bangor, Maine

By 1937, Al Brady had become one of the nation's worst criminals. Just 26 years old, Brady already had four murders and over 150 robberies to his credit. After becoming Public Enemy Number One, Brady attempted to lose the FBI by taking up residence in the relative sleepiness of Bangor, Maine. However, Brady blew his own cover when he and his gang tried to order Thompson submachine guns from a local sporting goods store. The owner became suspicious, alerted the Feds, and soon the town was crawling with undercover agents.

Upon returning to the sporting goods shop on September 21, 1937, two of Brady's gang were arrested. Seeing this from their getaway car, Brady and an accomplice opened fire. Sixty shots later, Brady was dead, as was his partner in the car. A plaque marks the exact site of the battle, and the manhole covers located in front of the plaque are the actual ones upon which Brady died.

Brawley, Tawana

Pavilion Apartments
24 Carnaby Street
Wappinger's Falls, New York

In November 1987, a 15-year-old girl named Tawana Brawley was discovered here at an apartment complex in upstate New York, covered with feces and racial slurs written in charcoal. Brawley, who is black, told police she had been abducted and raped by six white law enforcement officers. Her case was ultimately thrown out in 1988 when a grand jury determined that her story was not credible on any level whatsoever.

Ten years after the incident, the three men who had advised Brawley — Al Sharpton, Alton Maddox, and lawyer C. Vernon Mason — were sued by one of the six men accused by Brawley — Steven Pagones, then a local prosecutor. The trial began in December 1997 and on July 13, 1998, a jury found the three advisors liable for defaming Pagones. The jury awarded Pagones $345,000 in damages — about two percent of the amount he originally sought. Sharpton was found liable for $65,000 of the total damages, Maddox for $95,000 and Mason for $185,000. (Brawley was initially discovered by a neighbor behind the building containing units 17, 19 and 21.)

Capone, Al

93 Palm Avenue
Palm Island, Florida

Gangster Al Capone died here on January 25, 1947, in his mansion in Biscayne Bay, near Miami. The notorious Capone ultimately expired from both the physical and mental damage caused by a long bout with syphilis. The home (built by St. Louis beer-brewing magnate Clarence Busch for $40,000) remains virtually the same as when Capone passed away. It is a private residence and is not open for tours.

The Central Park Jogger

Along the 102nd Street cross-drive near Loch Ravine
Central Park
New York City, New York

On the night of April 19, 1989, "wilding" entered the vocabulary of New Yorkers as groups of (mostly) teenage black and Hispanic men roamed through New York City's Central Park, robbing, assaulting and raping random victims. One of the victims was a 28-year-old white women who was beaten, raped, hit in the head with a rock, and left for dead. At first she wasn't expected to live. Then, after coming out of a 12-day coma, she was thought to have suffered severe brain damage. However, she miraculously recovered over the years and went on to write a book about the event. Eventually, the convictions of her attackers were overturned when another man confessed to the crime.

Chambers, Robert

Dorrian's Red Hand
1616 Second Avenue
New York City, New York
212-772-6660

This is the Upper East Side bar where convicted "Preppie Murderer" Robert Chambers picked up his victim-to-be, Jennifer Levin, on August 26, 1986. Soon after, the pair went to a secluded part of Central Park called "Cleopatra's Needle," near 5th Avenue and East

82nd Street. Chambers' lawyers claimed that they were having sex together and that their rough play went too far, resulting in Ms. Levin's death. Chambers, however, discarded that defense and pled guilty. He received a sentence of 5 to 15 years and was released in February 2003.

Close, Bill

KTSP-TV
511 West Adams
Phoenix, Arizona

On the night of May 28, 1982, a mentally disturbed cement finisher named Joe Billie Gwin entered the KTSP-TV studio with a gun and demanded that he be allowed to deliver an urgent message on live television. After five hours of negotiating, police agreed to let him go on air. At 9:30 P.M., Gwin, holding his pistol at the head of newscaster Bill Close, forced Close to read Gwin's incoherent statement on racism, homosexuality and World War III. Gwin was arrested immediately afterwards.

Dalton Gang

Dalton Gang Hideout

502 South Pearlette Street (four blocks south of US 54)
Meade, Kansas
620-873-2731

At one time this was the house of Eva Dalton and her husband, John Wipple. That was until the early 1890s when Eva's siblings, Bob, Emmett and Gratton Dalton, the mythi-

cal Dalton Brothers, moved in. The gang dug a 95-foot-long tunnel under the house to their hideout in the barn. The house still stands as originally built in 1887, but the tunnel has been enlarged and restored and the barn has been rebuilt (it now houses a museum).

The hideout and escape tunnel are visited by thousands of people every year. The Meade County Historical Society maintains the property, and the museum displays Dalton Gang photographs and newspaper clippings, period clothing, civil war artifacts, a barbed wire collection, many guns and some natural oddities as well. A small admission is charged for adults; children are admitted free.

Dalton Gang

Death Alley

812 1/2 Walnut Street
Coffeyville, Kansas

Around 9:30 A.M., the morning of October 5, 1892, five members of the Dalton Gang (Gratton Dalton, Emmett Dalton, Bob Dalton, Bill Powers and Dick Broadwell) rode into the small town of Coffeyville, Kansas. Their objective was to achieve financial security and make outlaw history by simultaneously robbing two banks. From the beginning, their audacious plan went astray. The hitching post where they intended to tie their horses had been torn down due to road repairs. This forced the gang to hitch their horses in a nearby alley – a fateful decision.

To disguise their identity (Coffeyville was the Dalton's hometown), two of the Daltons wore false beards and wigs. Despite this, the gang was recognized as they crossed the town's wide plaza, split up and entered the two banks. Suspicious townspeople watched through the banks' front windows as the robbers pulled their guns. Someone on the street shouted, "The bank is being robbed!" and the citizens quickly armed themselves – taking up firing positions around the buildings. The ensuing firefight lasted less than 15 minutes. Four townspeople lost their lives, four members of the Dalton Gang were gunned down, and this small Kansas town became part of history.

Today, you can walk the same path taken by the Daltons in 1892 as they attempted to rob the two banks. Markers show the location of the three Coffeyville citizens – Lucius Baldwin, George Cubine and Charles Brown – who were killed in the gunfire north of Isham Hardware, and a fourth marker in "Death Alley" shows the location where Marshall Connelly was killed. Also in the alley you will see the old jail which has replicas of the Daltons as they were laid out following their death. Three of the Daltons were killed in the alley – the fourth died while attempting to flee Coffeyville. Look closely at the north brick wall in Death Alley to see bullet holes from the gun battle.

Condon Bank

809 Walnut Street
Coffeyville, Kansas
800-626-3357

This is one of the two banks the Dalton Gang attempted to rob in the Dalton Raid in 1892. Built in 1890 by Luther Perkins, the building was owned by First National Bank and occupied by the Condon Bank in 1892. Over the years, the building has been home to many offices and today is occupied by the Community Relations Department of the Coffeyville Area Chamber of Commerce.

The D.C. Snipers
Maryland; Washington, D.C.; and Virginia

For three long weeks they terrorized the nation, most specifically Maryland, Washington, D.C., Virginia (and now it is also believed, Alabama). Finally, 42-year-old John Allen Muhammad, a veteran of the Gulf War in 1991, and his stepson, 17-year-old John Lee Malvo, were caught sleeping in their own car, a Chevrolet Caprice, at an Interstate 70 rest area near Middletown, Maryland.

After receiving a tip, members of the police task force investigating the recent sniper attacks blocked off the highway exit and arrested the men. Police found a gun in the suspects' car; the criminals had supposedly shot it 13 times, killing 10 innocent people, and wounding three. Police also found a scope and a tripod. The ensuing investigation reported that the criminals probably shot the victims without even leaving the car, as there was an opening in the trunk that would allow them to lie hidden and shoot the victims.

Below are the exact dates and locations of each shooting. As of this writing, both men have been convicted of these crimes. John Allen Muhammad was sentenced to death for his part in the sniper spree; accomplice Lee Boyd Malvo was sentenced to life in prison without parole.

October 2, 2002 – 13850 Georgia Avenue
Aspen Hill, Maryland
Windows shot at Michael's craft store.

October 2, 2002 – 2201 Randolph Road
Wheaton, Maryland
Man killed at Shoppers Food Warehouse.

October 3, 2002 – 11411 Rockville Pike
White Flint, Maryland
Man killed while cutting grass at auto dealership.

October 3, 2002 – Aspen Hill Road and Connecticut Avenue
Aspen Hill, Maryland
Man killed at Mobil gas station.

October 3, 2002 – 3701 Rossmoor Boulevard
Norbeck, Maryland
Woman killed outside post office.

The D.C. Snipers
Maryland; Washington, D.C.; and Virginia

October 3, 2002 – Knowles and Connecticut Avenue
Kensington, Maryland
Woman killed at gas station.

October 3, 2002 – Georgia Avenue and Kalmia Road
Washington, D.C.
Man killed while standing on the street.

October 4, 2002
Fredericksburg, Virginia
Woman wounded in Michael's craft store.

October 7, 2002 – 4901 Collington Road
Bowie, Maryland
13-year-old boy wounded as he is dropped off at school.

October 9, 2002 – 7203 Sudley Road
Manassas, Virginia
Man killed at Sunoco gas station.

October 11, 2002 – US 1 and Market Street
Massaponax, Virginia
Man killed at Exxon gas station.

October 14, 2002 – Arlington Boulevard and Patrick Henry Drive
Falls Church, Virginia
Woman killed at Home Depot.

October 19, 2002 – SR 54 & I-95
Ashland, Virginia
Man wounded at Ponderosa Steak House. This is near the site where the suspects
called the FBI from a payphone; they also left the note that helped lead to their capture
behind the Ponderosa. It was not the first time they'd left a communique. At a shooting
scene on October 7th, the sniper reportedly left a tarot death card inscribed, "Dear
Policeman, I am God."

October 22, 2002 – 14100 block of Grand Pre Road
Aspen Hills, Virginia
Man killed.

Ferguson, Colin

Merillon Avenue Train Station
Nassau Boulevard and Merillon Avenue, just South of Jericho Turnpike
(Route 25)
Garden City, New York

On December 7, 1993, a deranged killer named Colin Ferguson marched up the aisle of a crowded, evening rush-hour Long Island Railroad car, arbitrarily shooting passengers as the train pulled into the Merillon Avenue station. Ferguson's shooting rampage killed six — four were pronounced dead on the scene — and injured more than a dozen others. In the end, after a bizarre trial in which Ferguson defended himself and actually questioned his shooting victims, he was sentenced to six consecutive life sentences — about 200 years of prison time.

Flores, Juan

Barton Mound
Southeast corner of I-405 and State Hwy 133
Two miles south of East Irvine, California

In 1857, the notorious outlaw Juan Flores, who had recently escaped from San Quentin prison, was being sought by lawman James Barton and his posse of five men. Near this

mound (now called Barton Mound), Flores surprised Barton and three of his men — all four were killed. (Sheriff Barton and Deputies Little, Baker and Daly became the first lawmen in Los Angeles County to lose their lives in the line of duty.)

When authorities in Los Angeles learned of the slaughter, a new posse was formed. Led by General Andrés Pico, the posse went on to trap Flores and his men on Flores Peak, located in the Tucker Wildlife Sanctuary, on the north side of Modjeska Canyon Road in Modjeska Canyon, California (about 20 miles from the Barton Mound site). Flores escaped that day by jumping from the peak, but was captured soon thereafter.

Floyd, Pretty Boy

Sprucevale Road between Beaver Creek State Park and Clarkson
Near East Liverpool, Ohio

The gangster Charles Arthur "Pretty Boy" Floyd was killed here on the farm of Mrs. Ellen Conkle. On October 19, 1934, Floyd had been spotted after robbing the Tiltonsville Peoples Bank with two other men. Police and FBI were put on alert throughout Ohio for the suspects. The following day a shootout between the criminals and the Wellsville, Ohio police ended in the capture of Richetti, Floyd's partner, but Floyd escaped.

On October 22, 1934, things would finally come to a fatal end for Pretty Boy Floyd. He entered the Conkle's house by posing as a lost hunter and asked for a ride to the bus. Ellen Conkle fed him (a meal for which Floyd paid one dollar), then sent her brother to drive him to the bus station. As they got into the car, two police cars sped by, and Floyd jumped from the car to hide behind a corncrib. Police spotted and recognized Floyd, who decided to flee. Ignoring the cop's demand to stop, he was shot in the arm. Continuing to run, he was shot again, only this time he fell to the ground. He dropped his gun, grabbed his right forearm where he had been hit, and died several moments later under an apple tree. (His body was taken to the Sturgis Funeral Home in East Liverpool.) A plaque placed by the East Liverpool Historical Society marks the exact spot where Floyd was shot.

Gein, Eddie

Near Plainfield, Wisconsin

On November 17, 1957, police in Plainfield, Wisconsin, arrived at the run-down farmhouse of one Eddie Gein, a suspect in the robbery of a local hardware store and subsequent disappearance of the owner, Bernice Worden. (Gein had been the last customer at the hardware store and had been witnessed lingering around the premises.)

Police found the desolate Gein farmhouse a gross tangle of cluttered chaos, with junk and old rotting food all over the place. But the worst was yet to come. The local sheriff, Arthur Schley, felt something brush against his jacket as he inspected the kitchen. To his shock, he then came face to face with a large, dangling carcass hanging upside down from the ceiling beams. The carcass (which turned out to be Bernice Worden) had been decapitated, slit open and gutted. Upon further inspection, the shocked deputies soon discovered that they were standing amidst a human corpse warehouse. The funny-looking bowl was the top of a human skull. The  lampshades and wastebasket were made from human skin. And there was more: An armchair made of human skin, a human head, four noses and a heart.

This bizarre scenario soon inspired Author Robert Bloch to write a story about Norman Bates, which became the central theme of Albert Hitchcock's classic thriller *Psycho*. In 1974, Tobe Hooper's horror flick *The Texas Chainsaw Massacre* was also loosely based on the Gein story. Years later, Gein was the inspiration for the serial killer Buffalo Bill in *The Silence of the Lambs*. (Like Eddie, Buffalo Bill treasured women's skin and wore it like clothing in an insane transvestite ritual.)

Gein eventually confessed to killing two women, who, he said, resembled his mother. (Police suspect he killed many more given the physical evidence.) Despite the evidence, he insisted he had not committed necrophilia or cannibalism, but merely decorated himself and his house with female body parts. Although police could only link him to the murders of the two women, he was suspected of having killed five other people, including his brother and two other men who had worked on the farm. Eddie Gein was found insane and committed to Central State Hospital at Waupon. In 1978, he was moved to the Mendota Mental Health Institute where he remained until his death in 1984; he was 77 years old. Today, there is nothing left of the farmhouse.

Gilmore, Gary

Sinclair Gas Station
168 East and 800 North
Orem, Utah

City Center Inn
150 West, 300 South
Provo, Utah

These are the locations where killer Gary Gilmore murdered two victims by shooting them in the head (after they complied with him to lie down). The killing spree took place on July 19, 1976 – just three months after Gilmore had been released from prison for prior offenses. Once captured, Gilmore refused to fight the execution sentence and on January 17, 1977, he was executed by firing squad. The Norman Mailer book about Gilmore, *Executioner's Song,* was made into a television mini-series starring Tommy Lee Jones.

Golden Dragon Massacre

Golden Dragon Restaurant
816 Washington Street
San Francisco, California
415-398-3920

On July 4, 1977, the Golden Dragon Restaurant was the site of a bloody assassination-attempt gone awry. It was the result of a long-standing feud between two notorious Chinatown gangs and resulted in the deaths of five innocent bystanders (including two tourists) with another 11 injured.

Grubman, Lizzie

Conscience Point Inn
1976 North Sea Road
Southampton, Long Island, New York
516-204-0600

It was here at this Long Island Club on July 7, 2001, that Lizzie Grubman, the high-profile New York celebrity publicist, made headlines when she backed her SUV into a crowd of clubgoers, severely injuring 16 of them. A bouncer at the club told her to move her father's Mercedes-Benz SUV from the fire lane. After calling the bouncer a piece of "white trash," she got in the SUV, fired it into reverse, and rammed into the bouncer and 15 other people. She then drove away without waiting for police to arrive. Eventually, Grubman was brought to trial and served 37 days in jail after pleading guilty to assault and leaving the scene. She offered a tearful apology in front of reporters and, after her release from jail, began a new job as a gossip and entertainment reporter for a New York radio station.

Hardin, John Wesley

**Acme Saloon
227 East San Antonio
El Paso, Texas**

On August 19, 1885, noted gunslinger John Wesley Hardin was in the Acme Saloon rolling dice for drinks, then turned to a friend and said, "Brown, you have four sixes to beat." At that instant, Constable John Selman approached and shot Hardin in the head, killing him instantly.

Hardin (who was rumored to be so mean he once shot a man for snoring) had killed upward of 30 people in his life, and fled with his family to Florida after killing a deputy sheriff in 1874. During that

flight, he killed at least one, and perhaps as many as five more victims, and was captured by Texas Rangers in Pensa-cola on July 23, 1877. On September 28, 1878, Hardin was sentenced to 25 years for the Brown County deputy's murder.

Pardoned on March 16, 1894, Hardin was admitted to the Texas bar soon after his release (he had studied law while in prison). In 1895, Hardin headed to El Paso to testify for the defense in a murder trial and, following the trial, he ended up staying and establishing a law practice.

Things seemed to be straightening out for the one-time killer until he became involved in an affair with one of his married female clients. The woman's husband found out about the affair and learning of this, Hardin supposedly hired some law officials to kill the husband. However, the plan backfired – it ended up that one of the hired gunmen, Constable John Selman, shot Hardin after he rolled the dice at the bar. (Today the building is known as the Old Lerner Store.)

James, Jesse

Nimrod Long and Company

296 South Main Street
Russellville, Kentucky

On the afternoon of March 20, 1868, the James Gang, comprised of outlaw Jesse James, his brother Frank James and four others, robbed Nimrod Long and Company, a local bank. The actual robbery scene is now a private home; the bank (now called The Old Southern Bank) moved down the street to Sixth and Main Streets and today features a lobby mural depicting the legendary heist.

First National Bank

Scriver Building
408 Division Street
Northfield, Minnesota
507-645-9268

Today this building houses the Northfield Historical Museum, but back on September 7, 1876, this was where the townspeople of Northfield rose up against the notorious James Gang when they attempted to rob the First National Bank.

James and his gang didn't realize how well-armed and well-prepared the people of Northfield were to do battle, but after killing the bank's cashier, they were engaged in seven minutes of bloody, dramatic gunfire with the townsfolk. The famous band of out-laws saw two of their own killed and several others hunted down over the course of the next 10 days. Only Jesse and Frank James escaped by heading to South Dakota. Thus, the humiliated gang made away with nothing that day, and was disbanded forever.

The James Farm

21216 James Farm Road
Kearney, Missouri 64060
816-628-6065

Outlaw Jesse James was shot and killed in this house on April 3, 1882, by Bob Ford, a member of the James gang. Ford killed James to collect a $10,000 reward offered by Governor Tom Crittenden. At the time, the 34-year-old Jesse James was living with his wife and two children under the assumed name of Tom Howard. Jesse was shot from behind while he stood on a chair to straighten a picture in his own home.

Today at the farm, visitors can see artifacts from James's grave including the coffin han-dles; a small tie pin Jesse James was wearing the day he was killed; a bullet removed from his right lung area; and a casting of his skull, showing the bullet hole behind his right ear. (The famous bullet hole from the fatal shot also remains under Plexiglas in the wall.)

Kansas City Massacre

Union Station Kansas City
30 West Pershing Road
Kansas City, Missouri
816-460-2020

On the morning of June 17, 1933, a bloodbath in front of Union Railway Station took the lives of four peace officers and their prisoner. The Kansas City Massacre involved the attempt by Charles Arthur "Pretty Boy" Floyd, Vernon Miller and Adam Richetti to free their friend, Frank Nash, a Federal prisoner. At the time, Nash was in the custody of several law enforcement officers who were returning him to the U.S. Penitentiary at Leavenworth, Kansas, from which he had escaped on October 19, 1930.

Six months after the massacre, Vernon Miller was murdered by fellow mobsters in Detroit. In October of 1934, "Pretty Boy" Floyd was killed in a shoot-out with FBI Agents on a farm in Ohio. Adam Richetti was arrested in 1934 and, after a trial and conviction for murder, was executed in the gas chamber at the Missouri State Penitentiary. (Note: Some of the bullet holes from the thunderous shootout are still visible near the train station's east entrance.)

Kelly, Machine Gun

327 Northwest 18th Street
Oklahoma City, Oklahoma

On Saturday, July 22, 1933, Mr. and Mrs. Charles F. Urschel, one of Oklahoma's wealthiest couples, were playing bridge with Mr. and Mrs. Walter R. Jarrett on a screened-in porch here at the posh Urschel home. Suddenly, two armed men burst in and hastily asked which of the two men was Charles Urschel. Perhaps from fright, neither couple uttered a word, and so the crooks remarked, "Well, we will take both of them."

One of the abductors was the notorious George "Machine Gun" Kelly; the other was his partner, Albert Bates. News of the sensational crime swept the nation and the government responded by sending agents from the Department of Justice's Bureau of Investigation, later called the FBI. After a ransom was paid, Urschel was released and the agents were quick to track down Machine Gun Kelly; Kelly's wife, Kathryn; and outlaw Harvey Bailey. (Jarrett had been hastily thrown from the car the day after the bold kidnapping.)

Eventually, George Kelly, his wife and 19 others were convicted in the case. When arrested in Memphis on September 26, 1933, Kelly was reported to have thrown his hands in the air and famously cried, "Don't shoot, G-men!" as he surrendered to FBI Agents.

Leopold and Loeb

Northwest corner of Dearborn Street and Hubbard Street
Chicago, Illinois

When Nathan Leopold and Richard Loeb were arrested for the thrill killing of 9-year-old Bobby Franks in 1923, they were held in the jail that was located here on the northwest corner of Dearborn and Hubbard, behind the County Courthouse. (The famous "trial-of-the-century," as it became known, was held in the fifth-floor courtroom of the nearby courthouse.) In 1990, the building was renovated and is now occupied by lawyers. The jail itself was torn down in the early 1930s.

Mackle, Barbara Jane

The Roadway Inn
1670 Claremont Road
Decatur, Georgia

On December 17, 1968, heiress Barbara Jane Mackle, a 20-year-old student at Emory College, was kidnapped from her off-campus housing here at the Roadway Inn. Sick with the Hong Kong Flu, Barbara was being cared for by her mother at the time of the kidnapping (her mother was gagged by the kidnappers). The young woman, daughter of an influential land developer, was taken 20 miles northeast of Atlanta to Berkeley Lake where she was buried in a specially fitted "coffin" that had an air pump, water, food and a battery-powered lamp (which burned out before she was rescued almost four days later). The kidnappers demanded and received $500,000 in ransom and then gave the FBI directions to rescue the young woman.

The kidnappers, Gary Steven Krist and Ruth Eisemann-Schier, were eventually arrested and convicted (Krist ended up confessing to several murders in Utah and Alaska) and Mackle returned home to Florida. (The event was made into a chilling made-for-television movie.) The burial site was located on South Berkeley Lake Road, approximately one mile south of City Hall, on the right, in Berkeley Lake, Georgia. There is now a medical center at this location.

Manson, Charles

Barker Ranch
Ballarat, California
(The "ghost" town of Ballarat is located 90 miles north of Barstow and
31 miles north of Trona. Barker Ranch is on Goler Canyon Road,
in Death Valley National Park. Four-wheel drive is recommended.
For exact directions call 760-786-3200.)

James Dean Died Here identified the most brutal Manson family landmarks around Southern California. But it was here, at Barker Ranch, that the evil mastermind and 24 members of his gang were finally captured in 1969. The local County Sheriff's Department and National Park law enforcement arrested Manson and his group thinking they were responsible for vandalizing a portion of the Death Valley National Park further north. It wasn't until later that they realized they had the infamous mass murder suspect and his faithful cult members in custody.

McCoy, Kid

2819 Leeward
Los Angeles, California

It was at this apartment building (unit 212) that boxer Kid McCoy (born Norman Selby) murdered his girlfriend. The onetime Welter and Middleweight Champion of the World, McCoy was paroled in 1932 and killed himself in 1940. McCoy's name is often credited with inspiring the expression "The Real McCoy."

Mobster Mayhem

Columbo, Joe

Columbus Circle
Southwest corner of Central Park
New York City, New York

On June 29, 1971, at an Italian-American rally here in Columbus Circle, famed mobster Joe Columbo was shot in the head and never regained consciousness – he died nearly seven years later. The hit was carried out by cameraman-turned-gunman Jerome Johnson, who was in turn shot by Joe Columbo's bodyguards.

Galante, Carmine

Joe and Mary's Italina Restaurant
205 Knickerbocker Street
Brooklyn, New York

This was the scene of one of the toughest, most brutal hits in mob history. Galante, a power hungry ex-hit-man, was having lunch with a cousin outside at this restaurant, when a group of ski-masked shooters wiped out everyone on the back patio. Even after all the shooting, the cigar remained in Galante's mouth after death, resulting in one of the most gory, sensational news photos ever. Today there is another restaurant at this location.

The Phantom Assassination

15th Street and Fifth Avenue
New York City, New York

One night in January 1943, the political refugee and labor leader Carlo Tresca was crossing the street here when someone came up and shot him three times, fatally wounding him. The killer hopped into a west facing car on 15th street and disappeared into the winter night, leaving the crime unsolved.

Mobster Mayhem

The Troutman Shootout

305 block of Troutman Avenue between Knickerbocker and Irving Avenues
Brooklyn, New York

It was on this dilapidated residential block in 1966 that famed Mafioso Bill Bonanno was to have a "sit-down" at the home of another mobster, Vito Bonventure. However, the meeting was derailed when, upon arriving on the block, Bonanno and his bodyguard were ambushed by rooftop snipers. A blistering gun battle broke out, but the two men escaped.

Moxley, Martha

38 Walsh Lane
Greenwich, Connecticut

On October 30, 1975, in the posh town of Greenwich, Connecticut, pretty 15-year-old Martha Moxley and her friends set out for a night of harmless pranks — spraying shaving cream and throwing eggs and toilet paper around the neighborhood — before stopping at the home of Tommy and Michael Skakel. Sadly, the night-before-Halloween ritual ended in death for Moxley.

The Skakel brothers were well known in the neighborhood for several reasons — their rowdy behavior, their general lack of discipline and also because they were the nephews of Ethel Skakel-Kennedy, widow of the late Senator Robert F. Kennedy. Both the Moxleys and Skakels lived near each other here in Belle Haven, a gated, tony section of Greenwich.

Sometime between 9:30 P.M. and 11:00 P.M. that night, Martha left the Skakel house, which was just about 150 yards away from hers. But Martha never made it home. Her body was discovered the next day under a tree in her backyard. She had been beaten so brutally with a six-iron golf club that the shaft had shattered. (A jagged piece of the club, which was eventually traced to the Skakels, was used to stab her through the neck.) Though the Skakels were questioned, back then a soft-leaning, seemingly intimidated police force did little to examine evidence that may have implicated the powerful family's sons.

Twenty-five years later, Michael Skakel was finally arrested for the murder, in part from light shed on the case by Detective Mark Fuhrman, who wrote a book outlining the evidence and presenting a theory against Skakel. On August 29, 2002, Michael Skakel (who had been tried and found guilty of the crime) was sentenced to 20 years to life in prison, where he remains today. (The Skakel house is located at 71 Otter Rock Drive, Greenwich, Connecticut.)

Nelson, Baby Face

Langendorf Park
235 Lions Drive
Barrington, Illinois

It was during a bloody shootout here in Langendorf Park on November 27, 1934, that outlaw Baby Face Nelson killed two FBI agents, and was mortally wounded himself (he escaped but was later found dead). The shootout occurred on the northwest edge of town at the north entrance to what was then called Barrington City Park. Special Agent Hollis and Inspector Cowley were killed during the gun battle that lasted only four or five minutes. Nelson, who was critically injured, was helped into Cowley's automobile by John Paul Chase, an accomplice. Guns and other articles were also transferred from Nelson's car to the agents' car.

Baby Face Nelson died about 8:00 P.M. that evening. In response to an anonymous telephone call, FBI Agents found his body the next day near a Niles Center, Illinois, cemetery (Niles Center is now known as Skokie). Today, a marker in the park sits exactly where the shootout took place.

The Night Stalker

Bristol Hotel
56 Mason Street
San Francisco, California
415-296-0980

This is where serial killer Richard Ramirez lived in 1985, at the height of the terror caused by his crimes. In fact, Ramirez was living here when he shot and killed 66-year-old Peter Pan on August 17, 1985. Pan, who was asleep in his home near Lake Merced the night of the shooting, was able to describe the attacker before dying, and his description helped form the profile that ultimately led to Ramirez's arrest near Los Angeles several weeks later. (Up until this attack, Ramirez had already killed more than a dozen people by home invasion in the Los Angeles area.)

Ramirez was convicted on September 20, 1989, of 13 murders and 30 felonies. Today, he is a Death Row inmate at San Quentin Prison, awaiting execution for the Los Angeles area crimes. (Unfortunately, he has not yet been tried for the murder of Pan and many others he is suspected to have killed or attacked.)

North Hollywood Shooting

Bank of America
6600 Laurel Canyon Boulevard
North Hollywood, California

On Friday, February 28, 1997, the Los Angeles Police Department experienced one of the most harrowing days on record – the North Hollywood Bank Shootout, which will long be remembered as one of the country's most shocking displays of extreme and violent

criminal behavior and an outstanding example of professional, heroic law enforcement. On that day, two men in full body armor held up a bank and then proceeded to shower a North Hollywood community with hundreds of armor-piercing AK-47 rounds.

Miraculously, of the 12 officers and eight civilian bystanders who were wounded, none were killed. This amazing fact is attributable to the bravery and heroic actions, on that infamous day, of the men and women of the Los Angeles Police Department. Ultimately, the two bank robbers where the only ones killed in the 44-minute shoot-out. Most of the gun battle was taped by media helicopters, including the death shots fired on the criminals.

Orr, John

Ole's Home Center
452 Fair Oaks Boulevard (now an OSH store)
South Pasadena, California

During the 1980s and early 1990s, Southern California was plagued by a series of mysterious fires, including a 1984 blaze that killed four people at this home center. During an arson investigator's conference in Los Angeles in 1987, another fire broke out.

Investigator Marvin Casey recovered a single fingerprint from the incendiary device and developed a theory that the fires were somehow connected to the conference. Later, after another conference and more fires, the forensic team finally identified the culprit and realized it was one of their own – John Orr, a fire captain and renowned arson investigator. In 1998, Orr was convicted of setting 20 fires, including the Ole's Home Center fire.

Packer, Alferd

630 Gunnison Avenue
Lake City, Colorado
(Just south of Alpine Miniature Golf)

Back in November 1873, a man named Alferd Packer was hired to lead a group of five men into the gold fields near this site. Several months later, Packer returned alone, suspiciously, with a tale that he'd become separated from his group in a snowstorm. Packer eventually admitted that he'd actually *eaten* his victims, claiming that he did so to stay alive once they'd died of exposure.

However, the evidence didn't quite support these claims. The bodies were all found at one campsite as opposed to being spread out along the trail as Packer had originally claimed. Under further questioning, Packer revised his story – he claimed that he returned to the group one day to find that four of the men had been murdered by the fifth man and that to defend himself, Packer had to kill the murderer to save his own life. Then, he stuck to the claim that he had resorted to cannibalism to stay alive.

Packer was sentenced to 40 years, but spent just five years in jail after a sympathetic reporter pushed to have his sentence reduced. The site of the killings and subsequent cannibalistic event was a remote outpost in the 1800s, but today it's just a few minutes south of the Lake City miniature golf course. A sign identifies the spot, which is marked by a small rock and a plaque that lists the victims.

Peterson, Laci

523 Covena Avenue
Modesto, California

On Christmas Eve, 2003, Laci Peterson, the pretty 27-year-old wife of Scott Peterson, disappeared from this Modesto home, prompting a nationwide search. When the body of Laci and her unborn child (she was eight months pregnant) were found four months later, Scott was charged with two counts of murder and, as of this writing, is on trial for the murders in Northern California.

From the start, public suspicion fell on her husband. Scott Peterson told detectives that he had last seen his wife on December 24th at 9:30 A.M. when he left their home in the La Loma neighborhood of Modesto for a solo fishing trip in Berkeley, about an hour-and-a-half drive away. Laci, he said, had plans to go grocery shopping and then walk their golden retriever in nearby East La Loma Park. But when he returned home that night, she was gone. Police are also interested in a Modesto storage facility where Scott kept his boat, which investigators believe was involved in the crime. The facility, Security Public Storage, is located at 1401 Woodland Avenue.

Rudolph, Eric

Save-A-Lot Grocery Store
4537 The Plaza
Murphy, North Carolina

The hunt for the 1996 "Olympic Bomber" finally ended May 31, 2003, at 3:30 A.M., when Jeff Postell, a 21-year-old rookie police officer, apprehended Eric Rudolph near a trash bin behind this Save-A-Lot grocery store.

The 36-year-old survivalist, who was on the FBI's 10 Most Wanted List, is suspected in the infamous 1996 Olympic Park bombing in Atlanta, as well as attacks at a gay nightclub and two abortion clinics. The Olympic bombing, the worst of his alleged attacks, killed 44-year old Alice Hawthorne and wounded more than 100.

Sacco and Vanzetti

South Braintree Square
Braintree, Massachusetts

At 3:00 P.M. on April 15, 1920, a paymaster and his guard were carrying a factory payroll of $15,776 here through the main street of South Braintree, Massachusetts. Suddenly, two men standing by a fence opened fire on them. The gunmen grabbed the cash boxes dropped by the mortally wounded pair and drove off. The bandit gang, numbering four or five in all, sped away, eluding their pursuers.

At first this brutal murder and robbery, not uncommon in post-World War I America, aroused only local interest. Three weeks later, on the evening of May 5, 1920, two Italian anarchists, Nicola Sacco and Bartolomeo Vanzetti, fell into a police trap that had been set for a suspect in the Braintree crime.

Although originally not thought to have been involved in this crime, both men were carrying guns at the time of their arrest and, when questioned by the authorities, they lied. As a result they were held and eventually indicted for the South Braintree crimes. (Vanzetti was also charged with an earlier holdup attempt that had taken place on December 24, 1919, in the nearby town of Bridgewater.) It remains one of the most controversial trials and outcomes in American history.

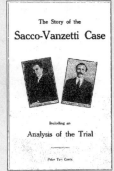

The Story of the

Sacco-Vanzetti Case

Including an

Analysis of the Trial

Smart, Elizabeth

10200 South State Street
Sandy, Utah

On June 5, 2003, teenager Elizabeth Smart was forcefully abducted from her bedroom in an affluent Salt Lake City suburb. Nine months later, Sandy Police received a call from two citizens reporting a possible sighting of the male suspect who was wanted for questioning by Salt Lake City Police in the Elizabeth Smart case. Officers responded and located a male and two females here on South State Street at the side of the road. Sandy officers questioned the three and determined one of them was Elizabeth Smart. All three were transported to the Sandy Police Department at 315 East 200 South Street where Smart was reunited with her family.

Spector, Phil

1700 South Grand View Drive
Alhambra, California

It was here in the 33-room, "Pyrenes Castle," owned by famed record producer Phil Spector, that actress Lana Clarkson was killed in the early hours of February 3, 2003. The next day the reclusive, eccentric industry veteran Phil Spector was arrested in connection with the shooting.

Spector is famous for creating the "Wall of Sound" effect that involved overdubbing scores of musicians to create a massive roar, which changed the way pop records were recorded. He produced hit records for Elvis Presley, Ike and Tina Turner, the Righteous Brothers and the last Beatles album, *Let It Be,* to name a few. As of this writing, Spector is awaiting trial for the crime.

Spencer, Brenda

Cleveland Elementary School
San Carlos, California

On January 16, 1979, 16-year-old Brenda Spencer fired a volley of bullets from her house toward the Cleveland Elementary School playground during a 6½-hour siege. She told a reporter she spoke to during the incident that she opened fire because, "I don't like Mondays. This livens up the day." Her attack killed two and wounded nine others, while making international headlines. One songwriter who took note was Boomtown Rats vocalist, Bob Geldof, who was inspired by the shooting to write the band's biggest hit, *I Don't Like Mondays.* Today, Brenda Spencer is serving a sentence of 25 years to life in prison.

Starkweather, Charles

Highway 25 at Ayers Parkland, the Natural Bridge Turnoff
About 12 miles west of Douglas, Wyoming

It was here in 1958, along this lonely stretch of highway, that cold-blooded killer Charles Starkweather and his girlfriend, Caril Ann Fugate, were finally captured, ending an eight-day murder spree during which the notorious pair killed 10 people. They were held in the Converse County jail before being returned to Nebraska, where the killings had begun.

Charles Starkweather commenced his reign of terror across the Nebraska farmlands on December 1, 1957, with the murder of Lincoln gas station attendant Robert Colvert. After robbing the gas station, Starkweather kidnapped Colvert and drove him to a secluded spot where he executed him with several shots to the head.

Almost two months later, the 19-year-old Starkweather, while waiting for 14-year-old Caril Ann to return home, murdered her mother and step-father with a rifle. When Caril Ann returned home, he strangled Caril Ann's two-year-old sister in her bed, after which he went to the kitchen where he prepared sandwiches for lunch. Charles Starkweather was electrocuted at the Nebraska State Penitentiary at midnight on June 24, 1959.

Swenson, Kari

Big Sky Ski and Summer Resort
1 Lone Mountain Trail
Big Sky, Montana
406-995-5000

It was in the parking lot of this ski resort, on July 15, 1984, that Olympic biathlon hope-ful Kari Swenson was kidnapped by deranged mountain man Don Nichols (who wanted Swenson as a wife for his son). Don and his son, Dan, held her hostage for 18 hours, chaining her to tree and torturing her.

After a search party discovered them, the two men made a run for it, but not before killing Alan Goldsten, a friend of Swenson's, who was leading the recovery party. Five months later the father/son pair were arrested and are currently incarcerated in Montana. The crime and ensuing recovery was made into the 1987 television movie *The Abduction of Kari Swenson* starring Tracy Pollan.

The Unabomber

Park Hotel
432 North Main Street
Helena, Montana
406-442-0960

It was here that Ted Kaczynski, the "Unabomber," stayed 31 times from 1980 to 1995. Typically, he would stay in room 119, which is located just to the right of the lobby, and it is believed he used the hotel as a stopping place immediately before and after every bomb that he set off. The hotel has since closed, but the building still stands and today is occupied by several other businesses.

Vigliotto, Giovanni

Mesa Wedding Chapel
465 East Broadway
Mesa, Arizona

Although bigamist Giovanni Vigliotto married more than 100 women over the course of 30 years, his reign of romance came to an end after being wed here on November 16, 1981. Soon after the wedding, Vigliotto danced off with his new bride's savings and, after almost committing suicide, the motivated bride tracked Vigliotto down. Her testimony (along with charges from several other brides) landed him in jail for the rest of his life.

Walker, Edwin

4011 Turtle Creek Boulevard
Dallas, Texas

After working at a few odd jobs in Fort Worth and Dallas, Lee Harvey Oswald moved his family to New Orleans in the spring of 1963. But before he left Texas, he purchased a rifle by mail with a telescopic sight. This gun (which was later used to shoot J.F.K.), is believed (and was documented in the Warren Commission) to have been used in Oswald's attempted assassination of retired Major General Edwin A. Walker. (Walker was a con-servative spokesman who was urging President Kennedy to send troops to oust Castro.) The assassination attempt occurred here at Walker's house in Dallas, Texas, on April 10, 1963. The shot allegedly fired by Oswald just missed Walker.

Celebrity Deaths and Infamous Celebrity Events

Albert, Marv

Ritz-Carlton Hotel
1250 South Hayes Street
Alexandria, Virginia

On February 12, 1997, NBC broadcaster Marv Albert was charged with biting the back of Vanessa Perhach and forcing her to perform oral sex on him at this Virginia hotel. It was the third time Albert had been with Perhach. Their first encounter was after a 1993 Knick's game in Miami and the second was in 1994, at a Hyatt Hotel in Dallas.

While those two occasions allegedly featured their own moments of strangeness, neither approached the intensity of what happened in Virginia. Eventually, Albert pled guilty to a misdemeanor charge of assault and battery and was given a 12-month suspended sentence. During the sentencing, Albert made a statement in court in which he apologized to Perhach and said, "There was some biting and rough sex in the past. I did not realize until her testimony that she thought I had caused her harm, and for that, I am sorry."

Bias, Len

Washington Hall (Southwest Quad B-5)
University of Maryland
College Park, Maryland
301-314-7484

This is the dorm where college basketball star Len Bias died on June 19, 1986. Just two days earlier, the Maryland forward (the Atlantic Coast Conference player of the year) had been selected by the NBA's Boston Celtics (who had the second pick of the draft). Autopsy tests revealed traces of cocaine in his system, and the resulting investigation led to charges against three people who admitted using drugs with Bias on the day of his death. This controversy prompted the resignation of Maryland coach Lefty Driesell.

Blandick, Clara

The Shelton Apartments
1735 North Wilcox
Hollywood, California

Character actress Clara Blandick was born June 4, 1880, on a ship in Hong Kong. Starting in 1914, and all through the 1920s and 1930s, she worked in hundreds of films, but it was her role as Auntie Em in 1939's *The Wizard of Oz* that most of us remember her by. Her last movie was 1950's *Key to the City*, and from that time on her health declined.

On Palm Sunday, April 15, 1962, Clara went to church near her home in Hollywood and, when she returned here to her apartment, she wrote a note saying she was about to take the greatest adventure of her life. She took an overdose of sleeping tablets and pulled a plastic bag over her head, thus ending her life. Clara Blandick was 80 years old.

Bonaduce, Danny

St. Croix Villas
100 East Fillmore Street
Phoenix, Arizona

This is the apartment where police found former Partridge Family "bassist" Danny Bonaduce hiding naked beneath a pile of clothes in a closet back in 1991. Bonaduce was arrested; he was on the lam for having allegedly beaten up a transvestite prostitute. Since then, Bonaduce has gone on to forge a successful career as a radio personality while also co-hosting a TV talk show for men.

Brown, James

430 Douglas Road
Beach Island, South Carolina

On July 7, 2000, an electric company repairman showed up here at the residence of the Godfather of Soul, James Brown. Brown allegedly swung a steak knife at the man and called him "you son-of-a-bitch white trash." No charges were filed against Brown, who had a history of run-ins with the law. (In 1988, Brown pleaded no contest to possession of PCP and pleaded guilty to carrying a gun and resisting arrest. He received a two-year suspended sentence and a $1,200 fine.)

Another time, Brown interrupted an insurance seminar at his headquarters in Georgia by waving a rifle and demanding to know who had used his personal bathroom. The subsequent police chase through two states ended with Brown being sentenced to a six-year jail term.

Bryant, Kobe

The Lodge and Spa at Cordillera
Eagle, Colorado
800-877-3529

On July 18, 2003, Los Angeles Laker basketball star Kobe Bryant was charged with sexually assaulting a 19-year-old woman in room 35 of this elegant resort hotel. Bryant denied the charge, saying he was guilty only of adultery. Bryant had been in Colorado to have arthroscopic surgery on his right knee at the Steadman Hawkins Clinic. As of this writing, the case has yet to go to court.

Capote, Truman

Towson Center at Towson University
Towson, Maryland

In 1977, writer Truman Capote made headlines when he showed up barely conscious at Towson University's public speaker series. Though he was warmly welcomed, Capote appeared at the podium and began cursing at everyone and anyone. The shocked audience watched as, after about 10 minutes, several people tried to escort Capote offstage. This only served to make Capote more irate, until the microphone was turned off and the lights dimmed, and he was dragged from the stage. The next day, a contrite Capote apologized and admitted to having been drunk.

Carey, Mariah

The TriBeCa Grand
2 Sixth Avenue
New York City, New York
212-519-6600

The TriBeCa Grand Hotel is where pop singer Mariah Carey had her much-publicized breakdown in July 2002. Though few details ever emerged, Carey, while staying in the hotel's penthouse suite, evidently snapped and began throwing plates and dishes around. She allegedly stepped on some shards of the broken glass, cutting her foot, and then asked to be taken to the suburban home of her mother, Patricia. Later on, Carey checked into a Connecticut psychiatric facility to recover.

Cassidy, Jack

1221 North Kings Road
Hollywood, California

Actor Jack Cassidy is perhaps best remembered for his stage appearances. He won the Tony award in 1963 for his role as Mr. Kinkaide in *She Loves Me* and remains one of the most nominated actors in Tony Award history. Cassidy had four sons — David (born in 1950 with then-wife Evelyn Ward) and Shaun (born 1958), Patrick (born 1962) and Ryan (born 1966) with then-wife Shirley Jones. Sadly, Cassidy died here in a fire in his fourth-floor penthouse apartment on December 12, 1976. He was just 49 years old.

Celebrity Air Disasters

Dubroff, Jessica

Cheyenne Airport
200 East 8th Avenue
Cheyenne, Wyoming

On April 11, 1996, seven-year-old pilot Jessica Dubroff was killed while attempting to set a record as the youngest to pilot a plane across the United States. The child died when her plane stalled (due to too much weight) and crashed just after take off from the Cheyenne, Wyoming airport. Her father and the pilot-in-command were also killed. They

had been flying into a thunderstorm at the time of the crash. Eerily, just that week in a *London Times* interview, Jessica said, "This started off as a father-daughter adventure, and it's gotten wonderfully out of hand . . . I'm going to fly till I die."

Graham, Bill

Highway 37, between Sears Point and Vallejo, California
(where Highway 37 passes Napa Creek)

On October 25, 1991, the famed concert promoter Bill Graham was killed here in a helicopter crash. Graham, who was 60 at the time, made a name for himself in the 1960s by promoting shows at San Francisco's Fillmore Auditorium and New York City's Fillmore East, and later in the '70s and '80s by promoting "mega-tours" for bands such as The Rolling Stones. Graham (and two others) died when his Bell 206B helicopter hit an electrical transmission tower and crashed during heavy rain and high winds.

Marciano, Rocky

Near Newton, Iowa

On August 31, 1969, 45-year-old former heavyweight champion boxer Rocky Marciano and two others died in the crash of a Cessna 172H airplane near Newton, Iowa. It had been a dark and rainy night and Marciano was just one day short of celebrating his 46th birthday. The pilot, who was not instrument-rated and had minimum night flying experience, took off at night despite warnings of a building storm front. Marciano was hitching a ride home to a planned birthday party.

Celebrity Air Disasters

Martin, Dino

Mount San Gorgonio, California (20 miles east of San Bernardino)

On the afternoon of March 21, 1987, an F-4C Phantom II fighter jet piloted by 35-year-old Dean Paul "Dino" Martin, son of actor/singer Dean Martin, slammed into a solid wall of granite at the 5,500-foot level of the Mount San Gorgonio foothills while on a routine training flight.

Martin, a California Air National Guard captain, was given permission by controllers to perform a "maximum climb" takeoff from March Air Force Base in Riverside County. Nine minutes after takeoff, while flying into clouds, the jet disappeared from radar. His weapons systems operator was also killed in the crash. Previously, Dino Martin's pop group had had one hit, "I'm a Fool," and it was his death that sent his father Dean into a downward spiral of depression from which many say he never recovered.

Reeves, Jim

**10 miles south of Nashville in a wooded area just off US 31
Near Nashville, Tennessee**

On July 31, 1964, country-western star Jim Reeves' Beechcraft Debonair crashed here in a wooded area during a heavy rainstorm. Reeves, who was piloting the plane, lost reference with the ground and experienced spatial disorientation. It took searchers two days to find the wreckage. (His manager was also killed in the crash.) The 39-year-old singer was coming home to Nashville after a business trip to Batesville, Arkansas. Voted into the Country Music Hall of Fame in 1967, Reeves continued to have hit records posthumously as recently as the 1970s and '80s.

Rockne, Knute

**10 miles south of Cottonwood Falls off Highway K-177
Near Bazaar, Kansas**

On March 31, 1931, legendary Notre Dame football coach Knute Rockne was one of eight killed when a Trans Continental & Western Airways Fokker F10A plane crashed during a heavy storm near Bazaar, Kansas. (One of the aircraft's wings separated in mid-flight.) The coach was just 43 years old. Today, a marker rests at the crash site in honor of Rockne. To visit the memorial, which sits off the road on private property, contact the Chase County Historical Society at 316-273-8500.

Celebrity Air Disasters

Smith, Samantha

Auburn-Lewiston Municipal Airport
80 Airport Drive
Auburn, Maine

On August 25, 1985, 13-year-old Samantha Smith, her father, and six others were killed when their Bar Harbor Airlines Beechcraft 99 crashed while trying to land here at Auburn, Maine. (On approach to Auburn, the plane missed the runway by 200 yards and crashed into the nearby woods.) Samantha was the young girl made famous for writing a letter to Soviet leader Yuri Andropov and then getting invited to visit Russia.

Stewart, Payne

Mina, South Dakota
(The crash site is located on a marshy pasture about two miles south of Mina, in Edmunds County, an area about 20 miles west of Aberdeen.)

On October 25, 1999, PGA golfer Payne Stewart, winner of the 1989 PGA Championship and two-time winner of the U.S. Open, died after his Lear jet lost pressure, causing everyone aboard to lose consciousness. He was only 42 years old.

Stewart, the two pilots, sports agents Van Ardan and Robert Fraley (who headed the sports management firm of Leader Enterprises) and golf course designer Bruce Borland were all killed when the private plane ran out of fuel and crashed here in a field outside Mina, after flying uncontrolled for several hours across the United States. Stewart had been on his way from Orlando, Florida to Dallas, Texas, to play in a golf tournament.

Todd, Michael

Zuni Mountains, near Grants, New Mexico

On March 22, 1958, Broadway and Hollywood producer Mike Todd, his biographer Art Cohn, a pilot and co-pilot were all killed when Todd's Lockheed Lodestar private plane, "The Lucky Liz" (named after Todd's wife, Elizabeth Taylor) crashed in bad weather in the Zuni Mountains of New Mexico.

During their flight, ice had developed on the wings, which created too much weight on the engines and caused the plane to crash. Todd had been on his way from Burbank to New York City to attend a Friars Club award meeting at which he was to receive the Showman of the Year award.

Celebrity Air Disasters

Turner, Curtis

About one mile northeast of Bell Township
Clearfield County, Pennsylvania

On October 4, 1970, 45-year-old NASCAR driver Curtis Turner and 51-year-old professional golfer Clarence King were both killed when Turner's Aero Commander private plane went into a tailspin and crashed into an abandoned strip mine.

Chapin, Harry

Long Island Expressway (near exit 40)
Long Island, New York

On July 18, 1981, fans waited in Eisenhower Park's Lakeside Theater (located in East Meadow) for a free concert by the popular troubadour Harry Chapin. But instead of hearing hits like "Cats in the Cradle" or "Taxi," fans were told by security that there wouldn't be a show that night — Chapin had been killed on his way to the venue, the victim of a fiery collision between his car and a tractor-trailer on the Long Island Expressway.

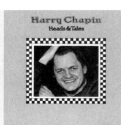

Chapin had been driving west in his blue Volkswagen Rabbit when he veered into the path of the truck. Chapin, historically a bad driver whose license had been revoked after several suspensions, was pulled alive from the wreckage but died soon after from massive internal bleeding.

Clapton, Eric

117 East 57th Street
New York City, New York

Tragically, it was here in 1991 that the 4-year-old son of rock star Eric Clapton plunged 48 stories to his death. He fell from a picture window apparently left open by a housekeeper who had just washed it. The boy wandered onto the ledge of a window that opened like a door before falling to the ground. The luxury duplex on the 52nd and 53rd floors did not have window guards, which are required by law. The event later inspired Clapton's beautiful song "Tears in Heaven."

Dandridge, Dorothy

8495 Fountain Avenue
Hollywood, California

Dorothy Dandridge was the first African-American woman to receive an Academy Award nomination for best actress for her performance in the 1954 film *Carmen Jones.* One of the era's most beautiful and charismatic stars, Dorothy Dandridge blazed a number of trails during her short life – including becoming the first African-American actress to achieve leading-role status.

However, in the years following her success with *Carmen Jones,* Dandridge had trouble finding film roles that suited her talents. In 1959's *Porgy and Bess* she did get to star as Bess opposite Sidney Poitier, but she then turned down the supporting role of Tuptim in *The King and I* because she refused to play a slave. As her film career and marriage

failed, Dandridge began drinking heavily and taking antidepressants; on September 8, 1965, she was found dead here in her Hollywood home, an apparent suicide from a drug overdose. She was only 41 years old.

Dick, Andy

Corner of Highland Avenue and Camrose Drive
Hancock Park area of Los Angeles, California

At about 10:45 A.M. on Sunday, May 15, 1999, actor Andy Dick lost control of his car and smashed into a utility pole here in Hancock Park while allegedly driving under the influence. He tried to run away from the scene, but witnesses caught up with him.

Police found pot and cocaine in Dick's car, and he was arrested on DUI and drug possession charges. Released on $10,000 bail, Dick later pleaded no contest to the charges and entered a two-year drug treatment program. (After completing the court-ordered drug program, a Los Angeles Superior Court judge officially dropped the charges against Dick.)

Divine

Regency Plaza Suites
7940 Hollywood Boulevard
Hollywood, California

On March 7, 1988, famed cross-dressing actor Divine (born Glen Milstead) – who was made famous by director John Waters in the movies *Pink Flamingos* and *Polyester*, among others – was in Los Angeles to tape an episode of the television show *Married . . . With Children.* The night before the shoot, Divine had dinner with friends and came back to room 261 of this hotel. When he didn't show up on the set the next morning, his manager, Bernard Jay, came to the room and found the 42-year-old Divine lying in bed – dead. He had apparently died in his sleep of heart failure.

Duel, Peter

2552 Glen Green Terrace
Hollywood Hills, California

On December 31, 1971, actor Peter Duel – star of the television series *Alias Smith and Jones* (he played Joshua Smith) – shot himself here at his home. He was just 31 years old; police ruled his death a suicide.

Entwistle, John

Hard Rock Hotel
4455 Paradise Road
Las Vegas, Nevada
800-851-1703

On June 27, 2002, John Entwistle, the quiet, rock steady bassist (and cofounder) of The Who died here at this hotel of an apparent heart attack. He was just 57 years old. Entwistle was in Vegas for an exhibit of his artwork, which was to be followed by a Who performance at the Joint on June 28th, the opening night of the group's U.S. tour.

"The Ox," as he was nicknamed, contributed such songs to The Who as "Boris the Spider" and "Whiskey Man." He also had a prolific solo career in the early-1970s, releasing *Smash Your Head Against the Wall* in 1971, followed by *Whistle Rhymes* (1972), *Rigor Mortis Sets In* (1973), *Mad Dog* (1975) and *Too Late the Hero* (1981). Entwistle's final release was 1999's live album *Left for Live*. Today, the hotel has yet to reveal the exact room where he died, in an effort to not attract undue attention from Entwistle's fans.

Entwistle, Peg

Hollywood Sign
Hollywood, California

On September 18, 1932, after a night of drinking and feeling depressed, struggling actress Peg Entwistle told her uncle that she was going to walk up Beachwood Drive to meet some friends at the local drug store. Instead, Peg clawed her way up the slope to the Hollywood sign (then named Hollywoodland, a real estate development) where she

took off her coat and placed it, along with her purse, at the base of the service ladder which led up the letter "H." She then made her way up the ladder to the top of the 50-foot-high letter. Upon reaching the top, she dove head-first into the ground, dying instantly. She was just 24 years old.

In a cruel twist, shortly after her death a letter from the Beverly Hills Playhouse arrived at her uncle's home declaring that the producers wanted her to star in their next production, which was centered around a young girl who commits suicide.

Farley, Chris

John Hancock Center
875 North Michigan Avenue
Chicago, Illinois

On December 18, 1997, 33-year-old actor/comedian Chris Farley died here in his apartment on the 60th floor of the John Hancock building. An autopsy indicated he died of an accidental overdose of cocaine and morphine, with coronary atherosclerosis – a narrowing of the heart arteries – a contributing factor.

Farley, who got his early comic training with Chicago's famous Second City comedy troupe, later became popular on *Saturday Night Live* and then moved into feature films, starring with comedian and pal David Spade in the movies *Tommy Boy* and *Black Sheep.*

Flynt, Larry

Gwinnett County Courthouse
Lawrenceville, Georgia

The date was March 6, 1978. On the opening day of his obscenity trial, controversial magazine publisher Larry Flynt was shot twice in the abdomen by an unidentified assailant in front of this Georgia courthouse, rendering Flynt permanently paralyzed from the waist down. (After the shooting, Flynt renounced God and moved to a Bel Air mansion once owned by Errol Flynn.) Though the assailant was never apprehended, white supremacist Joseph Paul Franklin is believed to have been the gunman. (Flynt's lawyer was also shot in the incident.)

George, Lowell

Marriott-Twin Bridges
333 Jefferson Davis Highway
Arlington, Virginia

The blues/rock band Little Feat was formed in 1970 by two alumni of Frank Zappa's Mothers of Invention – innovative slide guitarist Lowell George and bassist Roy Estrada. The group disbanded in 1978 after several near-hits and critically acclaimed albums, including the popular live set *Waiting for Columbus.* Lowell George then recorded a solo album, *Thanks I'll Eat It Here,* and went out on the road to promote it in 1979.

But excess caught up with the overweight, overindulging George who succumbed to a heart attack on June 29, 1979 at this hotel. (The Marriott-Twin Bridges in Arlington, the very first Marriott to be opened, was demolished in 1990.) George had performed the night before in Washington at the Lisner Auditorium, located on the campus of The George Washington University at 730 21st Street, N.W. Ironically, this is where Little Feat's *Waiting for Columbus* had been recorded.

Gifford, Frank

Regency Hotel
540 Park Avenue
New York City, New York
212-759-4100

This is the hotel where shapely flight attendant Suzen Johnson set up former football great Frank Gifford in a hidden-camera-equipped room. The ensuing tape, which was backed by *The Globe* newspaper, created a ton of embarrassing publicity not just for Gifford and his girlfriend, but for the former Giant's perky wife, Kathi Lee, who had a habit of presenting her marriage as ideal. *The Globe* printed photos of the affair, which Gifford admitted to having. Speaking later on *The Larry King Show*, Gifford said his marriage "Is probably much stronger because of what happened."

Graves, Teresa

3437 West 78th Place
Hyde Park area of Los Angeles, California

Actress Teresa Graves died at her home in a fire that occurred around midnight on October 10, 2002. One of the first black actresses to star in her own TV series, Teresa started out as a regular on *Rowan & Martin's Laugh-In* in the 1960s. In the early '70s, she was a fixture in "Blackploitation" films like *Shaft, Superfly* and *Cleopatra Jones,* which became so popular that ABC-TV created the movie *Get Christie Love* starring Graves as a "funky" black police woman. The movie spawned the short-lived television series of the same name in 1974.

Hardin, Tim

625 North Orange
Hollywood, California

Tim Hardin was a gentle, soulful 1960's singer/songwriter who has achieved much of his recognition through covers of his songs by other singers – including Rod Stewart (who covered "Reason to Believe"), Nico (who covered "Eulogy to Lenny Bruce" on her first album), Scott Walker (who sang "Lady Came from Baltimore"), Fred Neil ("Green Rocky Road" has been credited to both him and Hardin), and of course, Bobby Darin, who made Hardin's "If I Were a Carpenter" a Top Ten hit in 1966. Beleaguered by a heroin habit from early in his career, Hardin died of a drug overdose at his house on December 29, 1980.

Harlow, Jean

512 North Palm Drive
Beverly Hills, California

She was born Harlean Carpentier in Kansas City, Missouri on March 3, 1911, but she is remembered as platinum-bombshell Jean Harlow. The actress's first big break came in 1930 when Howard Hughes remade his 1927 *Hell's Angels* with sound, replacing the heav-

ily-accented Swede, Greta Nissen, with this woman who, after her divorce in 1929, had adopted her mother's maiden name – Jean Harlow. She went on to star in many other films with such actors as Spencer Tracy and Clark Gable, and it was here at this modest home that she came down with uremic poisoning in 1937. She died June 7th of cerebral edema at the young age of 26.

Heche, Anne

Highway 33 and Nebraska Avenue
Cantua Creek
About 40 miles west of Fresno, California

In was here, in rural western Fresno county, that actress Anne Heche wandered confused and disoriented down a remote dirt road before seeking help from a farm worker's family. Hours after news of her breakup with comedian Ellen DeGeneres was made public, Heche apparently abandoned her Toyota SUV near Highway 33 and Nebraska Avenue outside the tiny community of Cantua Creek. She walked about a mile before arriving at a nearby home, where residents called the sheriff's office for help. Sheriff's deputies later reported that Heche – star of such films as *Six Days, Seven Nights* and 1998's *Psycho* – cooperated with them and then asked for an ambulance. Heche has yet to offer a clear explanation of the bizarre event.

Hexum, Jon-Eric

20th Century FOX
10201 W. Pico Boulevard
Los Angeles, California

On October 18, 1984, between takes on the set of the CBS series *Cover Up*, up-and-coming actor Jon-Eric Hexum was fatally injured by a prop gun that discharged either during a bit of accidental horseplay, as was first suggested, or through a mere act of negligence, as later suspicions indicated. According to detectives, Hexum had loaded three empty cartridges and two gunpowder-filled blanks into a high-powered handgun before saying, "Let's see if I've got one for me," and fired the gun. The force of the blank round's explosion fractured the actor's skull near his right temple.

Holiday, Billie

Mark Twain Hotel (now the Ramada Inn Union Square)
345 Taylor Street
San Francisco, California

On January 22, 1949, jazz great Billie Holiday was busted here in a raid on room 203. Holiday, then just 29 years old, was in town with her manager-boyfriend, John Levy, for an engagement at Cafe Society Uptown on Fillmore Street, when she was arrested for possession of opium (Holiday's drug bouts were already legendary – she had previously spent 10 months in a federal slammer in West Virginia on a heroin charge in 1947).

Billie Holiday was eventually acquitted on June 3, 1949, after her defense team convinced the jury that she had been framed. Today, a plaque and assorted artwork at the hotel bear quiet homage to the great singer.

Hoon, Shannon

440 St. Charles Avenue
New Orleans, Louisiana

The tour bus for the band Blind Melon was parked here, in the lot next to the Hotel Inter-Continental, on October 21, 1995, when pal and fellow Hoosier Axl Rose of Guns 'n Roses discovered singer Shannon Hoon's dead body on board. It is suspected that drugs were responsible for the 28-year-old's death.

Idol, Billy

Corner of Gordon Avenue and Fountain Avenue
Hollywood, California

On February 6, 1990, rocker Billy Idol crashed his motorcycle here at this Hollywood intersection at about 8:00 A.M. He had just finished his *Charmed Life* album, and wound up breaking both an arm and a leg. The accident forced the cancellation of his original role in *The Doors*, but director Oliver Stone found another part for Idol – the character of Cat who is actually portrayed on crutches. Five leg operations later, Idol rebounded from the accident and embarked upon an extensive world tour in August 1990.

Jackson, Michael

4641 Hayvenhurst Avenue
Encino, California

In November 1993, police searched singer Michael Jackson's famous family compound here in the San Fernando Valley, looking for evidence that might support charges of child molestation against Jackson. (The criminal case was eventually dropped for lack of evidence.) Michael Jackson later settled the civil lawsuit out of court for a reported $20 million, while insisting that he was innocent of any and all charges.

Michael's sister LaToya Jackson had earlier alleged that she had been abused as a child by her father at this same Jackson family home, though the rest of the family heatedly denied all of her explosive charges.

Jam Master Jay

490-10 Merrick Boulevard
Queens, New York

On October 30, 2002, legendary hip-hop DJ Jam Master Jay (born Jason Mizell) of the seminal rap group Run-DMC was shot and killed while working here in his 24/7 recording studio. The crime was a brutal execution-style murder that stunned music fans around the world. According to police, two men entered the second floor of the building around 7:30 P.M. and committed the murder. Jay was just 37 years old and left behind a wife and three sons. To date, nobody has been arrested in connection with the case.

James, Rick

8115 Mulholland Terrace (just west of Laurel Canyon and north of Mulholland Drive)
Los Angeles, California

In 1991, "Superfreak" singer Rick James and his girlfriend, Tanya Anne Hijazi, were arrested here and charged with imprisoning and torturing a 24-year-old woman. Eventually, James received a five-year sentence and today has been rehabbed and is back making music. James, who had a string of hits in the early 1980s, had also become addicted to crack over the years, which seemed to play a part in his outrageous behavior.

Jolson, Al

St. Francis Hotel
335 Powell Street
San Francisco, California
415-397-7000

On October 23, 1950, "The World's Greatest Entertainer" was at this famed San Francisco hotel preparing for an appearance on Bing Crosby's radio show. While playing cards with friends in his private suite, the 64-year-old Al Jolson began complaining of indigestion. When two doctors arrived, Jolson tried joking with them. Then he felt for his own pulse, looked up and quietly said, "Oh, I'm going." His eyes closed a moment later, and attempts to revive him proved useless. Jolson was dead from a heart attack.

Joplin, Janis

Barney's Beanery
8447 Santa Monica Boulevard
Hollywood California
323-654-2287

On October 4, 1970, Janis Joplin (a regular at this classic Los Angeles haunt) sat at her favorite booth (number 34) and downed two screwdrivers before heading up to the Landmark Hotel, where she died later that evening of a heroin overdose. Barney's Beanery was also a favorite spot of Jim Morrison, who hung out here with Joplin and Jimi Hendrix, among many others.

Kinnison, Sam

US 95
Near Goffs, California

The manic comedian Sam Kinnison, who started out as a preacher and traveled all over the southern U.S. doing tent-based revivals, was killed near here on April 10, 1992. A long-time hard drinker and drug user, the recently reformed Kinnison was ironically killed when a drunk driver smashed head on into his car as he was en route to the Riverside Hotel in Laughlin, Nevada. (Look for a handmade marker along the side of the road that identifies the exact site.)

Kitaen, Tawny

Newport Beach Police Station
870 Santa Barbara Drive
Newport Beach, California

On April 1, 2003, B-movie actress Tawny Kitaen was arrested and charged with spousal abuse and battery after authorities said she attacked her husband, former Cleveland Indians pitcher Chuck Finley, as the two were driving home from dinner. The much-circulated mug shot, which showed a noticeably unglamorous Kitaen, was shot here at the Newport Beach Police Station when she was booked.

Landis, Carole

1465 Capri Drive
Beverly Hills, California

This is the home where actress Carole Landis (who starred in *One Million BC* and *Topper Returns,* among many other films) killed herself in 1948 by taking an overdose of pills. It was rumored that the 29-year-old Landis was heartbroken over her breakup with actor Rex Harrision, who was then married to Lilli Palmer.

Lawrence, Martin

Ventura Boulevard near Sepulveda Boulevard
Sherman Oaks, California

In May 1996, actor/comedian Martin Lawrence was detained by police and hospitalized after he was found carrying a gun and yelling and screaming in the middle of this busy intersection. He was admitted to nearby Sherman Oaks Hospital and released to the custody of his physician, who said Lawrence failed to take prescribed medication and had suffered a seizure. His doctor said Lawrence was suffering from "complete exhaustion and dehydration," according to a publicist's statement.

One witness said Lawrence was shouting obscenities and yelling something like, "Fight, don't give up, fight the power." He later admitted to using marijuana and undergoing treatment for depression. A few months later, while trying to board a plane at Burbank Airport, Lawrence was stopped by authorities who found a pistol in his possession. Lawrence later pleaded no contest to misdemeanor gun possession and received two years of probation.

Led Zeppelin

Edgewater Inn
Pier 67
2411 Alaskan Way
Seattle Washington
800-624-0670

Located on the edge of beautiful Puget Sound, this hotel (now called simply "The Edgewater") is the site of the infamous 1969 Led Zeppelin "Shark Incident." On July 25th, Zeppelin checked into the hotel, which back then was a favorite with musicians because guests could fish from their rooms. (Zeppelin was in town to play at the Seattle Pops Festival scheduled for July 25-27 at Woodenville, Washington.) The band caught some red snapper, and then, though versions vary, partook in some unseemly behavior with a 17-year-old redhead named Jackie in room 242. (Members of the band Vanilla Fudge were also present.)

Lee, Brandon

Carolco Studios (now Screen Gems)
1223 North 23rd Street
Wilmington, North Carolina

On March 31, 1993, 28-year-old actor Brandon Lee (son of martial arts legend Bruce Lee) died during the filming of *The Crow*. While filming a scene where he gets shot, the cap of a blank became lodged in his spine after penetrating his abdomen. He was rushed to the New Hanover Regional Medical Center located at 2131 South 17th Street.

Doctors worked for five hours, but were unable to save Lee, who was pronounced dead at 1:04 P.M. the following day. (Brandon's last sane words were supposedly, "Bang! Bang! Don't forget to send flowers!" – he was telling another actor to remember to bring the flowers for his character's upcoming funeral scene.) His body was flown to Seattle to be buried beside his father in Lake View Cemetery.

Lopez, Jennifer

Club New York
252 West 43rd Street
New York City, New York

Actress/singer Jennifer Lopez and her then-boyfriend – rapper and record company mogul Sean "Puffy" Combs – were arrested near this popular nightclub on the morning of December 27, 1999, and charged with criminal possession of a weapon and stolen property. The two were detained after fleeing the club where three people were wound-

ed in a shootout. According to police reports, Combs and Lopez were in the back seat of a Lincoln Navigator that was pulled over after it allegedly ran at least one red light; during a search of the vehicle, cops found a 9 mm pistol.

Others in the SUV – bodyguard Anthony "Wolf" Jones and driver Wardel Fenderson – were arrested on weapons and stolen property charges. Combs was found not guilty after the case went to court and the jury also found Combs' protégé, Jamal "Shyne" Barrow, 21, not guilty of attempted murder (however, they convicted him of reckless endangerment and assault). Jones was acquitted of gun possession and bribery charges, while Fenderson became a witness for the prosecution.

Madonna

6970 Wildlife Road
Malibu, California

On August 16, 1985, Madonna married actor Sean Penn at this palatial, clifftop home that was owned by Dan Unger, a friend of the Penn family. Penn, outraged at the massive press attention on the wedding day, spelled out an expletive in the sand in 20-foot-high letters as a message to the paparazzi helicopters.

Matuszak, John

3429 Oak Glen
Hollywood Hills, California

Football star and actor John Matuszak, who starred for the Oakland Raiders from 1976-1981, died here of AIDS on June 17, 1989, at age 38. Matuszak tried movies after football and wound up with good parts in the football-oriented *North Dallas Forty*, *Ice Pirates* and *Goonies*, among others.

Murphy, Eddie

Santa Monica Boulevard at Formosa Avenue
West Hollywood, California

In May 1997, actor/comedian Eddie Murphy was stopped in his car by police here at this intersection at about 4:45 A.M. The cops arrested his passenger, identified as a transsexual prostitute. Murphy himself was not arrested; he had done nothing illegal.

Undercover officers say they saw Murphy stop his Toyota Land Cruiser in an area they call a "prostitution abatement zone" – and pick up 21-year-old transsexual Atisone Seiuli. They followed the pair in an unmarked car for a few blocks before pulling them over. Seiuli was then busted on an outstanding warrant for prostitution. According to Murphy's attorney, the actor was just trying to do a good deed. Apparently, he couldn't sleep and so he drove down from his home in the Hollywood Hills to a newsstand for some magazines. On his way back, he spotted what looked to him like a disoriented woman and he stopped to offer her help.

Osbourne, Ozzie

The Alamo
300 Alamo Plaza
San Antonio, Texas
210-225-1391

We know of Ozzie's famous exploits of biting the head off of bats and pigeons, but this hallowed American landmark was the scene of another classic Ozzie moment back in the early 1980s. It was here at the Alamo that, after donning one of his wife's dresses, he wandered out in a drunken state and relieved himself in public. (Contrary to myth, not on the actual Alamo wall, but on a monument called the Cenotaph in Alamo Plaza, across the street from the landmark.) Ozzie was arrested and banned from appearing in the city.

Pollock, Jackson

Pollock-Krasner House and Study Center
30 Fireplace Road
East Hampton, New York
631-324-4929

On August 11, 1956 (less than a year after James Dean died in a car crash), artist Jackson Pollock was killed near his Long Island home here on Fireplace Road while driving intoxicated. In 1945, Pollock moved out here to a small homestead in The Springs, a rural hamlet near East Hampton, Long Island. Soon after establishing this secluded studio in the country, he would go on to pioneer the now-famous spontaneous pouring technique for which he became world-renowned.

This same property, now the Pollock-Krasner House and Study Center, would be Pollock's home for the rest of his life, and the site of his most innovative and influential work. The facility is open at various times throughout the year for tours and allows for a fascinating glimpse into the world of one of America's most noted artists. The exact crash site where Pollock was killed can no longer be visited because it is now on private land, but the location is approximately one mile west of the Pollock-Krasner House and Study Center, on Fireplace Road.

Prefontaine, Steve

Near the intersection of Skyline Boulevard and Birch Lane
Eugene, Oregon

One of the leading American distance runners of the early 1970s, the charismatic Steve Prefontaine won seven NCAA championships while running for the University of Oregon from 1969-73 (three in cross-country, four in the three-mile race) and finished fourth in the 1,500 meter race at the 1972 Munich Olympics. Prefontaine also set more than a dozen American records at distances from 2000 meters to 6 miles and, in 1974, became the first athlete to sign a contract with Nike.

But his life ended tragically on May 30, 1975, when the 24-year-old Prefontaine crashed his 1973 MGB near this intersection on the east side of Eugene. Today, the site is marked by a rock with a makeshift shrine, a plaque and a statue of Prefontaine. Note: This memorial is located on a dangerous corner with no parking or shoulder.

Prevost, Marie

6230 Afton Place
Hollywood, California

 Marie Prevost had been one of the silent film era's leading stars, and one of director Mack Sennet's original bathing beauties through the 1920s. She was featured in dozens of films and her career was flourishing until tragedy struck in 1926 when Prevost's mother was killed in a car accident. Prevost was devastated and, supposedly, this led to the drinking problem that ultimately killed her.

The advent of sound spelled the end of many silent film careers and Prevost was no exception. Relegated to secondary roles, she still stayed busy, appearing in 23 films from 1930–1936. However, her drinking took over and her finances began to disappear. Living in poverty, Marie Prevost died at this address of alcoholism and malnutrition on January 21, 1937. She was just 38 years old.

Puckett, Kirby

Redstone American Grill
8000 Eden Road
Eden Prairie, Minnesota

On September 6, 2002, 43-year-old former Twins outfielder Kirby Puckett allegedly groped a woman after pulling her into the bathroom of this restaurant. Puckett was charged with false imprisonment, fifth-degree criminal sexual conduct and fifth-degree assault, but was found not guilty after the case went to trial.

Ray, Margaret

Near Hotchkiss in west-central Colorado

This is where Margaret Ray, the woman who went to prison for repeatedly stalking David Letterman, was struck and killed by a train in an apparent suicide. Ray, age 46, was last seen by the engineer and conductor of the westbound Union Pacific coal train kneeling by the tracks; she did not respond to the train's whistle.

Ray had spent her last few years in and around Delta County, after spending various terms in prison, jail and mental institutions over the years for harassing Letterman and, more recently, former astronaut Story Musgrave. She was first arrested in 1988 while driving Letterman's Porsche near the Lincoln Tunnel in New York City.

Riggins, John

National Press Club
529 14th Street NW
Washington, D.C.

It was at the 1985 National Press Club's Salute to Congress that football great John Riggins drunkenly told Supreme Court Justice Sandra Day O'Connor to "loosen up" because she was "too tight" when the two met at dinner. Riggins then fell asleep under the table. The incident created a national stir.

Ryder, Winona

Saks Fifth Avenue
9600 Wilshire Boulevard
Beverly Hills, California
310-275-4211

On December 12, 2001, 30-year-old actress Winona Ryder was arrested for allegedly shoplifting clothing and other items valued at about $5,500 from this Saks Fifth Avenue store in Beverly Hills, California. (Ryder was also suspected of stealing from two other high-end department stores before being arrested on theft and vandalism charges at Saks.) At the time of her arrest, police also charged her with illegal possession of a painkilling drug. This charge was later dropped because she did indeed have a prescription for that drug (though she apparently hadn't obtained those specific pills using the prescription).

Eventually, Winona Ryder was sentenced to three years probation and 480 hours of community service for theft and vandalism convictions in connection to her shoplifting spree. Though she could have faced three years behind bars, the sentence came as no surprise since prosecutors did not seek jail time for the actress.

Scala, Gia

7944 Woodrow Wilson Drive
Hollywood Hills, California

Born in England, actress Gia Scala was raised in Rome by her Italian father. As a teenager she moved to New York and began to study at the Actors' Studio. She was spotted by an agent while appearing on a game show in the mid-1950s and put under contract at Universal Studios, thus starting her screen career. Her most celebrated role was as the traitorous underground fighter in *The Guns of Navarrone* (1961). In 1966, she portrayed a lady scientist trapped in the stomach of a whale on the fanciful TV series *Voyage to the Bottom of the Sea.*

After that, things began to spiral downward as drink and drugs took over. Her marriage to actor Don Burnett ended and, at one point, she threw herself off the Waterloo Bridge in London. (She would have drowned had a passing lorrie driver not pulled her out of the water.) Her addiction led to numerous arrests, and her bouts with depression got so severe she was forced to undergo frequent psychiatric observations. On April 30, 1972, Gia was found dead here at her Hollywood Hills home of an overdose of alcohol and sleeping pills. It was ruled a suicide.

Shakur, Tupac

Quad Recording Studios
723 Seventh Avenue
New York City, New York
212-730-1035

On November 29, 1994, a Manhattan jury had convened to deliberate charges of sodomy, sexual abuse and weapons possession against 23-year-old Tupac Shakur and his code-fendant, 24-year-old Charles Fuller. They stood accused of molesting a 19-year-old woman in Tupac's $750-a-night, 38th-floor Parker Meridien Hotel suite on November 18, 1993.

After the first day of deliberations, Tupac went on to Times Square's Quad Recording Studio to record a track with Uptown Records' Little Shawn. At 12:20 A.M., Tupac and his three-man entourage swept past a man sitting on a desk in the entranceway to this office building where Quad is located. The man got up from the desk as two other men came in the door, and the three followed Tupac and his crew to the elevator, pulled out guns, and hollered, "Give up the jewelry, and get on the floor!"

While his friends lay on the floor, Tupac cursed at the holdup men and lunged for one of the guns. The rapper was shot at least four times. His friends dragged the severely wounded Tupac into the elevator and up to the eighth-floor studio to administer first aid. Tupac survived this shooting, but was subsequently shot and killed in Las Vegas on September 13, 1996.

Simpson, O.J.

10600 block of Southwest 92nd Avenue
Miami, Florida

On December 4, 2000, while driving westbound on Southwest 106th Street approaching 92nd Avenue, former football great and accused murderer O.J. Simpson ran a stop sign and became involved in an altercation with another motorist. The driver, 55-year-old Jeffrey Pattinson, claimed Simpson grabbed his glasses and scratched him.

According to police, Pattinson said that he saw a black Lincoln Navigator drive past a stop sign in this suburban community of Kendall. Pattinson said that he "flicked his lights" at the sports utility vehicle. The Navigator stopped and its driver exited the vehicle and walked toward the other car. The men supposedly argued, then Simpson allegedly reached inside the car and pulled off the victim's glasses, causing a small scratch on his face.

Sprewell, Latrell

Oakland Convention Center Garage (fifth floor above the garage)
Broadway and 10th Street
Oakland, California

In December 1997, at the practice facility of the Golden State Warriors basketball team, NBA guard Latrell Sprewell attacked his coach, P.J. Carlissimo. It has not been made clear what started this attack, but according to witnesses Sprewell first ran to the sideline and began choking his coach. Sprewell then left the gym for 20 minutes and returned, at which point he threw several punches at the coach before being restrained. Reports differ on whether these punches landed. Sprewell was initially given a one-year suspension which was cut to the remaining 68 games of the 1997–98 season by an arbitrator.

Strickland, David

Oasis Motel
1731 Las Vegas Boulevard South
Las Vegas, Nevada

In March 1999, 29-year-old actor David Strickland was found hanging from a bed sheet that was tied around a ceiling beam in room 20 of this Las Vegas Motel. Strickland, who among other roles played the nice-guy rock critic on the NBC sitcom *Suddenly Susan,* had checked into the $64-a-night room at about 4:00 A.M. that same day. It is believed that the actor, who had been arrested for cocaine possession the year before, had been scheduled for a court-mandated progress report (he was on parole) hearing in Los Angeles the day he died.

Tilden, Bill

2025 North Argyle
Hollywood Hills, California

One of the greatest tennis players of all time, William "Big Bill" Tilden achieved spectacular success on the courts only to suffer an equally spectacular fall when his homosexuality and yen for underage boys became publicly known. In 1920, Tilden became the first American to win the men's singles title at Wimbledon, a title he won again 1921 and in 1930. During the 1920s he also won seven U.S. Open championships, seven U.S. clay court titles, and six U.S. doubles championships, among many other tournaments and titles.

In the 1930s he moved to Hollywood where he acted and wrote books, and it was also during this time that his lifestyle proved to be his downfall. In 1946, Tilden was arrested and convicted of contributing to the delinquency of a minor. Although the young man – a teenage prostitute – had consented to Tilden's advances, Tilden was nevertheless sentenced to prison where he served seven months of a one-year term. In 1949, Tilden was

arrested again for approaching a 16-year-old hitchhiker and sentenced to another year in prison (he served ten months).

His reputation all but ruined, friends turned on Tilden and his last years were spent living on handouts. He died of a heart attack at age 60 on June 5, 1953, at his apartment. His net worth was valued at only a few hundred dollars.

Tyson, Mike

Canterbury Hotel
123 South Illinois Street
Indianapolis, Indiana
866-809-9330

In the wee hours of July 19, 1991, boxer Mike Tyson led 18-year-old beauty pageant contestant Desiree Washington to room 606 of this hotel. Washington ended up charging Tyson with rape, and the boxer was found guilty and sentenced to 10 years in prison. However, Tyson was released on May 9, 1995, after serving three years. He went on to reclaim his two championship belts with wins over Frank Bruno and Bruce Seldon in 1996. (Tyson also went on to bite off a piece of rival Evander Holyfield's ear in a 1997 match and returned to jail in 1999 for assaulting two motorists during a 1998 traffic dispute.)

West, Dottie

Briley Parkway (Opryland exit)
Nashville, Tennessee

On August 30, 1991, legendary country singer Dottie West (then 58 years old) was killed while riding with her 81-year-old neighbor, George Thackston. Dottie had left her condo that night to perform at the Grand Old Opry, but when her car stalled in front of the old Belle Mead Theater on Harding Road, she flagged down a passing car, driven by the elderly Thackston.

While trying to make up for lost time on their way to the concert, Thackston took the 25 MPH exit at 55 MPH and the 1982 Plymouth Reliant went airborne for 165 feet before striking an embankment. Dottie West died five days later on the operating table. (Thackston survived the crash.)

Williams, Hank

Andrew Johnson Hotel
912 South Gay Street
Knoxville, Tennessee

Hank Williams' death at age 29 remains a mystery to this day. On December 30, 1952, Hank Williams packed up his '52 Cadillac and later that morning Charles Carr, a 19-year-old college freshman hired by Williams as a driver, and Williams began their journey from Montgomery, Alabama to Charleston, West Virginia, where Williams was scheduled to make an appearance. They made it to Knoxville, Tennessee around 10:30 A.M. the next day and, as the poor weather made traveling difficult, Carr checked himself and Williams into the Andrew Johnson Hotel.

That evening, Williams called for a doctor after experiencing convulsions. Charles Carr had by now phoned the promoter to let him know they would not be making it to Charleston in time for the appearance. The promoter, A.V. Bamford, insisted that they show up for a matinee the next day in Canton, Ohio. With that, Charles Carr had the porters transport the now unconscious body of Williams to the car. Given the reports of wheezing and lifelessness as they left, it is likely Williams died right then, in the Andrew Johnson Hotel. Later the next morning, Charles reached back to pull Williams' coat over his body, when he noticed Hank was ice cold and not breathing. Panicked, in the early morning hours of January 1, 1953, Carr stopped the car at Glen Burdette's 24-hour Pure Oil service station and called the police. At 6:00 A.M., Dr. Diego Nunniri pronounced the 29-year-old Williams dead. The Andrew Johnson Hotel, where Williams likely died, remains standing. (It is no longer a hotel – today it is simply called the Andrew Johnson office building.)

Let's Go to the Movies

Airport

**Minneapolis-St. Paul International Airport
4300 Glumack Drive
Minneapolis, Minnesota**

1970's *Airport* starring Burt Lancaster, Dean Martin and George Kennedy was the first of the true celebrity-infused disaster movies. Though interiors for the movie were shot at Universal Studios in Hollywood, a real Boeing 707 was actually landed in a snowstorm here for the movie's most intense sequences.

All About Eve

**445 Geary Street
San Francisco, California**

The Curran Theatre poses as a Broadway theater in New York in Joseph Mankiewicz's 1950 classic about a calculating ingenue, *All About Eve*. Starring Bette Davis, Anne Baxter, Gary Merrill, George Sanders and Celeste Holm, *All About Eve* won six Oscars and features an early appearance by Marilyn Monroe. In addition, the theater where we first meet the calculating Eve, waiting in the rain by the backstage door, is the John Golden Theater in New York City at 252 West 45th Street (at 8th Avenue).

Allen, Woody

Since he started as a serious filmmaker, Woody Allen has loyally utilized the city of New York as the perfect backdrop for his movies. The cafes, parks, restaurants, museums and apartments all seem to function as characters of their own – living, breathing props that help accent the poignant comedy and bittersweet mini-dramas that have become Allen's hallmark. To walk certain streets while having a particularly intense or humorous conversation with someone is to feel as if you've stumbled into a Woody Allen movie, thanks to the many cinematic milieus he's created over the years.

Annie Hall

Annie's apartment
70th Street between Lexington and Park Avenues
New York City, New York

Diane Keaton's exact apartment address remains a bit of a mystery, though it certainly was located here on 70th.

Beekman Cinema

1254 Second Avenue
New York City, New York

This is where Alvy Singer (Woody) is accosted by a fan who recognizes him (when Annie is late for the movie and Alvy is waiting outside for her).

The Thalia Cinema

250 West 95th Street
New York City, New York

Torn down in 1987, this was where Alvy bumped into Annie (as she takes her new boyfriend to see *The Sorrow and the Pity*) at the bittersweet ending to *Annie Hall.*

Manhattan

Elaine's Restaurant
1703 Second Ave
East 88th and East 89th Street
New York City, New York

Long an actual Wood Allen hangout in real life, this is where *Manhattan* opens, as the foursome has drinks and Woody waxes on about the trials of dating a 17-year old.

Allen, Woody

John's Pizzeria

278 Bleecker Street
New York City, New York

This Greenwich Village restaurant is where Mariel Hemingway tells Woody Allen that she is off to London to study.

Queensboro Bridge

New York City, New York
Riverview Terrace on Sutton Square, just beneath the 59th Street Bridge

The most famous scene from the movie (pictured on the film's poster), this is where Woody and Diane Keaton watch the sun come up. (There's no longer a bench located where the pair sat.)

Broadway Danny Rose

The Carnegie Deli
854 Seventh Avenue
New York City, New York
1-800-334-5606

This 1984 effort focused on the career of Danny Rose, a small-time Broadway talent agent whose roster of hopeless, hapless clients and bad luck sends him on a series of adventures, recalled by some old Borscht belt comedians who trade Danny Rose stories here at New York's most famous deli.

Hannah and Her Sisters

Pomander Walk
260-266 West 95th Street
(Through to 94th Street)
New York City, New York

An architect played by Sam Waterston takes Dianne Wiest and Carrie Fisher on a favorite building tour, including a walk through this beautiful (but not public) mock-Tudor village.

Allen, Woody

The Langham

135 Central Park West
New York City, New York

This was Mia Farrow's apartment in this 1986 smash, where the Thanksgiving dinners were held each year.

St. Regis-Sheraton Hotel

2 East 55th Street
New York City, New York
212-529-5333

This is where Michael Caine and Barbara Hershey conduct their affair after meeting at the Pageant Print and Book Store (now the Pageant Bar and Grill) located at 109 East Ninth Street in the East Village.

Crimes and Misdemeanors

Bleecker Street Cinema
144 Bleecker Street
New York City, New York

Now a video store, this Greenwich Village site is where Allen takes his niece to see movies in this 1989 classic tale of morals, ethics and values. (This former theater was also where Aidan Quinn worked as a projectionist in the Madonna movie, *Desperately Seeking Susan*.)

Outside of New York

Sleeper
Located in Mount Vernon Canyon on Genesee Mountain Road overlooking I-70 near Exit 254.
Genesee, Colorado (near Denver)

The 7,500-square-foot home on three levels was designed as a sculpture first, and as a house second (it's called "Sculptured House"). The architectural curiosity, built in 1963, was featured in Woody Allen's 1973 film, *Sleeper*.

Any Which Way but Loose

Royal Host Motel
930 East Colfax Avenue
Denver, Colorado

Clint Eastwood starred in the hit movie about a drifter and his pet chimpanzee cruising around in a pickup truck. Much of the movie was filmed here on Colfax Avenue, primarily East Colfax Avenue. In one scene, Eastwood stays at the Royal Host Motel, and rides the glass elevator to the curb before sauntering east toward the 7-11 right across the street.

Bad News Bears

Mason Park
10500 Mason Avenue
Chatsworth, California

This community park was actually built for the 1976, spot-on Little League movie *Bad New Bears* starring Walter Matthau and Tatum O'Neal. The tale of an underdog team of misfits led by a broken-down coach, its characters and scenarios about hyper-competitive parents and sandlot lessons remain timeless. This field was also used for parts of the sequel, *Bad News Bears in Breaking Training.*

Back to the Future

4 Westmoreland Place
Pasadena, California

Robert Zemeckis's charming 1985 smash features many actual locations around the Los Angeles area, including this highly visible landmark: Doc Emmett's house is the famous Gamble House. Built in 1908, the house is open to the public (818-793-3334 for more information). The exterior of Doc's workshop, where he keeps the time-traveling DeLorean car, is the Gamble House bookshop, located along the main house. But the interior of the workshop was shot at the similarly historic RR Blacker House at 1177 Hillcrest Avenue in Pasadena.

Basic Instinct

2930 Vallejo Street
San Francisco, California

It is here in the Pacific Heights area of San Francisco where Sharon Stone's character (Catherine Trammel) lives in the controversial 1992 potboiler, which co-stars Michael Douglas. The steamy thriller written by Joe Eszterhas and directed by Paul Verhoeven had several well-publicized run-ins with gay rights groups throughout the city who protested the portrayal of gays in the movie.

Being There

Biltmore Estate
Asheville, North Carolina
800-543-2961

The Biltmore Estate has been featured in numerous Hollywood movies, including *Hannibal, My Fellow Americans, Richie Rich, Patch Adams, The Swan,* and *Private Eyes,* but perhaps most famously, this was where Chance the gardener (Peter Sellers) ended up in 1979's understated classic, *Being There.* The Biltmore House is a 225-room chateau built in the 1890s for the Vanderbilts. It has seven restaurants, eight shops and is open for public tours. The entrance to the Biltmore Estate is off U.S. 25 just north of Interstate 40 in Asheville.

Big

FAO Schwartz
745 Fifth Avenue
New York City, New York

This is where Tom Hanks (playing Josh) dances on a giant keyboard in Penny Marshall's 1988 comedy hit, *Big.* Interestingly, the part was originally intended for Robert De Niro. The store declared bankruptcy in 2003 and, as of this writing, many changes are being made to this location.

The Big Chill

Tidalholm, 1 Laurens Street
Beaufort, South Carolina

Kevin Costner's suicide brought the characters of the movie to this house in the 1983 soul-searcher from Lawrence Kasden. However, Costner ended up being cut from the final film. The house served as Kevin Kline's mansion where everyone gathers for Costner's wake. Built here along the coast in 1853, the house is not open to the public.

Blade Runner

Bradbury building
304 South Broadway (at 3rd Street)
Los Angeles, California

One of L.A.'s true architectural treasures, this 1893 structure was Harrison Ford's home in the movie *Blade Runner*. Over the years it's been used for hundreds of other movies, TV shows and commercials. The interior of the Bradbury Building features marble stairs, ornate iron railings and open-cage elevators providing access to the various office floors. Today, it's the oldest remaining commercial building in the city.

Blossom Room

The Roosevelt Hotel
7000 Hollywood Boulevard
Los Angeles, California
1-800-950-7667

In this ballroom directly off the lobby, the first Academy Awards (then called Merit Awards) were given out on May 16, 1929 for performances and work covering a two-year

 period. (The night was hosted by Douglas Fairbanks.) The Blossom Room has been used for hundreds of other entertainment-related functions over the years and remains just as busy today as it was back in the glory years of Hollywood.

Buckskin Joe Frontier Town & Railway

1193 Fremont County Road 3A
Cañon City, Colorado
(Take U.S. Highway 50 eight miles west of Cañon City to the Royal Gorge Road.)
Buckskin Joe is open from May 1st through the last weekend of September.
During the main summer season the town is open from 9:00 A.M. to 6:30 P.M.

This was a real 1800's Western mining camp named for a prospector called Joe who wore buckskin. In 1957, the sole remaining building and the name were moved from Park County near Alma to Fremont County near Cañon City and a western main street was built, creating the perfect movie-location site. Films made here include *Cat Ballou, The Cowboys, Comes a Horseman, True Grit* and many more.

Butch Cassidy and the Sundance Kid

Grafton, Utah
Grafton is located in eastern Washington County about two miles west of Rockville and just south of the Virgin River.

This ghost town was used for several scenes in the 1969 film starring Paul Newman and Robert Redford — in particular, the famous "Raindrops Keep Fallin' on My Head" scene. It was also where Katherine Ross's house was located. The film about the famous out-law pair won four Academy Awards, including Best Song ("Raindrops Keep Fallin' on My Head") and Best Screenplay.

Chinatown

Echo Park Lake
1632 Bellevue Avenue
Los Angles, California

In the 1974 noir classic *Chinatown*, private eye Jack Nicholson rows out on this lake to shoot pictures of a man who is cheating on his wife. Directed by Roman Polanski, this dark and brooding film featured Nicholson as J.J. Gittes, a Raymond Chandleresque character who, during a routine straying-spouse investigation, finds himself drawn  deeper and deeper into a web of clues and corruption. Also starring Faye Dunaway and John Huston, *Chinatown* screenwriter Robert Towne won the Oscar that year.

Citizen Kane

Oheka Castle
135 West Gate Drive
Huntington, New York (Long Island)

Though much of this 1941 tour-de-force directed by (and starring) Orsen Welles was shot at RKO Studio (780 Gower Street, Hollywood, California), in the movie a "fake" documentary depicting Xanadu is actually showing this 1919 estate on Long Island.

City Slickers

Cool Water Ranch
Durango, Colorado

In 1991's *City Slickers,* Norman the lovable calf is swept down the river at Cool Water Ranch, CR105 between Bayfield and Vallecito Lake. (Ask at the ranch office for permission to enter.) You can also get a glimpse of the ranch shown toward the end of the movie. Take U.S. Highway 160 west 2 miles from Durango to Lightner Creek Road and turn right. Go two miles to the end of the road. It's the ranch on the left and it's private property, so trespassing is not allowed.

The "Cliffhanger"

New Jersey cliffs
Fort Lee, New Jersey

Most people are familiar with the movie term "cliffhanger," used to describe a movie filled with suspense, danger, and "seat-of-your pants" thrills. But did you know that the term originated out of the early serials filmed here on the New Jersey Palisades in Fort Lee — the birthplace of the motion picture industry in America?

Corbett-Fitzsimmons Movie

901 East Musser Street
Carson City, Nevada

On St. Patrick's Day in 1897, the very first motion picture footage taken in Nevada was shot in Carson City during the heavyweight prizefight between "Gentleman Jim" Corbett and British challenger Bob Fitzsimmons. (Fitzsimmons went on to knock Corbett out in the 14th round.) Today at the site of the huge arena, a plaque commemorates the historic event. (It's right next to the Carson City Sheriff's office.)

Dazed and Confused

Bedichek Middle School
6800 Bill Hughes Road
Austin, Texas

Richard Linklater's 1993 nostalgic homage to high school life in the mid-1970's was centered here at this real high school in Austin, the director's hometown. The movie featured early performances by (among others) Matthew McConaughey (his first movie), Parker Posie and Ben Affleck.

Dirty Harry

Kezar Stadium
Kezar Drive in Golden Gate Park
San Francisco, California

This is where Harry Callahan (Clint Eastwood) shoots the psycho killer (who lives here in the stadium) and steps on his leg at midfield. Kezar Stadium was built in 1922, and the San Francisco Forty-Niners played here from 1946-1970. The original stadium was demolished in 1989 after an earthquake, but a new one was rebuilt on the same site.

Duck Soup

**Arden Villa
1145 Arden Road
Los Angeles, California**

This classic 1933 Marx Brothers comedy saw most of its action (centered on the fictional country of Freedonia) shot at Paramount Studios, but they went on location to Arden Villa for the famous garden party scene where Groucho Marx (as Rufus T. Firefly) insults Margaret Dumont over and over again. The home is a private residence and was also used as the Carrington mansion in the TV series *Dynasty*.

Father of the Bride

**843 South El Morino
Pasadena, California**

This was Steve Martin and Diane Keaton's home in the 1991 remake of the 1950 film starring Spencer Tracy. (In this version, the actual wedding takes place at The Trinity Baptist Church at 2040 West Jefferson Boulevard in Los Angeles, California.)

First Movie Studio in Hollywood

**6121 Sunset Boulevard
Hollywood, California**

In the early 1900s, motion picture production companies from New York and New Jersey started moving west to California because the good weather and longer days allowed for more productive shooting. (Although electric lights did exist at that time, the best source of illumination for film production was natural sunlight.)

In 1911, the first movie studio in the Hollywood area was founded here by David Horsley for the Nestor Company, in an old roadhouse called the Blondeau Tavern. Until the 1930s, the Nestor Company cranked out a ton of one-reel westerns and comedies before closing shop. In 1936, CBS razed the old studios and built Columbia Square, which was the home of many famous radio shows including *Burns and Allen, Our Miss Brooks* and

Edgar Bergen and Charlie McCarthy. Today, Columbia Square is home to a pair of radio stations and the local CBS-TV news station. A plaque marking this site as the first movie studio in Hollywood can be found in the middle of the block on Sunset between El Centro and Gower.

48 Hours

Torchy's
218½ West Fifth Street
Los Angles, California

This is the downtown nightspot where wise-cracking cop Eddie Murphy dresses down a bunch of beer drinking rednecks in the 1982 comedy *48 Hours* co-starring Nick Nolte. It is no longer a nightclub; it has since been converted into a discount store.

Giant

The Ryan Ranch
Marfa, Texas
About 500 miles southwest of Dallas in Presidio County otherwise known as Big Bend Country. The two closest towns are Alpine and Fort Davis. The Big Bend National Park and the Rio Grande River are also nearby, and Mexico is just an hour's drive south.

Marfa is known primarily for its famous Marfa Mystery Lights and as the location for the shooting of the classic movie *Giant*, with Rock Hudson, Elizabeth Taylor, Dennis Hopper and James Dean. There's even a James Dean memorial here by *Giant*'s ruins of Reata (near the Ryan Ranch), where director George Stevens shot the 1956 epic.

In this tiny Texan town you'll also find the Hotel Paisano, which was home to stars Elizabeth Taylor, Rock Hudson and James Dean during the filming of *Giant*. The hotel is located in downtown Marfa on Highway 17, one block South of the Courthouse and just north of the intersection of State Highway 90 (1-866-729-3669). Note: You can ask for directions to the *Giant* site at the hotel.

Godfather II

Fleur du lac
4OOO West Lake Boulevard (on Lake Tahoe)
Homewood, California

Originally the palatial summer estate of Henry J. Kaiser (Kaiser Aluminum) and built in 1939, Fleur du Lac lies just north of Homewood and just south of Eagle Rock. Though the

grounds and original buildings were used in the filming of the movie *Godfather II* (as the family's lakeside estate), shortly after the movie was made a developer purchased the property and demolished the old main house to make room for an exclusive condo development. The only structures used in the movie that still remain are the complex of old native stone boathouses with their wrought iron gates. Although Fleur du Lac is private property and no one is allowed ashore there, the boathouses and multi-million dollar condominiums are easily viewed from the lake.

Gone With the Wind

Bidwell Park
Manzanita Avenue
Chico, California

From Chico, California, take West Sacramento Avenue 5 miles until it intersects with River Road. Big Chico Creek (the area of much of the filming) is to the left.

Dozens of movies have been filmed here over the years, including the scene in *Gone With the Wind* where Gerald O'Hara (Thomas Mitchell) makes his first horseback ride. The park, which features towering oaks and many creeks was also popularized in the original *Adventures of Robin Hood* starring Errol Flynn in 1937.

Hairspray

Mergenthaler Vocational Technical School
3500 Hillen Road
Baltimore, Maryland

John Waters' last vehicle for his star Divine (before it became a smash musical on Broadway), this comedy (also starring Ricki Lake) used this high school as its primary backdrop.

Heaven Can Wait

Malibu Canyon/Las Virgenes Road
Malibu, California

Warren Beatty's 1978 remake of 1941's *Here Comes Mr. Jordan* garnered nine Academy Award nominations including Best Picture, Best Actor (Warren Beatty), Best Director (Beatty/Buck Henry) and Best Adapted Screenplay (Elaine May/Warren Beatty). This tunnel is where Beatty (as L.A. Rams quarterback Joe Pendleton) is riding his bike when he gets killed near the beginning of the film, thus sending him to heaven where he meets Buck Henry and James  Mason. It is located about 3 1/3 miles up Los Virgenes Road from Pacific Coast Highway.

In a Lonely Place

1300-1308 North Harper Avenue
West Hollywood, California

Humphrey Bogart stars in this dark, 1950 film noir classic about a gritty screenwriter who *may* have committed murder. In the film, Bogart's character lives in a secluded enclave of European-esque apartments, which is the Villa Primavera complex. Today, it retains the same tucked-away charm it displayed in the film.

Intolerance set

Intersection of Sunset Boulevard and Hollywood Boulevard
Hollywood, California

On this site in 1916, movie director D.W. Griffith erected the biggest set ever constructed for a movie. *Intolerance* featured a re-creation of ancient Babylon and for the shots he needed, Griffith hired a mob of 4,000 extras gathered from the skid rows of the Los Angeles area.

Released in 1916, the movie failed to perform and as a result, there was not even money left to remove the elaborate movie set, which was finally condemned by the Los Angeles

Fire Department and razed in 1930. Today at the intersection of Hollywood Boulevard and Highland Avenue (6801 Hollywood Boulevard; 323-467-6412) there is a replica of the *Intolerance* set, right near the Kodak Theatre, home to the Academy Awards. The Vista Theater is now located at the actual site of the original set.

King of Comedy

Paramount Plaza
1633 Broadway 50th Street and Broadway Avenue
New York City, New York

Martin Scorcese's brilliant tale of celebrity stalking and obsession featured Jerry Lewis and Robert De Niro in two of their most interesting roles to date. This building is where Lewis (as talk show host Jerry Langford) kept his offices (and where De Niro and co-star Sandra Bernhard kidnap Lewis).

Lethal Weapon

8431 Santa Monica Boulevard (one block east of La Cienega)
West Hollywood, California

In the original *Lethal Weapon*, this is the building where tortured cop Mel Gibson attempts to talk a suicidal man off the building's ledge. Eventually, they both end up taking a wild jump onto an inflated air bag.

Lost Weekend

PJ Clarke's Saloon
915 Third Avenue
New York City, New York
212-317-1616

The grim, 1945 classic from Billy Wilder starring Ray Milland was shot here at this Manhattan institution — a legendary bar that's been in the neighborhood for almost 130 years. In addition, Milland's depressing journey along Third Avenue (from 55th Street near the bar to 110th Street) in desperate search of a pawnbroker was shot with a camera hidden inside a bakery truck.

Moonstruck

Cammareri's Bakery
502 Henry Street
Brooklyn, New York
718-875-1283

John Patrick Shanley won the Oscar for Best Original Screenplay, Olympia Dukakis the Oscar and the Golden Globe for Best Supporting Actress and Cher the Oscar and the Golden Globe for Best Actress in this 1987 charmer about love, jealousy and family among Italians in Brooklyn, New York. Now the Read Rail restaurant, this building (and a real former bakery) is where Nicholas Cage worked (and cut off his thumb).

The Munchkins

Culver City Hotel
9400 Culver Boulevard
Culver City, California
310-838-3547

When the 1939 classic *The Wizard of Oz* was being filmed at nearby MGM Studios, 124 midgets (who played the "Munchkins" in the film) stayed here at the old Culver City Hotel. According to legend, the Munchkins' ribald, drunken shenanigans ruled the entire time they resided here. Their stay even helped inspire the 1981 movie comedy *Under the Rainbow* (starring Chevy Chase and Carrie Fisher), which was actually shot at the hotel.

In addition to Munchkin mayhem, the recently refurbished Culver City Hotel was also seen in several Laurel & Hardy silents, a few "Our Gang" comedies, and in the Arnold Schwarzenegger movie *The Last Action Hero*.

Nashville

Parthenon
Centennial Park
2500 West End Avenue
Nashville, Tennessee

This is where the Replacement Party political rally was filmed in Robert Altman's brilliant 1975 satire, *Nashville*. The building is the only full-scale replica of the original Parthenon in Athens, Greece. Nashville's long-standing reputation as the "Athens of the South," partially because of its many colleges and universities, is one reason for its being located here.

Network

New York Public Library
Fifth Avenue between 40th and 42nd Streets
New York City, New York

Though Paddy Chayevsky's 1976 wickedly dark satire on American broadcasting was mostly shot in Toronto, one of the key scenes was filmed at this venerable New York landmark building. Here in the library, in a conference room, is where anchorman Howard Beal (played by Peter Finch, who posthumously won the Best Actor Oscar for this role), gets lectured by the fiery businessman played by Ned Beatty, who instills the fear of God in Finch.

North by Northwest

The Pratt Estate
Welwyn Preserve
Crescent Beach Road
Glencove, New York

This once-regal estate was where Cary Grant got mixed up with the bad guys in Hitchcock's 1959 classic, *North by Northwest.* (The original *Sabrina* with William Holden, Audrey Hepburn and Humphrey Bogart was also shot here.) Today, the estate grounds are open to the public as a nature preserve.

On the Waterfront

400 Willow Avenue
Hoboken, New Jersey

Our Lady of Grace church was featured in this 1954 Elia Kazan classic starring Marlon Brando. However, Stevens Park, which appears to be located in front of the church in the movie, actually sits four blocks away at 400 Hudson Street.

A Place in the Sun

Cascade Lake
Emerald Bay Road
Lake Tahoe, California

Based on real events known as "The Gillette Murders," this 1951 classic stars Montgomery Clift and Elizabeth Taylor as star-crossed lovers, but things get dicey when Clift's other relationship with Shelly Winters goes south. This is the lake where Clift gets rid of Winters, committing the ultimate crime that results in the film's dramatic climax.

Play Misty for Me

KRML
Carmel Rancho Shopping Center
26135 Carmel Rancho Boulevard
Carmel, California

KRML, the radio station where Clint Eastwood spun records in this, the original cinematic tale of fatal attraction, was originally located here. KRML Jazz Radio (1410 AM or 92.5 FM) still exists, though it's moved to Crossroads Shopping Center, Highway 1 at Rio Road in Carmel.

Rain Man

Big 8$ Motel – Room 117
1705 East 66th Highway
El Reno, Oklahoma

 This is the tiny, Route 66 motel made famous in *Rain Man,* the touching 1988 classic from Barry Levinson. It was here that Dustin Hoffman became concerned about burning the baby with hot water. Note: Another recognizable site from the film is the train station where Tom Cruise bid farewell to Dustn Hoffman in the finale. It is the historic Santa Ana Train Station located at 1000 East Santa Ana Boulevard in Santa Ana, California.

Rebel Without a Cause

Santa Monica High School
601 Pico Boulevard
Santa Monica, California

 In this 1955 classic, Santa Monica High stood in for James Dean's new high school (called Dawson High in the film). It's been featured in other movies as well, and it was Leonardo DiCaprio's real-life high school.

Reservoir Dogs

Pat and Lorraine's Coffee Shop
4720 Eagle Rock Boulevard
Los Angeles, California
213-256-9269

This is the diner where the Dogs bantered on about both Madonna lyrics and the ethics of tipping in Quentin Tarantino's 1992 offbeat film starring Harvey Keitel and Tim Roth. Just east in a district called Highland Park is where the robbery of Karina was filmed.

Rocky

Richfield Coliseum
2923 Streetsboro Road
Richfield, Ohio

This was where, on March 24, 1975, a young, impressionable and not-yet-famous Sylvester Stallone witnessed the now-famous Chuck Wepner/Muhammad Ali fight. Wepner, the scrappy underdog nicknamed the "Bayonne Bleeder," went the distance, 15 rounds with Ali, but lost the fight. After that bout, Stallone was inspired to write the screenplay for the movie *Rocky*, the story of which he claimed to have based on Wepner's life (culminating with the fight). The Richfield Coliseum was torn down in 1999 and today the site sits in the middle of the Cuyahoga Valley National Recreation Area.

Roman Scandals

The Colorado Street Bridge
Pasadena, California
(West of Orange Grove Boulevard, just south of the 134 freeway.)

Though in the 1930s it held the dubious distinction of being called "Suicide Bridge" due to the almost 100 death jumps which occurred here, this beautiful span gained interna-

tional fame in the 1933 Eddie Cantor classic, *Roman Scandals,* which also starred a young Lucille Ball. The bridge, built in 1913, is part of the historic Arroyo Seco, the first freeway in California.

Roxanne

Town of Nelson
British Columbia, Canada
(Nelson is located at the junction of Highway 6 and Highway 3A, at the western
tip of the West Arm of Kootenay Lake, 26 miles northeast of Castlegar.)

Steve Martin's charming update of Edmund Rostand's book *Cyrano de Bergerac* was
adapted by Martin himself. After producers could not find a satisfactory ski town in
America, they headed up to this picturesque town in British
Columbia, Canada. (The fire engine used in the movie at the
time was the actual fire engine used by the volunteer fire
department there in Nelson.) Local walking tours are given in
this town of about 10,000 which documents many of the film
sites from *Roxanne*.

Shane

Gros Ventre Road (just west of Kelly)
Grand Teton National Park
Near Jackson Hole, Wyoming

This was the actual cabin used in the 1951 George Stevens' classic western about a mysterious stranger who turns up to aid a family of
homesteaders. The film starred Alan Ladd and
Jean Arthur, and closed famously with Ladd riding off into the Teton as young Brandon de Wilde
yelled, "Shane!"

The Shawshank Redemption

Ohio State Reformatory
Mansfield, Ohio
419-522-2644

This 1880's landmark (closed as a prison in 1990) now offers
"ghost tours" of its gothic grounds. It also served as
"Shawshank State Prison" in the 1994 Tim Robbins film, *The
Shawshank Redemption*. The moving, uplifting film (based on
a novella by Stephen King, *Rita Hayworth and the
Shawshank Redemption*) is widely held as one of the finest
of the 1990s.

Spiderman

Rockwell/Boeing/NASA Defense plant
Bellflower Boulevard and Imperial Highway
Downey, California

In the scene where news photographer Peter Parker (Tobey McGuire) is covering a "World Unity Festival" in Times Square when the crowd is attacked by the evil Green Goblin (Willem Dafoe), Spiderman springs into action, and the fight between the super-hero and the Green Goblin ensues. Some of the broader establishing shots were actual-ly done in Times Square, but most of the "World Unity Festival" scenes were shot on a huge re-creation of Times Square, constructed at an old defense plant on this historic 160-acre lot.

It was here where the Apollo Command and Service Module was built (for the first mis-sion to the moon in 1969) and also where the original Space Shuttle components were constructed. The now-empty lot is bordered by Bellflower Boulevard on the east, Lakewood Boulevard on the west, Imperial Highway on the south and Stewart and Gray Roads on the north.

The Stepford Wives

Westport, Connecticut

This spooky 1975 cult classic stars Katharine Ross as Joanna, a woman who moves to Stepford, Connecticut along with her husband (Peter Masterson) and her best friend, Bobbie (Paula Prentiss). As the two women meet the other housewives who live in Stepford, they begin to notice that all of them are interested only in cooking, cleaning, and pleasing their husbands. Joanna and Bobbie are alarmed further when their hus-bands join the mysterious Stepford Men's Club, which convenes in a heavily guarded mansion. Westport, which served as "Stepford," is on the southern coast of Connecticut.

Superman

News Building
220 East 42nd Street
New York City, New York

In Richard Donner's 1978 version of *Superman* starring Christopher Reeve, Margot Kidder and Gene Hackman, the Daily Planet building was actually this former *Daily News* building in Manhattan, one of the city's most classic art-deco structures.

The Taking of Pelham One Two Three

Park Avenue South between East 27th and East 28th Street
New York City, New York

In the 1970's film *The Taking of Pelham One Two Three,* the ransom for the hijacked subway train is delivered to this station. Interestingly, this was also the site of the first recorded real-life subway crime, when a $500 diamond stick-pin was stolen on opening day, October 27, 1904.

10

All Saints Episcopal/Anglican Church
504 North Camden Drive
Beverly Hills, California

This is where the wedding scene in the 1979 male-menopause comedy *10,* was shot; the place where Dudley Moore first eyes the beautiful Bo Derek. Moore has been tailing bride-to-be Bo in his car, and as he watches her he loses sight of the police car which he then hits (This exact accident scene was filmed on Camden, on the west side of the church.) There's more Hollywood history at this church — it's where the 1957 funeral of Humphrey Bogart was held. Note: the resort where *10*'s famous beach scene was filmed is called Puerto Las Hadas and is located on the Bay of Manzanillo, Mexico.

Texas Chainsaw Massacre

Quick Hill Road
Round Rock, Texas

Tobe Hooper's 1973 cult classic (shot in 16mm) has inspired dozens, if not hundreds of slasher films over the years (and was recently remade itself). The farmhouse featured in the original is now gone, but it once stood here on Quick Hill road off I-35, approximately 10 miles north of Austin.

Them!

Sixth Street Viaduct
Los Angeles, California

In the kitschy 1954 horror classic, *Them!*, giant ants (made big thanks to nuclear testing) emerge from this viaduct just east of downtown L.A., which spans the Los Angeles River at Sixth Street.

Titanic

SS Jeremiah O'Brien/National Liberty Ship Memorial
Pier 45
Fishermen's Wharf
San Francisco, California

The Triple Expansion Engine is where James Cameron filmed the engine room scenes for his 1997 blockbuster. Most of the remainder of the movie was shot on a set in Rosarito Beach in Mexico, just south of Tijuana.

Trona Pinnacles

Trona, California
The Trona Pinnacles National Natural Landmark is located about 10 miles west of Trona, a small town in the Mojave Desert.

The Trona Pinnacles have posed as other planet terrains in many movies and TV shows, including *Lost in Space, Star Wars* and *Star Trek IV*. The Pinnacles were formed by algae from when this place was filled with water. Some of them are nearly 60-feet tall.

The Usual Suspects

Angels Gate Park
South Gaffey Street
San Pedro, California

The huge bell where the suspects meet up with Redfoot is the Korean Bell of Friendship in San Pedro, California. The bell, presented by Korea during the U.S. bicentennial celebrations in 1976, is on a scenic bluff overlooking the harbor of San Pedro to the east and the Palos Verdes Peninsula to the west.

War of the Worlds

St. Brendans Catholic Church
310 South Van Ness Avenue
Los Angeles, California

In the final scene of 1953's *War of the Worlds*, this is where the desperate people of Los Angeles gathered to pray (while outside the doors, Martian ships blast their way through the streets of Los Angeles). This adaptation of the classic H.G. Wells story won the 1953 Oscar for Special Effects. Note: The Hollywood United Methodist Church (6817 Franklin Avenue in Hollywood) is commonly misidentified as the church used in this movie. However, this Hollywood church was used in *Back to the Future*, *Sister Act* and *That Thing You Do*, among many others.

Whatever Happened to Baby Jane?

172 North McCadden Place
Los Angeles, California

This creepy 1962 flick starring Bette Davis and Joan Crawford was shot here at this house in the Hancock Park section of Los Angeles and looks pretty much exactly as it did in the movie.

Vertigo

Alfred Hitchcock's 1958 film *Vertigo* is considered by many to be one of his greatest, most spellbinding works. Featuring James Stewart as a retired detective and Kim Novak in a unique double role, the eerie, romantic, complex tale used several locations in San Francisco that remain almost the same today as they were in the film.

Ernie's Restaurant
847 Montgomery Street at Jackson Street
San Francisco, California

A favorite real-life haunt of Hitchcock's (back when it was called Ernie's), this is the restaurant where James Stewart falls hopelessly in love with Kim Novak. When it was the Essex Supper Club until recently, one could notice that while much of the interior had changed since then, the bar area where Stewart catches sight of her remained virtually unchanged. As of this writing, it remains closed, but the building is still there.

Mission Dolores
320 Dolores Street
Mission District (at 16th Street)
San Francisco, California

Dating back to 1791, the mission is the oldest building in San Francisco and is now a museum. In *Vertigo*, it is the cemetery where Kim Novak (Madeleine) visits Carlotta Valdes' grave (alas, a studio prop). Founded in 1776, it was the third in a chain of 21 California missions, and it served the area's original inhabitants, the Ohlone Indians.

900 Lombard Street (corner of Jones Street)
Russian Hill
San Francisco, California

Located just down the hill from the famous "crookedest" street in the world (the world-famous Lombard street), this was Scottie's home (played by Jimmy Stewart) in *Vertigo*.

Nob Hill area of San Francisco

In this upscale area, you will find Madeleine's apartment building, The Brocklebank Apartments, located at 1000 Mason across from the Fairmont Hotel. The Empire Hotel, where Judy lived, is located at 940 Sutter Street, near Hyde. (Note – Hitchcock told fellow director Francois Truffaut that he had Judy live in the Hotel Empire because of its big, green neon sign. The name has changed, but the building is still there.)

Rock 'n' Roll, R&B, and the Blues

Aerosmith

1325 Commonwealth Avenue #2B
Boston, Massachusetts

This building was pictured in the 1991 video for the classic song "Sweet Emotion," and it was here from 1970 to 1972 that the band members of Aerosmith lived, wrote, played, and ate (and maybe even slept a little) until being signed by Columbia Records.

"There were six of us in the group, some of us were living in the kitchen, eating brown rice and Campbell's soup. Those days, you know, when a quart of beer was heaven. It was hard times and it was really good. During lunch we would set up all our equipment outside of BU [Boston University] in the main square and just start wailing. That's basically how we got billed. We never got much publicity in the magazines and newspapers." (Steven Tyler speaking to *Circus Magazine* in June 1975.)

Album Covers

Beach Boys – *Surfin' Safari*

Paradise Cove (just north of Malibu on
Pacific Coast Highway)
Malibu, California

On a chilly morning in 1962, the Beach Boys posed here on
this stretch of California beach for the cover of their first
album. (The site is open to the public, but there is a charge
for entry.)

Browne, Jackson – *Late for the Sky*

215 South Lucerne Street
Hollywood, California

Jackson Browne's third album, 1974's classic *Late for the
Sky,* had its title track featured in Martin Scorcese's film *Taxi
Driver.* The album also boasted other Browne standards "For
a Dancer" and "Farther On." The house featured on the cover
is in the up-
scale Hancock
Park section of Los Angeles.

Creedence Clearwater Revival– *Willie and the Poor Boys*

3218 Peralta Street
Oakland, California

This is where Creedence shot the cover of their fourth
album, 1970's *Willie and the Poor Boys.* The art direction was
an effective representation of the smash single, "Down on
the Corner."

Album Covers

Crosby, Stills and Nash – *Crosby, Stills and Nash*

North of 809 Palm Avenue
West Hollywood, California

The house where famed rock photographer Henry Diltz shot CSN's 1969 debut album cover is long gone from this site. The album featured "Suite: Judy Blue Eyes," "Marrakesh Express" and "Guinnevere" among others. Interestingly, after the album cover was shot, it was pointed out that the singers were posed as Nash, Stills and Crosby. When they returned to re-shoot, the house had been demolished, so they settled for the photo they had.

The Doors – *Strange Days*

150-158 East 36th Street between Lexington and Third Avenues
New York City, New York

This dark, 1967 classic featured the bluesy "Love Me Two Times" and the dramatic "People Are Strange." A mysterious, surreal cover, it was photographed in this New York City courtyard known as Sniffen Court. (The original mid-18th century stables in the courtyard were converted to housing in the 1910s.)

Album Covers

Dr. John – *Dr. John's Gumbo*

Farmer John Company
Soto Street and Vernon
Vernon, California

Dr. John and his band cook through a dozen New Orleans classics on this 1972 gem, featuring the tunes

of Professor Longhair, Huey Smith, Earl King and Ray Charles. The cover was shot in front of the huge mural adorning the wall of The Farmer John Company (also seen in the movie *Carrie*).

Lewis, Huey and the News – *Sports*

2 A.M. Club
382 Miller Avenue
Mill Valley, California
415-388-6036

"The Heart of Rock & Roll," "Heart and Soul," "I Want A New Drug" – these were the songs that launched Huey Lewis and the News on a national scale in 1983. The cover of their smash album *Sports* was shot at this popular Mill Valley bar, the 2 A.M. Club

McCartney, Paul – *Run Devil Run*

Miller's Rexall Drugs
87 Broad Street
Atlanta, Georgia

When Paul McCartney was passing through Atlanta, he saw Miller's Rexall Drugs, and the store inspired the title of his 1999 album. McCartney had been in town with two of his children. (His daughter Heather was unveiling her household creations at a trade show at the Americas Mart Atlanta.) After wandering into this funkier district of town, McCartney saw a bottle of bath salts called "Run Devil Run" in a Rexall shop window. He thought it was a good title for a song – then it became the name of the album (and inspired the album cover art as well).

Album Covers

Pink Floyd – *Wish You Were Here*

Warner Brothers Studios
4210 West Olive Avenue
Burbank, California

Considered by many to be the ultimate Pink Floyd effort, 1975's *Wish You Were Here* is a thematic LP dedicated to Pink Floyd's original frontman, Syd Barrett, who'd burned out years before. The famous cover photo was shot on the lot at Warner Brothers Studios in Burbank, with a guy who was actually on fire (not a photo after-effect). Though the studio is private, VIP tours are offered and while on the tour it is possible to view this location.

Ronstadt, Linda – *Livin' in the U.S.A.*

Irv's Burgers
8289 Santa Monica Boulevard
West Hollywood, California

The inner sleeve of Linda Ronstadt's 1978 smash LP *Livin' in the U.S.A.* featured the singer sitting here at Irv's Burgers.

Album Covers

Spirit – *The Family That Plays Together*

**Sunset Highland Motel
6830 Sunset Boulevard
Hollywood, California**

The classic 1968 release from this popular California band featured the FM staple "I Got a Line on You." The cover was shot at the Sunset Highland Motel, just across from Hollywood High School. (On January 2, 1997, Spirit guitarist and bandleader Randy California – born Randy Craig Wolfe – drowned off the coast of Molokai, Hawaii.)

The Sweet – *Desolation Boulevard*

**8852 Sunset Boulevard
Hollywood, California**

The Sweet shot the cover of this 1975 album near the front of a Los Angeles rock 'n' roll club called The Central. Today it's the site of The Viper Room, where River Phoenix died.

The Youngbloods – *Elephant Mountain*

**Elephant Mountain
Marin County, California**

Released in April 1969, this was the third Youngbloods' LP and their first after the departure of founder Jerry Corbitt. Produced by Charlie Daniels, the album featured an eclectic mix of jazz, blues, country and rock from the group who sang the smash hit "Get Together." The cover featured the scenic landscape of Northern California's Elephant Mountain.

American Sound Studio

827 Thomas Street (at Chelsea Street)
Memphis, Tennessee

From 1967 to 1970, 120 top-20 songs were recorded at the studio that was once located here. Dusty Springfield, Bobby Womack, and Elvis all worked here (this is where the King recorded "Suspicious Minds," "Kentucky Rain" and "In the Ghetto") and it was also here that the Box Tops recorded "The Letter," the biggest-selling single of 1967–68. The original structure has been torn down – today there is an auto parts store at this location.

The Band

8841 Evanview Drive
West Hollywood, California

Sammy Davis, Jr., once lived here, but this is also where The Band cut their brilliant second album, *The Band,* in 1969. The album featured the songs "Across the Great Divide," "The Night They Drove Old Dixie Down," and "Up on Cripple Creek."

Berry, Chuck

Berry Park
Buckner Road
Wentzville (suburb of St. Louis), Missouri

In the 1950s, rock 'n' roll icon Chuck Berry bought this 30-acre parcel of land with the intent of turning it into a full-fledged recreation site. A public pool and fishing spot opened in 1960, but that was about as far as the grand vision got. Berry Park has remained as Berry's homebase and several interesting scenes from the movie of Berry's life, *Hail! Hail! Rock 'n' Roll* (with Keith Richards) were shot here. It is no longer open to the public, but can be found by driving south on Interstate 70 to Highway Z (Church Street). After passing Highway N, head west on Buckner Road.

The Blues

The W.C. Handy House

Issaquena Street
Clarksdale, Mississippi

W.C. Handy lived in Clarksdale from 1903 to 1905, and it was during these formative years that he collected many blues songs. Though he was by no means a Delta blues-man, Handy is referred to by many as the "Father of the Blues" because of the love and attention he gave the music, and also because he helped bring blues music to the world.

Handy was a student of music as a child, playing the cornet, and later travelling the South with dance bands, playing minstrel and tent shows. Handy had heard something akin to the blues as early as 1892, but it was while waiting for an overdue train in Tutwiler, Mississippi, in 1902 or 1903 that he heard a shadowy bluesman playing slide guitar and singing about "goin' where the Southern crosses the Dog," (which referred to the junction of the Southern and the Yazoo and Mississippi Valley railroads farther south near Moorhead). Handy called it "the weirdest music I had ever heard," but from that moment on the seed had been planted — it was the true "Birth of the Blues."

W.C. Handy left Clarksdale and settled in Memphis, Tennessee, around 1909, using Beale Street's Pee Wee's Saloon as his headquarters. His greatest contributions to blues music were his compositions "Memphis Blues," "St. Louis Blues," "Yellow Dog Blues" and "Beale Street Blues." Handy died in New York City in 1958 and is today honored with the annual W.C. Handy Awards — the Blues Foundation's equivalent to the Grammy's. (His house is no longer located at this vacant site.)

Tutwiler Train Station

Tutwiler, Mississippi
(about 15 miles down Highway 49 from Clarksdale)

A plaque here and a commemorative mural near the foundation of the old train station mark where W. C. Handy made his remarkable blues discovery in 1902 or 1903. Handy wrote later of falling asleep while waiting for a late night train and being awakened by the sound of a lone figure playing a guitar by using the edge of a pocketknife as a slide, and singing about the place "where the Southern crosses the Dog."

The Blues

"Where the Southern Crosses the Dog"

Train station
Moorehead, Mississippi

The actual site the bluesman was singing about is located here in the tiny town of Moorehead, where the two railroad lines that were prominent in the Delta at the turn of the century meet. The Southern and the Yazoo and Mississippi Valley (known as the Yellow Dog) railroads cross at right angles here in Moorehead, and some Blues experts say that *this* was actually the crossroads where Robert Johnson made the deal to sell his soul – not the more famous crossroads where Highways 61 and 49 meet in Clarksdale. A sign commemorates the exact spot "where the Southern crosses the Dog," a location made famous by W.C. Handy in his song "Yellow Dog Blues."

W.C. Handy House II

352 Beale Street
Memphis, Tennessee
901-522-1556

This is the W.C. Handy house which was originally located at 659 Jennette Place. It was here that the Father of the Blues wrote such classics as "Yellow Dog Blues" and "Beale Street Blues." Items that belonged to Handy are featured in this turn-of-the-20th-century frame house.

Smith, Bessie

G.T. Thomas Hospital (now the Riverside Hotel)
615 Sunflower Avenue
Clarksdale, Mississippi

Bessie Smith, known as the *Empress of the Blues,* died here in 1937 after an infamous auto accident on Highway 61, outside of town. She was in a car driven by her companion (and Lionel Hampton's uncle) Richard Morgan. In the accident, Smith was critically injured. A doctor arrived and ordered that she be taken to a "colored" hospital in Clarksdale, However, she had lost a lot of blood and ended up dying at the hospital – she was just 43 years old.

Around the time of her death, John Hammond wrote in *Down Beat* magazine that she might have died because she was initially refused entrance to a white hospital and her treatment was delayed while she was taken to a black hospital. Although Hammond later recanted his story, playwright Edward Albee went ahead and wrote the play *The Death of Bessie Smith,* which forever branded the story in the public's mind.

The Blues

Johnson, Robert

109 Young Street
Greenwood, Mississippi

On the night of Saturday, August 13, 1938, blues legend Robert Johnson was playing guitar in a juke joint located on the outskirts of Greenwood, Mississippi – in the back room of a place called the Shaples General Store at Three Forks. (The store, which is gone now, was located where highways 82 and 49E cross today.) Legend says this is when Johnson was poisoned by a jealous husband with either strychnine or lye.

In the middle of the night, Johnson was supposedly taken to a house in nearby Greenwood, where his condition worsened. Three days later, on August 16th, he died at the house that stood at this address (a new house now stands in its place). Johnson was buried in the Mt. Zion churchyard before being re-interred in the nearby Mt. Payne graveyard.

Blues Alley

Clarksdale, Mississippi

Blues Alley is the name for Clarksdale's Historic Blues District. It is here that you'll find Clarksdale Station, the newly renovated passenger depot of the old Illinois Central Railroad and, just about a hundred yards away, the Delta Blues Museum.

The station is extremely significant to the history of the blues. After all, this is where many famous blues musicians such as Muddy Waters boarded the train to Chicago, seeking jobs and a potential career in music. The Delta Blues Museum houses a collection of memorabilia from B.B. King, Sonny Boy Williamson, Bessie Smith and Muddy Waters, along with many other exhibits. The Delta Blues Museum is located at #1 Blues Alley, Clarksdale, Mississippi (662-627-6820).

Bowie, David

Cleveland Public Hall Convention Center
500 Lakeside Avenue
Cleveland, Ohio

David Bowie made his American concert debut here in Cleveland on September 22, 1972, when he premiered his outrageously revolutionary *Ziggy Stardust* show with the Spiders from Mars at the Cleveland Music Hall. The orange-haired Bowie, who sailed over to America due to a fear of flying, almost saw the show cancelled by his manager, Tony DeFries, over the size of the piano that was provided in the 3,500-seat hall. However, a new piano was borrowed from the Cleveland Symphony Orchestra and the show went on. (The band Fumbal opened the show.) A post-concert party was held that night at the Hollenden House Hotel, which was located in Cleveland at 610 Superior Avenue. (Bowie would return to play this venue in 1974 during his elaborate *Diamond Dogs* tour.)

Brown, James

WIBB Radio
830 Mulberry Street
Macon, Georgia

In 1955, this was the location of WIBB 1280 AM, a local radio station that allowed a young singer named James Brown to cut a demo of what became his first hit single, "Please Please Please." A DJ at the station, Hamp Swain, played the song over and over until it caught fire, thus putting James Brown on the map. Today, the building still exists, but it's an insurance office, not a radio station.

The Doors

The Warehouse
1820 Tchoupitoulas Street
New Orleans, Louisiana

From 1969 to 1982, a former coffee storage warehouse hosted many memorable rock concerts, including shows from Bowie to Bob Dylan. It was here on December 12, 1970, that The Doors played their final public performance – a supposed disaster that found front man Jim Morrison smashing a hole in the middle of the stage with the mike stand. The building has since been razed.

Dylan, Bob

Birthplace

519 North 3rd Avenue East
Duluth, Minnesota

Dylan was born Robert Allen Zimmerman on May 24, 1941, in Duluth, and spent his first six years in this port city at the end of Lake Superior. The Zimmermans lived on the top floor of this house, which incidentally was auctioned off on eBay in 2001 for $94,600. When Dylan was in kindergarten, his family moved to his mother's hometown of Hibbing, a mining town about 75 miles north of Duluth.

Childhood Home

2425 7th Avenue East
Hibbing, Minnesota

For most of Dylan's life in Hibbing, he lived here. He graduated from Hibbing High School in 1959 (the 1959 yearbook is locked in a cabinet at Hibbing Public Library) and moved to Minneapolis to attend the University of Minnesota. In 1960, he dropped out of the University and moved to New York City. His first album, *Bob Dylan,* was released in 1962. That year, he legally changed his name from Robert Allen Zimmerman to Bob Dylan. A collection relating to Dylan's life and accomplishments is located at the Hibbing Public Library at 2020 East 5th Avenue.

The Ten O'Clock Scholar

416 14th Avenue SE
Minneapolis, Minnesota

Robert Zimmerman entered the arts school of the University of Minnesota, located in Minneapolis, in the fall of 1959. While a student at the University, he performed his first solo shows here at the "Ten O'Clock Scholar," a local coffeehouse. In October 1959, Robert Zimmerman went in to the coffeehouse to see if he could play there. When asked his name by owner David Lee, he responded "Bob Dylan." He maintained a regular job playing at the "Scholar" until May 1960. Today, the site is a video store parking lot.

Colorado Home

1736 East 17th Avenue
Denver, Colorado

Bob Dylan lived at this address for a short period in the early 1960s – around the time he was playing regularly at the legendary Satire Lounge located at 1920 East Colfax Avenue. Incidentally, the Satire Lounge was also the starting point for Tommy and Dick Smothers, better known as The Smothers Brothers (they lived in the only apartment above the Satire). Judy Collins also played here many times – she attended East High School just a few blocks away.

Dylan, Bob

Meeting with Woody Guthrie

Greystone Park Psychiatric Hospital
West Hanover Avenue
Morris Plains, New Jersey

When Bob Dylan first came east in February 1961, he headed straight here to visit his hero, the long-ailing Woody Guthrie, famous singer, ballad-maker and poet. This marked the beginning of a deep friendship between the two singers. Although separated by 30 years and two generations, they were united on many personal and artistic levels. Woody Guthrie was eventually transferred to Brooklyn State Hospital, where he spent the rest of his life. The Greystone Hospital still houses some patients, but many of the buildings are vacant and in need of repair.

Cedar Street Tavern

82 University Place
New York City, New York
212-741-9754

An old-fashioned tavern that was once a popular watering hole of artists such as Jackson Pollock, Willem de Kooning and Mark Rothko in the 1950s, by the '60s it had become a favorite Dylan hangout.

First Professional Gig

Gerde's Folk City
11 West 4th Street
New York City, New York

This former folk music landmark is where Bob Dylan played his first professional gig on April 11, 1961, supporting blues legend John Lee Hooker. He played here again on September 26th of that same year, a show that was reviewed by Robert Shelton in the *New York Times*. The rave review helped set the Dylan legend in full motion. The site is today occupied by the Hebrew Union College.

Dylan, Bob

White Horse Tavern

567 Hudson Street (at 11th Street)
New York City, New York
212-243-9260

This 18th-century bar was a popular Dylan haunt back in 1961, where he would come to hear the Clancy Brothers play. It's also famous as the place where the Welsh poet Dylan Thomas ate his last meal before drinking himself to death. His last words were supposedly, "I've had 19 straight whiskies. I believe that's the record." He died later that night. Founded in 1880, the White House Tavern is the second oldest bar in New York City.

Suze Rotolo

One Sheridan Square
New York City, New York

Formerly the location of the legendary club called Cafe Society Downtown, it was above this little theatre that the Rotolos lived (mother Mary, a widow, and her two daughters, Carla and Suze). 17-year-old Suze Rotolo had fallen for Dylan after seeing him play at a folk music day at the Riverside Church on July 29, 1961. Dylan crashed at a friend's place here on the fourth floor and soon, he and Suze were lovers. It's believed that after Suze left Dylan in May 1962, the heartache inspired him to compose such classic love songs as "Tomorrow Is a Long Time" and "Don't Think Twice, It's All Right."

The Freewheelin' Bob Dylan

161 West Fourth Street
New York City, New York

Dylan and his girlfriend, Suze Rotolo, first lived here in an apartment between Jones Street and Sixth Avenue. They moved here in December 1961 just after Dylan had finished recording his debut album for Columbia. Outside the apartment, in the middle of West Fourth Street, Dylan and Suze were photographed together in February 1963 for the cover of *The Freewheelin' Bob Dylan* album by Columbia staff photographer Don Hunstein (even though they had been separated for seven months at that point). The shot features Dylan and Suze walking toward West 4th with the camera facing Bleecker Street.

Dylan, Bob

Hotel Earle

163 Waverly Place
New York City, New York
212-777-9515

In the early 1960s, Dylan lived at this one-time run-down hotel (now the much nicer Washington Square Hotel) in room 305. Dylan pal and fellow musician Ramblin' Jack Elliott lived in room 312 and Red Indian folksinger Peter LaFarge lived in room 306 – LaFarge wrote "The Ballad of Ira Hayes," eventually recorded by both Johnny Cash and Dylan.

"A Hard Rain's A-Gonna Fall"

Village Gate
158 Bleecker Street
New York City, New York

In 1962, in the basement apartment of the renowned Village Gate theater, Dylan wrote the song "A Hard Rain's A-Gonna Fall." (The small apartment was then occupied by Chip Monck, later to become one of the most sought-after lighting directors in rock music.) Today, the Village Gate still presents music and theater; it's now called The Village Theater.

A.J. Weberman

94 MacDougal Street
New York City, New York

When the Dylan family left Woodstock in 1970, they moved into this tasteful Greenwich Village townhouse. It was here that Dylan found himself constantly (and infamously) harangued by the seemingly obsessed Dylan expert, A.J. Weberman. It was outside this very house that Weberman made off with the Dylan family's garbage for further study of the legend.

"Blowin' in the Wind"

The Commons
130 West 3rd Street
New York City, New York
212-533-4790

Dylan played here at The Commons, a sprawling basement club, within a week of his arrival in New York City. It was also here, in 1962, that Dylan started writing a song. After finishing it, he took it over to Folk City and played it for Gil Turner, who thought it was incredible. Gil got up on the stage and played it for the audience, while Bob stood in the shadows at the bar – which is how the world first heard the Dylan classic, "Blowin' in the Wind."

Dylan, Bob

"Masters of War"

Gaslight Cafe/Kettle of Fish Bar
116 MacDougal Street
New York City, New York

One of young Dylan's favorite haunts, the Gaslight was originally a "basket house," where performers were paid the proceeds of a passed-around basket. Opened in 1958 by John Mitchell – legendary pioneer of Greenwich Village coffeehouses – the Gaslight had already become a showcase for beat poets Allen Ginsberg and Gregory Corso. However, it was transformed into a folk club when Sam Hood took it over. It was here that Dylan premiered "Masters of War" and many other of his songs. The Kettle of Fish Bar, located upstairs above the Gaslight, was also a regular drinking hangout for Dylan and other bohemian artists of the day.

The Bitter End

147 Bleecker Street at La Guardia Place
New York City, New York

When Dylan started hanging out again in Greenwich in the summer of 1975, he made several appearances here with the likes of Patti Smith, Ramblin' Jack Elliot, Bobby Neuwirth and others before hitting the road with the Rolling Thunder Revue tour. The club is now called The Other End.

Blood on the Tracks

Sound 80
2709 East 25th Street
Minneapolis, Minnesota

At this one-time recording studio called Sound 80, Bob Dylan recorded his classic mid-1970's album, *Blood on the Tracks,* which featured both "Tangled Up In Blue" and "Idiot Wind," among others. The popular studio had also been used by Leo Kottke and Cat Stevens; the 1980 dance hit "Funkytown" was also cut here. Today, the building where so much musical history was made is used by Orfield Laboratories for testing products' acoustical properties.

Hard Rock Café

300 East 5th Street
Los Angeles, California

This was where photographer Henry Diltz shot the back of The Doors 1969 album, *Morrison Hotel*. (The front cover had been shot a few blocks away at a place called The Morrison Hotel.) The flophouse bar is long gone in this tough L.A. neighborhood.

Says Diltz: "I guess sometime the next year after the album came out with that picture on the back, they got a call from England and this guy says, 'Hello. Would you mind if we use that name on the back of your album? We're starting a cafe over here in London and we would like to use that name.' And they said no, go ahead, and that was the beginning of it. Now every time I go into a Hard Rock Cafe, whatever city I'm in, I always feel like I should get a free hamburger."

Harrison, George

Hard Day's Nite Bed and Breakfast
113 McCann Street
Benton, Illinois
618-438-2328

This was once the house of Louise Harrison, George Harrison's sister, and it's where the first Beatle ever stayed in the United States. Louise Harrison lived in the house in 1963 (until 1968), and shortly before the Beatles exploded in the U.S., Harrison made a trip here. He wanted to see his sister, but he also needed a break from insane Beatlemania that had already kicked in overseas. When George took his summer vacation, it is said he spent his time picnicking and performing with a local band, The Four Vests. George left in September and returned to the United States the following February to appear on *The Ed Sullivan Show*.

In 1996, Benton decided to make a parking lot next to Benton Consolidated High School, where the house resides. Three couples came together to buy the house and with the help of Louise, convinced the town that it should survive as a historical site. Today, it lives on as the Hard Day's Night Bed and Breakfast, replete with a Beatles mini-museum inside. At the Franklin County Jail Museum, one of the rooms is dedicated to George's Benton stay, primarily his visit to the WFRX 1300 radio station in West Frankfort. On display are the turntables that first brought Beatles records to the American airwaves. The museum is located 1/2 mile off I-57 on Route 14 in Benton (618-932-6159).

Hendrix, Jimi

Haleakala Crater
Maui, Hawaii
Directions: Park headquarters and the 10,023 foot summit can be reached from
Kahului via Route 37 to 377 to 378.

Haleakala is an active, but not currently erupting, volcano on the island of Maui that last
released its fury in 1790. And it was here on July 30, 1970 that Jimi Hendrix erupted, performing his last ever American show. This concert was supposed to be part of the film
Rainbow Bridge, but little of the concert footage was used in the film and *none* of the
audio was used on the
soundtrack album (this is a
widely bootlegged show
among Hendrix fans). After
this concert, Hendrix went
on to play a handful of dates
in Europe and died later that
year in his sleep, on September 18th, at the Samar-
kand Hotel in London. He
was just 27 years old.

Holly, Buddy

KDAV Radio (now KRFE AM 580)
6602 Martin Luther King Boulevard
Lubbock, Texas
806-745-1197

Today it's an easy listening station, but back in 1953 Buddy Holly did a weekly radio show
here with his partner Bob Montgomery. It's believed by many that KDAV was the first
full-time country music station in the United States.

Buddy Holly and Montgomery were initially given a chance to perform on the air during

The Sunday Party. This later evolved into a regular slot at 2:30 P.M. every Sunday for what by
then had become a trio (Holly, Montgomery,
and bassist Larry Welborn). The segment was
called *The Buddy and Bob Show* and featured a
unique blend of Country and Western and
Rhythm and Blues. Tours are offered today, so
you can get a chance to see the actual studio
where Buddy Holly cut his very first records.

Joplin, Janis

**Harvard Stadium
North Harvard Street
Cambridge, Massachusetts**

Janis Joplin performed the last concert of her life here with her Full Tilt Boogie Band on August 12, 1970 in front of 40,000 people. She was to die less than two months later on October 4th, in Los Angeles at the Landmark Hotel.

KISS

**10 East 23rd Street
New York City, New York**

Back in the pre-makeup days of 1972, this is where the band KISS (Gene Simmons, Paul Stanley, Ace Frehley and Peter Criss) got together to start rehearsing, up in a loft on the fourth floor. Today it is the site of Cosmic Comics.

Led Zeppelin

**Auditorium Arena
1245 Champa Street
Denver, Colorado
303-893-4000**

On December 26, 1968 Led Zeppelin played its first-ever American show at Denver's Auditorium Arena. The set list included "Train Kept A Rollin'," "Dazed and Confused," "You Shook Me," "Babe I'm Gonna Leave You" and "Communication Breakdown." The tour lasted into February and took the band from Denver to Cleveland to New York to Toronto. Now part of the Denver Center for the Performing Arts, the Auditorium Arena has hosted everything from the Democratic National Convention to auto shows to countless other concerts.

"Louie Louie"

142 West 54th Street
Los Angeles, California

The is the actual house where R&B singer Richard Berry wrote the classic garage band anthem, "Louie, Louie" in 1955. He recorded it himself in 1956, but it wasn't until The Kingsmen cut it in 1963 that the song became widely known. (Note – Berry had sung lead on The Coasters classic song, "Riot in Cellblock Number 9.")

McCartney, Linda

Memorial Stadium
Gayley Road
UC Berkeley Campus
Berkeley, California

An infamous tape in the early 1990s surfaced, purported to be the warblings of Linda McCartney singing background for her husband during an appearance here in 1990. The painfully off-key vocals during the Beatle classic "Hey Jude" became widely circulated and remains a bit of a comedy classic.

Media Sound

311 West 57th Street
New York City, New York
212-307-7228

Today, it's Le Bar Bat Restaurant, but this former Baptist church was once Media Sound Recording Studios, where the Rolling Stones recorded *Tattoo You,* where John Lennon recorded *Walls and Bridges,* where Lou Reed cut *New York* and where Marc Bolan/T. Rex recorded *Electric Warrior* (which featured the single, "Bang a Gong").

Metallica

3140 Carlson Boulevard
El Cerrito, California

This Bay-area house is where the band Metallica lived together from 1983 to 1986. During this time they wrote and rehearsed the albums *Ride the Lightning* and *Master of Puppets* in the garage before recording both sets. Perhaps the ultimate heavy metal landmark.

Morrison, Jim

8216½ Norton Avenue
West Hollywood, California

This was Doors lead singer Jim Morrison's last residence. He lived here in 1970 with Pamela Morrison (who was never legally married to the singer). It was here where Chuck Berry came to visit Morrison, an event that supposedly stunned him in the best of ways.

Rendezvous Ballroom

Between Washington and Palm Avenues
(Along what is now Ocean Front Boulevard)
Balboa, California

Originally built in 1928, the Rendezvous Ballroom was a huge, two-story dancehall that over the years hosted Artie Shaw, Ozzie Nelson, Benny Goodman, Guy Lombardo, Bob Crosby, Tommy Dorsey, Stan Kenton and many other music legends of the day.

But it was in the late 1950s and early 1960s that a musical revolution began at this spot, because that's when seminal surf guitarist Dick Dale and his group the Del-Tones began playing here. Their numerous appearances at the ballroom are considered by many to be what became the birth of true "Surf" music (Dale's sound even inspired a dance – "The Surfer Stomp"). In 1966, the Rendezvous Ballroom burned to the ground and today a plaque can be found at the site.

Rock 'n' Roll Festivals

Atlantic City Pop Festival

Atlantic City Racetrack
4501 Black Horse Pike
Mays Landing, New Jersey
609-641-2190

From August 1–3, 1969, 110,000 people attended this festival at the Atlantic City Racetrack — a sort of tune up for Woodstock. Thirty or so bands played, many of whom then headed up to play Woodstock the next week. The show featured (among others) Joan Baez, Arlo Guthrie, Tim Harden, Richie Havens, Ravi Shankar, Sweetwater, Canned Heat, Creedence Clearwater Revival, The Grateful Dead, The Jefferson Airplane, Mountain, The Who, The Band, Blood Sweat & Tears, Joe Cocker, Crosby Stills & Nash, Santana, Jimi Hendrix, Ten Years After, Johnny Winter and Sha Na Na.

Atlanta Pop Festival

Atlanta Motor Speedway
1500 Highway 41
Byron, Georgia

From July 3–5, 1970, here in the tiny central Georgia town of Byron (10 miles south of Macon), smack in the middle of a pecan grove (and on what was then known as the Middle Georgia Raceway) somewhere between 350,000 to 500,000 people witnessed the second annual Atlanta International Pop Festival. Exactly like Woodstock the previous summer (but with more people), the event was promoted as "three days of peace, love and music." On the bill were Jimi Hendrix, the Allman Brothers, Jethro Tull, B.B. King, Ravi Shankar, 10 Years After, Johnny Winter, John Sebastian and others. (Tickets for the music festival were $14.)

Devonshire Downs Racetrack

Devonshire Street just west of Zelzah Avenue
Northridge, California

This site, a former racetrack, is probably best known for hosting the famed Newport '69 music festival from June 20-22. Despite the name "Newport," the show (which drew about 150,000 fans) actually took place out in the San Fernando Valley. On the bill were Jethro Tull, Jimi Hendrix, The Animals, Led Zeppelin, Creedence Clearwater Revival, The Chambers Brothers, Johnny Winters, the Young Rascals, Booker T. & MG's, Three Dog Night, The Byrds, The Grassroots, Marvin Gaye and Mother Earth. The site is now a shopping center.

Rock 'n' Roll Festivals

Festival for Peace

Shea Stadium
123-01 Roosevelt Avenue
Flushing, New York

The Summer Festival for Peace was held here on August 5, 1970, and the scorching hot weather may have played a part in why the festival drew an undersized crowd. However, those in attendance were treated to performances by Jimi Hendrix, Janis Joplin, Poco, Steppenwolf, James Gang, Janis Joplin, The Rascals, Johnny Winter, Ten Wheel Drive, Tom Paxton, Dionne Warwick, Paul Simon and several others. An underpublicized, underdocumented event, it was one of the more diverse lineups featured during the spate of music festivals held in the wake of Woodstock.

Mount Pocono Festival

Pocono International Speedway
Long Pond, Pennsylvania

Held July 8-9, 1972, over 200,000 fans attended this muddy two-day festival which featured (among others) Emerson, Lake and Palmer, Humble Pie, Three Dog Night, Rod Stewart & The Faces, Mother Night, Cactus, Edgar Winter, The J. Geils Band and Black Sabbath. The festival was marred on Saturday by a three-hour rain delay.

Newport Pop Festival

Orange County Fairgrounds
88 Fair Avenue
Costa Mesa, California

On August 4-5, 1968, over 140,000 pre-Woodstock fans gathered here to watch (among others) Tiny Tim, The Jefferson Airplane, Country Joe and the Fish, The Grateful Dead, The Chambers Brothers, Charles Lloyd, James Cotton Blues Band, Quicksilver Messenger Service, The Byrds, Alice Cooper, Steppenwolf, Sonny and Cher, Canned Heat, Electric Flag, Butterfield Blues Band, Eric Burdon and the Animals, Blue Cheer, Iron Butterfly, Illinois Speed Press and Things To Come. Admission was just $5.50 per day and the festival was produced by "Humble" Harvey Miller, a top Los Angeles disk jockey. The site still hosts the popular Orange County Fair each year.

Rock 'n' Roll Festivals

Texas International Pop Festival

Dallas International Motor Speedway
Lewisville, Texas

This track, which closed down in 1973, was located on Interstate 35 East just north of Dallas. Over Labor Day weekend, 1969, (just two weeks after Woodstock) 120,000 fans converged on the small town of Lewisville for the Texas Pop Festival. They were treated

to performances by a diverse range of artists including B.B. King, Canned Heat, Chicago, Delaney & Bonnie & Friends, Freddie King, Grand Funk Railroad, Herbie Mann, Incredible String Band, James Cotton Blues Band, Janis Joplin, Johnny Winter, Led Zeppelin, The Nazz, The Quarry, Rotary Connection, Sam & Dave, Santana, Shiva's Headband, Sly & the Family Stone, Space Opera, Spirit, Sweetwater, Ten Years After and Tony Joe White.

Toronto Rock and Roll Revival

Varsity Stadium
277 Bloor Street West
Toronto, Canada

According to Ringo Starr, it was Lennon's first-ever solo performance – the famed Plastic Ono Band concert here at Toronto's Varsity Stadium on September 13, 1969 – that proved to be the end of the Beatles' career. With the exception of the famous rooftop concert at Apple Headquarters, this was Lennon's first live appearance since 1966. After the concert, Lennon returned to London with his mind made up to quit. Starr is quoted as saying "After (John Lennon's) Plastic Ono Band's debut in Toronto we had a meeting in Saville Row where John finally brought it to a head. He said: `Well, that's it lads, let's end it.'"

The show, billed as The Toronto Rock and Roll Revival, also featured The Doors, Chuck Berry, Little Richard, Bo Diddley, Alice Cooper and others, and for Lennon, resulted in the album *Live Peace in Toronto* and the single "Cold Turkey." The stadium has since been torn down, but the field remains.

"Rock Around the Clock"

Pythian Temple Studios
135 West 70th Street
New York City, New York

In April of 1954, Bill Haley and the Comets entered a recording studio here and recorded the seminal rock and roll classic, "Rock Around the Clock," which held down the Number One spot for eight weeks and went on to sell 45 million copies worldwide. Haley, who performed on the revival circuit throughout the 1960s and '70s, did get to see his signature song become a U.S. hit for the second time in 1974 when "Rock Around the Clock" appeared on the soundtrack for both the George Lucas film *American Graffiti* and the hit TV show *Happy Days*.

When Haley recorded his landmark tune, this building was a meeting hall for the Knights of Pythias, and Decca records used the building's ballroom as a recording studio. The building still maintains its odd, temple-like appearance, but it is now a condo. Haley suffered and died from a heart attack at his home in Harlingen, Texas on February 9, 1981.

The Rolling Stones

RCA Records

6363 Sunset Boulevard
Hollywood, California

From the early 1960s through the early 1990s, some of the most famous records of all time were recorded in this building. Elvis was here in the '70s, The Monkees recorded here, The Jefferson Airplane, etc. But the band that perhaps did the most damage was the Rolling Stones, who recorded (among other songs) "Satisfaction," "Paint it Black," "19th Nervous Breakdown" and "Let's Spend the Night Together" at this location. Today, the building houses the Los Angeles Film School.

The Rolling Stones

"Memory Motel"

692 Montauk Highway
Montauk (Long Island), New York
631-668-2702

The Memory Motel is a small (13 rooms) motel and bar immortalized by the Rolling Stones in the pretty ballad of the same name (which appeared on the band's 1976 album *Black and Blue*). During the mid-1970s, the Rolling Stones — and in particular Mick Jagger — were regulars out on the remote reaches of Montauk, hanging out with artist Andy Warhol at his nearby compound, among other places.

Jagger spent time at the motel because it had a pool table and a decent jukebox, and one night while here he supposedly was inspired to write the beautiful song about "Hannah, a honey of a girl," and where they spent "a lonely night at the Memory Motel." (Rumor has it he actually wrote part of the tune at the bar.)

Reckless Driving

Fordyce, Arkansas
(Near 100 South Main Street)

Fordyce (population about 5,000) is located at the intersection of two U.S. Highways, 79 and 167, and State Highway 8. On July 5, 1975, police pulled over a rented Chevy after the car swerved on the roadway. Among the car's occupants were guitarists Keith Richards and Ron Wood of the Rolling Stones. Richards was later charged with reckless driving and possession of a knife and his bodyguard Fred Sessler was charged with possession of a controlled substance. (Richards was released on $160 bail and later paid a fine.)

The Rolling Stones

Keith Richards' Heroin Bust

Harbour Castle Westin
1 Harbour Square
Toronto, Canada
416-869-1600

On February 27, 1977, Royal Canadian Mounted Police crashed into suite 2223 in this hotel and found five grams of cocaine, 22 grams of heroin, and Keith Richards, who was promptly arrested. After a six-month court battle, stunningly, Richards got off with a slap on the wrist (the Stones were made to play a charity show in Toronto to benefit the blind). The arrest followed club gigs at the El Mocambo, where the Stones had recorded portions of their 1977 concert album, *Love You Live.* The El Mocambo Club is located at 494 Spadina Avenue, Toronto, Ontario M5R3G1 (416-968-2001).

"Waiting on a Friend"

132 1st Avenue
New York City, New York

At one time this bar was called the St. Marks Bar & Grill, and in the 1981 video for their hit, "Waiting on a Friend," Mick Jagger and Keith Richards meet the rest of the Rolling Stones here (after Mick waited for Keith on the stoop of the building seen on the cover of Led Zeppelin's *Physical Graffiti* album). The band was filmed performing in this tiny space for the rest of the day, and for years the bar sold T-shirts commemorating the event.

Long View Farm

Stoddard Road
North Brookfield, Massachusetts

This rustic, isolated recording studio was home to the Rolling Stones from August though September 1981, as they rehearsed and prepared for their upcoming world tour. (Mick Jagger even invited several local high school kids up here to interview him for their school paper, creating a press opportunity that no national media got to enjoy.) Long View Farm was a former dairy farm that had been converted to a recording studio, and Stevie Wonder, J Geils, Motley Crue and James Taylor are just a few of the artists who have recorded here in the beautiful Massachusetts countryside.

The Rolling Stones

Sir Morgan's Cove

89 Green Street
Worcester, Massachusetts
508-363-1888

On September 14, 1981 the Rolling Stones played a surprise concert here at this small club (now called Lucky Dog Music Hall) on the heels of launching their massive 1981 tour of the United States. The Stones were nearing the end of a six-week stay at Long View Farm, where they were rehearsing for their upcoming tour that would showcase the album, *Tattoo You*.

Local radio station WAAF announced the show and handled the 350 tickets for the lucky fans, who got to witness the first live Stones show in three years, a nearly two-hour set that opened with "Under My Thumb" and included such classics as "Satisfaction," "Honky Tonk Woman," and "Tumblin' Dice." The next Stones show would be a little more than a week later in front of 90,000 people at Philadelphia's J.F.K. stadium.

Checkerboard Lounge

423 East 43rd Street
Chicago, Illinois

This historic south-side blues mecca was once owned by musical legends Buddy Guy and Junior Wells. The Rolling Stones have regularly showed up to jam after hours with the likes of Muddy Waters, as was famously documented on photos hanging throughout the popular club. Today it is closed.

Rubin, Rick

Weinstein Residence Hall
5-11 University Place
New York City, New York

It was in this dorm building, room 203 to be exact, that Rick Rubin started his influential Def Jam Records with Russell Simmons while a student at New York University. His work with L.L. Cool J, the Beastie Boys and Jazzy Jay attracted the attention of Columbia Records, who, just one year later, paid Rubin more than half a million dollars for a distribution deal.

Sigma Sound Studios

212 North 12th Street
Philadelphia, Pennsylvania
215-561-3660

When engineer Joe Tarsia took over this studio in 1968, it all but marked the birth of the sound known as "Philadelphia Soul." The Stylistics, O Jays, Delfonics, the Spinners, Harold Melvin and the Blue Notes and many others all created early 1970's magic here (David Bowie even recorded *Young Americans* at Sigma). The studio continues as a force today, though TSOP (The Sound of Philadelphia, as it was called) has yet to be equaled in terms of commercial impact.

Spencer, Jeremy

Hollywood Hawaiian Hotel
Corner of Yucca Street and Grace Avenue
Hollywood, California

In 1971, a pre-Stevie Nicks/Lindsay Buckingham version of Fleetwood Mac rolled into Hollywood, two weeks into their American tour. While staying at the Hawaiian Hotel, guitarist Jeremy Spencer went for a stroll to buy some newspapers at a bookstore on Hollywood Boulevard. He was approached by a member of a religious group called The Children of God and almost instantly fell under their spell.

When the guitarist failed to show up for that evening's gig, the police were contacted, and after five worry-filled days Spencer was traced to the Children of God headquarters at a warehouse in downtown L.A. In order to get in to see Spencer, Fleetwood Mac manager Clifford Davis had to make up a story about Jeremy's wife, Fiona, being seriously

ill. According to a Fleetwood Mac roadie who was at the scene, Spencer "was walking around in a daze like a zombie . . . he'd been brainwashed. It nearly killed me to see him." His head had been shaved and he now answered to the biblical name "Jonathan."

In the course of a three-hour talk (during which members of the cult rubbed Jeremy's arms and chanted "Jesus loves you"), Spencer explained that he had tired of the hedonistic rock and roll lifestyle and that he was through with the group.

With six weeks left on the tour, Fleetwood Mac persuaded eccentric former guitarist Peter Green to fly in and finish the tour. Today, it is believed that Jeremy Spencer is still involved with the Children of God, and he is still playing and composing music. As for the Hawaiian Hotel, the building still exists, only now it's the Princess Grace Apartments.

Springsteen, Bruce

The Student Prince
911 Kingsley Street
Asbury Park, New Jersey

It was here in the summer of 1971 that Bruce Springsteen first met the man who became one of the foundations of the E Street Band, and the ultimate onstage foil for Springsteen – sax player Clarence Clemons.

Stern, Howard

WRNW-FM
55 Woodside Avenue
Briarcliff Manor, New York

After graduating from Boston College in 1976, legendary radio personality Howard Stern started working as a DJ for the progressive FM station WRNW in Briarcliff, New York (located in Westchester County). This was his first real on-air job, and while here he eventually took over several other duties, including both program and production direction. Stern lasted about two years at WRNW before moving to Hartford, Connecticut, to work for WCCC. In Stern's autobiographical movie, *Private Parts* (based on his wildly successful book), you can actually see the building where WRNW used to exist, as Stern used the exterior in the movie. (Today, it houses other businesses.)

Surf Music

Bel Air Club
312 Catalina Avenue
Redondo Beach, California

Thought to be the birthplace of surf music, this is where a band called The Belairs played regularly in 1961 to the beach crowd. Their catchy instrumentals caught on, especially a tune called *Mr. Moto,* which became a local hit and eventually inspired the Beach Boys. An office is now located at the site.

Turner, Ike and Tina

4263 Olympiad Drive
Baldwin Hills, California

In this L.A. suburb, the Turners lived throughout their heyday years in the 1960s and '70s. It was the center of much of the torment Tina Turner allegedly suffered at the hands of her husband, and in fact the house was also used in the film about Tina Turner, *What's Love Got to Do with It,* starring actress Angela Bassett.

The Village Studios

1616 Butler Avenue
West Los Angeles, California
310-478-8227

This former Masonic Temple (built in 1922) has played host to some of rock and roll's most important recordings, including the Rolling Stones' *Goat's Head Soup*, Eric Clapton's *After Midnight* (as well as his Grammy Award-winning "Tears in Heaven,") most Steely Dan records (including *Aja*) and works by Rikki Lee Jones, Bob Dylan, The Red Hot Chili Peppers, and many more. It was also here in 1978 that Studio D was famously renovated for Fleetwood Mac's legendary recording of *Tusk*. (Eric Clapton was also photographed here for his first solo album.)

Wilson, Brian

10452 Bellagio Road
Beverly Hills, California

The musical genius Brian Wilson once painted this mansion purple, much to the ire of his neighbors. It also contained the home studio where he recorded much of the albums *Smile, Wild Honey, Friends, 20/20, Sunflower* and *Surf's Up.*

The Who

Brooklyn Fox Theater
Intersection of Flatbush and Fulton
Brooklyn, New York

On March 25, 1967, The Who made their United States debut here in Brooklyn, as part of a Murray The K Rock and Roll Festival. After a series of shows throughout the week, the band returned during the summer for a more extended tour of the east and south. The vintage Brooklyn Fox Theater, which had been built in 1928, was torn down in 1970.

Channel Surfing

The Andy Griffith Show

Mount Airy, North Carolina (35 miles northwest of Winston-Salem)
1-800-576-0231

Mayberry

Located at the foot of the Blue Ridge Mountains in western North Carolina, Mount Airy is where actor Andy Griffith grew up, and it's also the place that inspired the town of Mayberry from Griffith's popular 1960's TV show. Today, fans of *The Andy Griffith Show* can visit Floyd's City Barber Shop, the Old Mayberry Jail, Snappy Lunch, and even Andy's childhood home in this town that proudly wraps itself in its celebrated legend.

An American Family

35 Woodale Lane
Santa Barbara, California

Reality TV may have been born in 1973 with Public Television's airing of the *cinema verité* miniseries, *An American Family*, the groundbreaking production that followed the lives of Bill and Pat Loud of Santa Barbara, California and their five children: Michele, Delilah, Grant, Kevin and Lance. More than 10 million viewers played voyeur as this fascinating real-life middle-class drama documented marital tensions leading to divorce, a son's gay lifestyle and the changing values of American families. This is the house where the program took place.

Bewitched

The Fisherman Statue
Stacey Boulevard
Gloucester, Massachusetts

This famous statue was the focus of a 1970 *Bewitched* episode, shot on location (as opposed to the usual on-set episodes). The storyline involved Elizabeth Montgomery's character, Samantha, visiting the New England area to attend a witches' convention in historic Salem. Her husband, Darrin Stephens (Dick Sargent), crossed paths with his mischievous cousin-in-law Serena the witch (Elizabeth Montgomery in a dual role) who turned him into the likeness of a local monument called "The Fisherman Statue" (official title "The Man at the Wheel").

While Darrin became the statue, Serena ran around town with the reincarnated image of the Fisherman Statue. For the role, actor Dick Sargent was dressed in a fisherman's raincoat and hat and then sprayed all over with a rusty green color to simulate the weather-worn, oxidized statue. As to why the cast traveled east on location to shoot, it's because their Hollywood stage burned down in April 1970. While they rebuilt the show's filming stage, the production shot four episodes on location.

Buffy the Vampire Slayer

2607 Glendower Avenue
Los Angeles, California

During the second and third season of the series, Angel the vampire lived on top of a hill here in the Griffith Park area. The well-known, much-filmed mansion is the Ennis-Brown house, a landmark home designed by Frank Lloyd Wright. (The same building was also featured in the 1959 horror classic *The House on Haunted Hill*, the 1981 sci-fi flick *Blade Runner* and on the David Lynch TV series *Twin Peaks*.) The Buffy house is located three blocks north of Torrance High at 1313 Cota Drive in Torrance. The scenes set at Sunnydale High School were actually shot on location at Torrance High School at 2200 West Carson Street in the South Bay section in the city of Torrance (this was also used as the *Beverly Hills 90210* high school.)

Cagney and Lacey

111 North Hope Street
Los Angeles, California

This is the Department of Water and Power building in Los Angeles, and it served as the exterior of the 14th Precinct of *Cagney and Lacey*. (The garage parking lot of this build-

ing was used for the shootout and chase scenes in the movie, *The Terminator*.) The show, starring Sharon Gless and Tyne Daly, aired on the CBS television network from 1982–88, and though rated in the list of top 25 programs only once during those years, it drew critical acclaim and established a substantial audience of fiercely loyal viewers who, on at least one occasion, helped save the program from cancellation by the network.

Dennis the Menace

830 South Madison Avenue
Pasadena, California

This was Jay North's home in *Dennis the Menace*, which ran from 1959-1963. The show was based on Hank Ketcham's cartoon of the same name, which first appeared in American newspapers in 1951. Forever dressed in his striped tee-shirt and dungarees, Dennis was the typical cute kid – intent on do-gooding but always ending up with trouble at hand. (Especially when it came to his neighbor, Mr. Wilson, played first by Joseph Kearns and then by Gale Gordon in the last season.)

Designing Women

1321 South Street (at 14th Street)
Little Rock, Arkansas

The exterior shots of the Sugarbaker Design Firm in the popular series *Designing Women* (1986–1993) was actually Villa Marre, a Little Rock museum. Built in 1881 by Angelo Marre and his wife Jennie Marre, this Victorian home is just a few blocks away from the Arkansas Governor's Mansion (former home of Bill and Hillary Clinton) located at 1800 Center Street (at 18th and Spring Streets).

Dragnet

Parker Center
150 North Los Angeles Street
Los Angeles, California

Parker Center, the real headquarters for the Los Angeles Police Department, has been

seen in many TV cop shows, most notably, *Dragnet*. The show aired on NBC-TV twice, from 1952–1959 and then from 1967–1970. Starring Jack Webb as Sergeant Joe Friday with Ben Alexander as Officer Frank Smith and Harry Morgan as Officer Bill Gannon (among others), the show also featured the famous *Dragnet* theme song by Walter Schumann (Miklos Rozsa's name was added to the credits later after a lawsuit).

Dynasty

1625 Broadway Street
Denver, Colorado

The twin towers known as the "World Trade Center" in downtown Denver served as the mythical location of oil baron offices in the bitchy nighttime soap, *Dynasty* (1981–1989). At the time, Denver was home base to many real-life oil companies.

Falcon Crest

Northern California's Wine Country

Though much of the nighttime soap opera *Falcon Crest* (1981-1990) was filmed in Hollywood, a good deal of the exterior footage was actually shot up in the California wine country. In 1992, the main winery seen in the saga of greed, The Spring Mountain Winery (2805 Spring Mountain Road, St. Helena, California), went as far as to market two wines with the "Falcon Crest" label. The house used as Richard Channing's home was located at Altamura Valley Winery (1700 Wooden Valley Road, Napa, California). Additionally, the stained-glass-windowed house seen on the show was located in the Napa Valley on the grounds of the real Inglenook Vineyards (1991 Street along St. Helena Highway in Rutherford, California).

The Forty Acres Backlot

Culver City, California
Triangular area between Higuera Street, Lucerne Avenue and Jefferson Boulevard
Culver City, California

Today it's an industrial park and a fire station, but from the early 1920s through the late 1960s this was one of the busiest backlots in Hollywood and home to some of TV's most beloved locations. Originally, this was The Culver City studio, opened in the early 1920s by Thomas H. Ince. The area featured a jungle (where the fire station is located today) which was seen in one of RKO's first movies, *The Bird of Paradise,* and used extensively for village scenes for the movies *Tarzan* and *King Kong.*

In 1935, David O. Selznick used the backlot property for the city of Atlanta, a railroad station, and the Tara mansion for the $4 million blockbuster movie, *Gone With the Wind.* (In fact, several of the buildings built for Atlanta that were spared found later life on television.)

In 1948, tycoon and movie producer Howard Hughes bought the studio, then it changed hands a few more times until 1956, when Desi Arnaz's Desilu Studios bought the studio buildings and backlot grounds, then affectionately known as "Forty Acres" (even though in reality the lot was just under 29 acres). And it was here on this triangle-shaped property adjacent to Ballona Creek that TV history was made for years.

Those houses that weren't torched in *Gone With the Wind* became part of the town of *Andy Griffith*'s Mayberry. Floyd's Barber Shop, the Jailhouse and even Andy's house were located here. In addition to *The Andy Griffith Show,* The 40 Acres Lot was used for *The Adventures of Superman, Ozzie and Harriet, The Green Hornet, The Untouchables, Gomer Pyle, Hogan's Heroes, Lassie, Batman,* and several episodes of *Star Trek.*

In fact, TV worlds collided here when *Star Trek* shot the episode entitled "City on the Edge of Forever." In this segment, TV fans saw William Shatner and Joan Collins walking down Main Street, passing in front of Floyd's Barber Shop after a trip back to the early 20th century. In 1976, the Forty Acres backlot was bulldozed and turned into an industrial park.

Friends

**Warner Bros. Studios
4210 West Olive Avenue
Burbank, California**

At the beginning of each episode of this popular sitcom, the entire cast of the series is seen dancing and goofing around in a fountain (to the tune of The Rembrandts' *I'll Be There for You*). Though one might assume the fountain is in New York where the series is based, it's actually on the lot where the show is taped at Warner Bros. in Burbank, California. You can see the fountain and other prominent *Friends*' landmarks on the VIP tour that they offer.

The Fugitive

**Los Angeles Produce Mart (near 7th and Central)
Los Angeles, California**

The 1967 airing of the final episode of *The Fugitive* (with David Janssen) drew the largest TV audience of any show up to that date. Set throughout Los Angeles, the thrilling final chase took Dr. Richard Kimble from this downtown area (where he memorably shielded his face from a cop by carrying a box of lettuce on his shoulder) to the Los Angeles Zoo (in Griffith Park). The series was in part inspired by the real murder of Marilyn Sheppard, whose husband Samuel Sheppard was thought by many to be the murderer (though he denied it vociferously, pointing the finger at a shadowy culprit – as did the character in the TV show).

Green Acres

**Moorpark Exit off the 101 Freeway
Thousand Oaks, California**

The rural opening credits sequence of *Green Acres,* including the farmhouse with the show's title on it, were shot here in Thousand Oaks, California, near the Moorpark exit off the 101 freeway. Now overrun with condominiums, strip malls, apartments and business warehouses, the former land which was "spreadin' out so far and wide" is today unrecognizable from the show. The country comedy ran on CBS-TV from 1965–1971 and was the spin-off of the popular rural comedy *Petticoat Junction*. Both series took place in the farming valley known as Hooterville.

Growing Pains

John Marshall High School
3939 Tracy Street
Los Angeles, California

Growing Pains (1985–1992) was set in the suburbs of Long Island, New York. Mike (Kirk Cameron) and Carol (Tracey Gold) both attended Thomas E. Dewey High School, which was actually located in the Los Feliz area of Los Angeles. In addition to Growing Pains, John Marshall High was also the location for a prom scene in Highway to Heaven, and was seen in LA Law and the movie Uncle Buck. The high school overlooks the Walt Disney studios.

Ironside

Hall of Justice
750 Kearny Street
San Francisco, California

Robert T. Ironside (Raymond Burr), who was paralyzed by an assassin's bullet, took up residence in the upper levels of the Old Hall of Justice in San Francisco and continued as a consultant for the police department. The real building used as Ironside's office and apartment was actually the old Hall of Justice. Sadly, after shooting the exterior shots of the Hall of Justice, it was demolished in 1967 despite the fact that the series ran from 1967–75. Today, the Kearny Street site is now the home of the Holiday Inn and Chinese Cultural Center.

Land of the Lost

1418 Descanso Drive
La Cañada/Flintridge (northwest of Pasadena), California
818-952-4400
(Descanso Gardens is located near the intersection of the 210 and 2 freeways. It is a 20-minute drive from downtown Los Angeles.)

The jungle tree house that played a key role in the kid's series, Land of the Lost was, until 1996, located in this pretty park (it was taken down for safety reasons). The show involved a family that's sucked into a portal and then ends up in a prehistoric world with dinosaurs and cavemen. (Descanso Gardens also doubled as the jungle in the series.) The show ran from 1974–1976 and starred Sharon Baird, Kathleen Coleman and Wesley Eure.

Laverne & Shirley

200 East Wells Street
Milwaukee, Wisconsin

The historic Milwaukee City Hall was featured prominently in the opening segment of *Laverne & Shirley* (1976-1983). Erected in the 1890s, the H.C. Koch & Company-designed building has become one of Milwaukee's most recognizable landmarks. As for the show, it was another example of a successful spin-off. On *Happy Days,* Laverne De Fazio and Shirley Feeney were two girls who were love interests of Richie Cunningham and Fonzie. Their occasional appearances led to this, their own series, which took place in the same city as *Happy Days* – Milwaukee, Wisconsin during the 1950s.

Little House on the Prairie

Big Sky Ranch
4927 Bennett Road
Simi Valley, California

Big Sky Movie Ranch is a 10,000+ acre ranch that was, and continues to be, a working cattle ranch and farm. Oil Tycoon J. Paul Getty bought the ranch in the early 1930s and renamed it "The Tapo Ranch." (He held it until the early 1980s.) Movie making history at the ranch dates back at least to the middle 1950s, when some exterior scenes for *Gunsmoke* were filmed here, and over the years hundreds of shoots have taken place at the ranch, from commercials to *Dallas* to *Highway to Heaven.* But the meadow was perhaps most famous for *Little House on the Prairie,* which, despite using locations throughout the state, did most of its filming here.

Unfortunately, many of the remaining sets (including the Jonathon Garvey house and barn, and the Laura Ingalls Wilder house and barn) are believed to have been severely damaged or all but destroyed in the devastating wildfires in the fall of 2003. *Little House on the Prairie* starring Michael Landon, Melissa Gilbert and Melissa Sue Anderson among others was based upon the series of *Little House* children's books, written by author Laura Ingalls Wilder, and the TV series came on the heels of a successful made-for-TV movie, which had aired in March 1974. The series ran from 1974-1984.

Mad About You

5 East 12th Street
New York City, New York

The 16-story, brick-faced building shown as the residence of Paul and Jamie Buchman (Paul Reiser and Helen Hunt) on the yuppie-angst comedy *Mad About You* (1992–1999) is located here in lower Manhattan.

Magnum P.I.

11435 18th Avenue
Oahu, Hawaii (North Shore)

The house shown as "Robin's Nest" was actually a private residence located off the Kalanianaole Highway near Wiamanalo Beach. When not at Robin's Nest, Magnum could many times be found at the King Kamehameha Beach Club (actually the Kahala Hilton at 5000 Kahala Avenue in Honolulu, Hawaii – renamed the Kahala Mandarin Oriental in the 1990s).

Married with Children

Clarence Buckingham Memorial Fountain
Grant Park between Michigan Avenue and Lake Shore Drive
Chicago, Illinois

At the beginning of each episode of the dysfunctional comedy *Married with Children,* a large fountain is shown as Frank Sinatra sings the bouncy theme song "Love and Marriage." The fountain (modeled after the Versailles' Latona Basin Fountain in France) is the famous Clarence Buckingham Memorial Fountain in Chicago. Dedicated in 1927, the fountain was a gift to the city of Chicago by Miss Kate Sturges Buckingham in mem-

ory of her brother Clarence. In addition to this television trivia, there's some music trivia here – The Buckingham Fountain supposedly inspired the name of The Buckingham's, a late-1960s and early-1970s pop band who recorded such hits as "Don't You Care" and "Kind of a Drag."

Melrose Place

4616 Greenwood Place
Los Angeles, California

The main setting for *Melrose Place* (1994–1999) was a fictitious apartment complex of the same name. The actual complex seen on the series is located here in the hip Los Feliz area of Los Angeles, about four blocks north of Franklin Avenue.

My Three Sons

837 5th Avenue
Los Angeles, California

The fictitious address for the Douglas' first seven seasons on the popular *My Three Sons* was 837 Mill Street in Bryant Park, but no state was ever mentioned. The real house used for location shots of the neighborhood is located at 837 (same house number) 5th Avenue in Los Angeles. Second to *The Adventures of Ozzie & Harriet* as television's longest-running family sitcom, *My Three Sons* was created by former *Leave It to Beaver* alumnus George Tibbles (it ran from 1960–1972 on CBS-TV.)

Designed as a vehicle for movie star Fred MacMurray, the actor initially wasn't interested in the show because of the time demands of doing a television series. So the producers agreed to film the show at a breakneck 65-day period per season. Because of this plan, scenes from many different episodes were shot in one day, all out of sequence, and then later had to be edited together into a coherent episode. (Co-star William Frawley was used to years of filming *I Love Lucy* in sequence, and never liked this disjointed method of filming.) This system was also employed for Brian Keith when he signed on to star in the series, *Family Affair*.

NYPD Blue

321 East 5th Street between 1st and 2nd Avenues
New York City, New York

NYPD Blue is set in the (fictional) 15th precinct. The NYPD "house" was really the exterior of the 9th Precinct house here in lower Manhattan. Producer Steven Bochco's show premiered on ABC-TV amid controversy in 1993. It was his intent to produce network television's first "R-rated" series, and the cinematic, innovative police drama remains a consistent model of finely crafted storytelling and an engaging, gritty style more than 10 years after its premier. The building was recently razed.

Paramount Ranch

1813 Cornell Road
Agoura, California

This ranch tucked in the mountains near Malibu (part of Malibu Creek State Park near where *M*A*S*H* was filmed) has been the location for many TV Westerns from *The Rifleman* to *Have Gun Will Travel*. More recently, *Dr. Quinn Medicine Woman* was shot here, and many of the old town sets still exist.

Perfect Strangers

1100 South Main Street
Los Angeles, California

This was Larry and Balki's apartment in the show *Perfect Strangers,* which ran on ABC-TV from 1986–1993 and starred Mark Linn-Baker and Bronson Pinchot. The upper floors of the building have since been knocked down but the original first floor remains.

The Real World

30 30th Street
Venice, California

When MTV's Gen-X reality show *The Real World* came to California during the show's second season in 1993, this beachside house was the residence they used. (House members included Jon, Tami, Beth, Dom, Irene Aaron and David.)

Remington Steele/Moonlighting

Century Plaza Towers
2040 Avenue of the Stars
Century City, California

The twin skyscrapers with the tall fountains out front were featured each week in both the TV detective-romance series *Remington Steele* (1982-1987) and *Moonlighting* (1985-1989). The buildings are known as the Century Plaza Towers, at the ABC Entertainment Center in Century City.

Room 222

Los Angeles High School
4650 West Olympic Boulevard
Los Angeles, California
323-937-3210

This show ran September 17, 1969 to January 11, 1974. Most, if not all, of the 113 episodes produced were filmed on location at Los Angeles High School in Los Angeles, California.

Some scenes were filmed at 20th Century Fox studios in Hollywood. The show, which starred Karen Valentine, Lloyd Haynes and Michael Constantine among others, never ranked above #25 in the Nielsen Ratings, but had a loyal following nonetheless. The show also broke ground uncommon for TV at the time, mixing race and politics into a high school setting which mirrored the issues of the Vietnam-era climate.

Seinfeld

129 West 81st Street
New York City, New York

If you visit this westside apartment building in New York, you'll notice it's not the one used in the actual show. That's because the exterior shot of Jerry's apartment used in the show is a façade building in Los Angeles. However, this is the address used in the show, and this is where Jerry actually lived while doing stand-up here in New York. The actual façade that was used is located at Paramount Studios:
5555 Melrose Ave.
Hollywood, California
323-956-5575

Though tours have not been offered since the 9/11 tragedy, back then guests could view the *Seinfeld* exterior, part of the famous "New York Street," a large block of brownstone façades that have featured prominently in the movies *Ghost* and *Sister Act,* as well as such TV shows as *I Love Lucy, Brooklyn Bridge* and *The Untouchables.* One very familiar spot on this New York Street is the basement apartment shared by Laverne and Shirley in their popular TV series of the same name. Near this area, one could also see a building that served as the high school in *Happy Days,* and the tree where Greg puffed on a cigarette in an episode of *The Brady Bunch.*

Three's Company

Santa Monica Pier
Colorado Boulevard and Ocean Avenue
Santa Monica, California

During opening credits of the long-running comedy *Three's Company* (1977-1984), the three main characters were seen frolicking on a boardwalk and riding bumper-cars. That sequence was shot here at the popular Santa Monica Pier before the larger, current amusement park was built. A subsequent opening sequence from the show (post-Suzanne Somers) featured the new trio riding a zoo tram and looking at flamingos. Those shots were filmed at the Los Angeles Zoo (5333 Zoo Drive in Griffith Park).

Twin Peaks

Snoqualmie, Washington (28 miles east of Seattle)

This was one the two towns used by director (and Northwest native) David Lynch as the settings for his offbeat TV series, *Twin Peaks* (the other was nearby North Bend). In the middle of Snoqualmie is the Big Log, the 39-ton log seen in the show's opening credits. A mile north of town is the Salish Lodge, the exterior for Twin Peak's Great Northern Lodge. It's located at 37807 Southeast Snoqualmie Falls Road (1-800-826-6124).

Vasquez Rocks Natural Area Park

10700 West Escondido Canyon Road
Agua Dulce, California
From Los Angeles, take Interstate 5 north to the Antelope Valley Freeway (14) north. Exit at Agua Dulce Canyon Road and turn left (north). After Agua Dulce Canyon Road makes a right turn, continue on it past where it turns left. This will put you onto Escondido Canyon Road. The entrance to Vasquez Rocks Park will be on the right.

This 745+ acre park location has been heavily used by television and commercials, including: *Have Gun, Will Travel; Star Trek; The Adventures of Champion; The Adventures of Rin Tin Tin; The Big Valley; Bonanza; Broken Arrow; Buffalo Bill, Jr.; The Cisco Kid; The High Chaparral; Johnny Ringo; Kung Fu; Maverick; Paradise; The Range Rider;* and *Wild, Wild West.* (*Star Trek* TV fans will recognize it from the "Arena" episode where Kirk fought the Gorn.)

Welcome Back Kotter

New Utrecht High School
1601 80th Street
Brooklyn, New York

This was the inspiration for Buchanan High School, home of Barbarino, Horschack and the Sweathogs on TV's *Welcome Back Kotter* (1975–1979) starring Gabe Kaplan and John Travolta (it was also used in the opening credits). The plot centered on Gabe Kotter, formerly a Sweathog, who returns to James Buchanan High as a teacher. He's assigned the remedial class, teaching the same colorful group of kids to which he once belonged.

The four main students in his class were Vinnie Barbarino, Freddie "Boom-Boom" Washington, Juan Luis Pedro Phillipo de Huevos Epstein, and Arnold Dingfelder Horschack. The high school is still around, and Curly of the Three Stooges once attended classes here before dropping out during the mid-1920s.

WKRP in Cincinnati

Tyler Davidson Fountain
Fountain Square
Fifth Street (between Vine and Walnut Streets)
Cincinnati, Ohio

In the beginning of each episode of the sitcom *WKRP in Cincinnati* (which aired on CBS from 1978–82), a bronze statue of a female standing on a pedestal in the middle of the fountain with water trickling from her fingers is featured. This is the Tyler Davidson Fountain located in the center of downtown Cincinnati, Ohio. Commissioned in 1871 by Henry Probasco to honor Tyler Davidson, his former partner in a hardware business, the 43-foot fountain is based on a design by August von Kreling.

The X-Files

Queen Mary
Long Beach Harbor
Long Beach, California

This was the ocean liner used in the *X-Files* episode where Mulder and Scully time-traveled back to Nazi Germany. (It was also the episode where they first kissed.) A popular site for many TV shows and movies, the venerable Queen Mary is now permanently docked in Long Beach, where it is open to the public.

The Write Stuff

The Algonquin Hotel

59 West 44th Street
New York, New York
212-840-6800

Immediately after World War I in 1919, writers Dorothy Parker, Robert Benchley and Robert E. Sherwood gathered in the Rose Room of the Algonquin Hotel with some literary friends to welcome back acerbic critic Alexander Woollcott from his service as a war correspondent. The lunch was intended as a put-down of the pretentious Woollcott, but it proved so enjoyable that someone suggested it become a regular event. This plan led to the daily, crazy exchange of ideas, wit and opinion that has become the stuff of literary legend.

George S. Kaufman, Heywood Broun, Edna Ferber and several others were also included in this esteemed group, which strongly influenced such writers as F. Scott Fitzgerald and Ernest Hemingway. Though the group became famously known as the "Algonquin Round Table," they referred to themselves as the "Vicious Circle."

"By force of character," observed drama critic Brooks Atkinson, "they changed the nature of American comedy and established the tastes of a new period in the arts and theatre." The Algonquin remains a popular hotel and hangout for writers, and people from all over the world still flock to the Rose Room to see where the group used to meet.

Austin, Mary

Market and Webster Streets
Independence, California.

The is the house where Mary Austin wrote her classic about California desert country, *Land of Little Rain,* in 1902. She lived here from 1892 to 1903. Austin, who became one of the great writers of the west, wrote eloquently about the landscape and nature she encountered here in the Owens Valley, and also accurately documented the plight of women in the area. The house is not open for tours.

Buck, Pearl S.

520 Dublin Road
Perkasie, Pennsylvania
215-249-0100

Set on 60 acres in Bucks County, the 19th-century Green Hills Farm is a testament to the woman who made it her home for 40 years, the great writer Pearl S. Buck. In this very house, the prolific Buck wrote nearly 100 novels, children's books and works of nonfiction while raising seven adopted children and caring for many others. She is probably most renowned for *The Good Earth,* her classic 1931 novel about peasant life in China. The 1835 stone farmhouse displays her Nobel and Pulitzer prizes and many personal mementos collected in China. Guided tours are offered.

Burroughs, Edgar Rice

18354 Ventura Boulevard
Tarzana, California

Famed Tarzan author Edgar Rice Burroughs actually became the founder of the city where he lived, Tarzana, when he sub-divided part of his 550-acre ranch bearing the same name. The famous ranch had been the home of *Los Angeles Times* publisher Gen. Harrison Gray Otis prior to his death in 1917, and it included a 4,500-square-foot hacienda, gardens, orchards, fields and 500 Angora goats. Burroughs described it as "one of the loveliest spots in the world" and re-named it Tarzana. After Burroughs died on Sunday, March 19, 1950, his ashes were buried under a stately tree in front of the Edgar Rice Burroughs, Inc. offices at 18354 Ventura Boulevard in Tarzana, where they remain today.

Cather, Willa

Pioneer Memorial and Educational Foundation
413 North Webster Street
Red Cloud, Nebraska
402-746-2653

Pulitzer Prize-winning author Willa Cather spent her formative years here in the prairie town of Red Cloud, Nebraska. Cather, who was born in Virginia in 1873 and moved with her family to live in Webster County at the age of nine, graduated from Red Cloud High School in 1899. She attended the University in Lincoln, Nebraska for five years, then moved to the east coast for the remainder of her life. (She died in 1947 and was buried in New Hampshire.)

However, the years in Red Cloud were important and formative years in the writer's life. Six of her twelve novels are set in the Red Cloud and Webster County of her youth, including *One of Ours,* which won the Pulitzer Prize in 1922. The Willa Cather Pioneer Memorial (WCPM) and Educational Foundation was founded in 1955, through the efforts of a small group of volunteers in Red Cloud, Nebraska, led by Mildred R. Bennett. The WCPM is a non-profit organization dedicated to promoting understanding and appreciation of the life, time, settings, and work of Willa Cather.

Chumley's

86 Bedford Street
New York City, New York
212-675-4449

The famous door leading to Chumley's — a former speakeasy and well-oiled literary hangout for Steinbeck, Fitzgerald, O'Neill, Dos Passos, Faulkner, Anais Nin, Orson Welles, Edna St. Vincent Millay, James Thurber and others — is unmarked to this day. Now a popular, cozy bar and restaurant, it can be seen in such films as *Reds*; *Bright Lights, Big City*; *Wolfen* and *Sweet and Lowdown.*

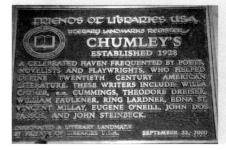

City Lights Bookstore

261 Columbus Avenue
San Francisco, California
415-362-8193

Founded by Lawrence Ferlinghetti in 1953, City Lights bookstore was the legendary cen-ter of the Beat movement. In 1955, City Lights began publishing the works of a daring new brand of cutting-edge writers and thinkers (including Alan Ginsberg's *Howl*) and went on to become an important meeting ground for many artists and writers. Today, City Lights remains one of the world's most vital literary landmarks, and an exception-ally unique bookstore.

Dickinson, Emily

The Homestead
280 Main Street
Amherst, Massachusetts
413-542-8161

Poet Emily Dickinson was born here in 1830. Although she and her family moved to another house in 1840, they returned to the Main Street residence in 1855, and the poet lived there until her death in 1886. It was after moving back here to the Homestead that Emily Dickinson began to write poetry in earnest.

During her most productive years, 1858 to 1865, she compiled her poems into small packets now termed "fascicles." Only 10 of her poems are known to have been published in her lifetime, all anonymously and presumably without her permission. The Dickinson Homestead is a National Historic Landmark owned by the Trustees of Amherst College, and is dedicated to educating the public about the life and work of one of America's greatest poets.

The Exorcist

3210 Bunker Hill Road
Mount Rainier, Maryland

William Peter Blatty's creepy novel *The Exorcist* was based on a real-life event that took place here in 1949. A 14-year-old boy who was seemingly possessed by evil spirits was the subject of a four-month exorcism. (Rumor has it that one of the practices was to play Frank Sinatra records backwards at just 16 rpm.) However, the "treatment" supposedly failed and the teenage boy was sent off to St. Louis for further help. (The original house has since been torn down.)

Faulkner, William

624 Pirate's Alley
New Orleans, Louisiana

This important literary landmark is where William Faulkner wrote his first book, *Soldier's Pay.* The house is now the site of Faulkner House Books, a bookstore specializing in southern literature. Faulkner House is a national literary landmark; the 27-year-old future Nobel Laureate rented rooms on the ground floor in 1925. The building was erected in 1840 by the widow of Jean Baptiste LeBranche on a site formerly occupied by part of the ward and buildings of the French Colonial Prison.

Fitzgerald, F. Scott

6 Gateway Drive
Great Neck Estates
Great Neck, New York

In 1922, a young writer named F. Scott Fitzgerald and his wife Zelda rented this stucco house in Great Neck Estates. The extravagant Fitzgerald drove a Rolls Royce and had three servants, maintaining a lifestyle that cost the then-enormous sum of $36,000 a year. Working in a room above the garage, he soon started working on a novel, inspired by the colorful "Roaring 20s" milieu he lived within. His main character, Jay Gatsby, lived in "West Egg," his fictitious name for Great Neck. Nearby Sands Point became East Egg.

Fitzgerald's great American novel, *The Great Gatsby,* was published in 1925 and interestingly, it was initially met with limited success (only 29,000 copies were published before his death). Eventually though, his books were translated into 35 languages, and in 2002 alone, over half a million copies of *The Great Gatsby* were sold.

Fitzgerald, F. Scott

1443 North Hayworth Avenue
Hollywood, California

This is where F. Scott Fitzgerald died from a heart attack on December 21, 1940, at the age of just 44. The home was not his, it was the apartment of his companion, journalist Sheila Graham. The author was staying there because of a bad heart condition which made it difficult for him to climb the stairs to his own second-floor apartment which was located nearby at 1403 North Laurel Avenue in Hollywood.

Frost, Robert

1/4 mile west of U.S. 7 on Buckhill Road
South Shaftsbury, Vermont

The renowned poet Robert Frost lived here at this farm in South Shaftsbury. The farm, known as "The Gully," was closely associated with the poet's life and work between 1929 and 1938. While this was his residence, he received two Pulitzer Prizes, in 1931 for *Collected Poems* and in 1937 for *A Further Range*. Frost wrote many of the poems found in the latter volume at The Gully. The private residence is today on the National Historic register.

Frost, Robert

Route 28
Derry, New Hampshire
603-432-3091
From I-93, take exit 4. Go east on 102 to Derry Traffic Circle, and then go south on Route 28 and follow the signs to the Robert Frost Farm Historic Site.

The Robert Frost Farm was home to Robert Frost and his family from 1900–1911. Frost was one of the nation's most acclaimed poets whose writings are said to be the epitome of New England, and he attributed many of his poems to memories that stemmed from the Derry years. The basic, two-story white clapboard farmhouse is very representative of New England in the 1880s. The Farm is open to visitors for tours during the spring and summer.

Hawthorne, Nathaniel

The House of the Seven Gables
54 Turner Street
Salem, Massachusetts
978-744-0991

This house was the inspiration for Nathaniel Hawthorne's novel, *The House of the Seven Gables*. Built in 1668, this is the oldest surviving 17th century wooden mansion in New England. Additionally, the home where Hawthorne was born was moved to The House of the Seven Gables and now lies just feet away from the mysterious mansion made famous in fiction. On the grounds visitors will also find the 1682 Hathaway House, the 1658 Reitre Beckett House, the Counting House, seaside period gardens and a panorama of Salem Harbor.

The guided tour includes an introductory audio-visual program, six rooms and a secret staircase in the Gables, and six rooms in Hawthorne's birthplace. Incidentally, Nathaniel Hawthorne actually wrote *The House of the Seven Gables* in a small clapboard cottage in 1850 and 1851 on the Tappan estate, which is now home to the Tanglewood (MA) summer music festival that attracts some 300,000 visitors every year. The actual cottage that's located there is a replica of the original that burned down in 1890. Not open to the public, it contains practice rooms for Tanglewood's student musicians.

Hemingway, Ernest

Windemere Cottage
Lake Grove Road/Walloon Lake
Near Petoskey, Michigan

It was here at this remote cottage in the woods that Ernest Hemingway spent most of his summers until the age of 21, and where he learned to hunt and fish and to first write serious fiction. Windemere, still owned by the Hemingway family, is closed to the public.

All told, Ernest Hemingway lived and worked in Kansas City for just over a year. His longest stint was six months, while he was a cub reporter on *The Kansas City Star* from October 18, 1917 to April 30, 1918. The rest of his time in Kansas City was comprised of a series of six-week stopovers between visits to Arkansas, Wyoming and Florida, during which time he completed two important pieces of literature: *A Farewell to Arms* and *Death in the Afternoon*. These are a few of the places with some Hemingway history in Kansas City.

Hemingway, Ernest

Aunt and Uncle's Home

3629 Warwick Boulevard
Kansas City, Missouri

This is where Hemingway's uncle Alfred Tyler Hemingway and aunt Arabell lived in 1917. Alfred Tyler used his pull with editor Henry Haskell to get Ernest a job writing at *The Kansas City Star* newspaper. Though Hemingway lived at a nearby boarding house (once located at 3733 Warwick), he would often visit this house for dinner with his relatives.

The Kansas City Star

1729 Grand Boulevard
Kansas City, Missouri

As a reporter here at *The Star*, Hemingway was responsible for covering fires, crimes, the General Hospital and whatever was happening at Union Station. Inside the lobby here at *The Star*, a World War I service plaque near the main entrance displays Hemingway's name (16th from the top, in the first row). The Nobel Prize-winning writer is also remembered in a vestibule display, as well as through the paper's Hemingway Writing Award, a national contest for high school journalists.

The Muehlebach Hotel

Southwest corner of 12th Street and Baltimore Avenue
Kansas City, Missouri

When working late on a story or if he was simply too tired to take the long trolley car home, Hemingway would crash in a bathtub in the Muehlebach's pressroom, using towels for a mattress. (In the novel, *Across the River and into the Trees,* Hemingway glorified the beds he slept on in this historic hotel during the winter of 1917.)

Riviera Apartments

229 Ward Parkway
Kansas City, Missouri

Back when it was called Riviera Apartments, Ernest and Pauline Hemingway awaited the arrival of their second son, Gregory Hancock. He was delivered via cesarean section by Dr. Guffey on November 12, 1931. To say thank you, Hemingway gave the doctor an original manuscript of *Death in the Afternoon.* (Which the doctor sold for $13,000 in 1958.)

Hemingway, Ernest

Villa De Cubero

State Road 124 at mile marker 14
Cubero, New Mexico
505-552-9511

The small community of Budville was named after H.N. "Bud" Rice, who opened an automobile service and touring business here in 1928. The Villa de Cubero, built in 1937, once operated as a famous roadside inn. It played host to many celebrities over the years, including Ernest Hemingway while he was writing *The Old Man and the Sea.* The motel closed in the 1980s, but the Villa De Cubero is still open as a grocery store and gas station. The actual room used by Hemingway still stands, and is used today as a storage space (and visible to tourists who ask the management to see it).

Hemingway Home and Museum

907 Whitehead Street
Old Town Key West, Florida
305-294-1136

Ernest Hemingway lived and wrote here for more than ten years. The house was built in 1851 by Asa Tift, a marine architect and salvage wrecker, and became Ernest

Hemingway's home in 1931. Today, the cozy abode still contains the furniture that "Papa" and his family used, and the cats that prowl the home and grounds are actually descendants of the cats he kept while he lived in the house.

The building where Hemingway had his studio was originally a carriage house; his studio was on the second floor. Today a stairway has been erected from the patio on the ground floor for tourists to gain access to the second floor writing studio. Incredibly, the studio remains precisely as it was back then – Hemingway's Royal typewriter, Cuban cigar-maker's chair, and the mementos he collected are all still in place. It was within this studio where he crafted *Death in the Afternoon, Green Hills of Africa, To Have And Have Not, For Whom The Bell Tolls,* and many of his most-famous short stories, such as "The Snows of Kilimanjaro" and "The Short, Happy Life of Francis Macomber."

Hemingway, Ernest

Hemingway's Suicide

East Canyon Run Boulevard
Ketchum, Idaho

Ernest Hemingway died here on July 2, 1961 (he and his wife, Mary, had moved here in 1959). Mary Hemingway first reported that her husband had accidentally shot himself while cleaning his gun. However, the official cause of death was then listed as suicide. (It was here that Hemingway finished his book, *For Whom the Bell Tolls*.)

Though the house is not regularly open to the public, on rare occasions there are opportunities to visit. The Hemingway Memorial, located in a grove of aspens and willows overlooking Trail Creek, features a bronze bust of the writer. Hemingway's gravesite, along with Mary's, is located in the Ketchum Cemetery. Other Hemingway-related sites in Ketchum include Michel's Christiania on Sun Valley Road (where the author had his last dinner on July 1, 1961), and Whiskey Jacques, a bar at 309 Walnut Avenue North.

The Hotel Monteleone

214 Rue Royal
New Orleans, Louisiana
1-800-535-9595

The Hotel Monteleone has the distinct honor of being dedicated as a Literary Landmark by the Friends of Libraries USA. Over the years, the hotel has housed many famous writ-

ers, such as Pulitzer Prize-winner Richard Ford, Tennessee Williams, Eudora Welty, William Faulkner, Sherwood Anderson, Truman Capote and many more. Interestingly, the Hotel Monteleone is actually featured in stories by both Welty and Ford, and Truman Capote claims to have been born while his parents were staying at the Hotel Monteleone.

There are countless other stories that continue to make the life of the Hotel Monteleone quite an interesting and intriguing landmark. With its 117-year history and wonderful French Quarter location, the Hotel Monteleone is the best place to begin experiencing the colorful literary history of New Orleans.

Hurston, Zora Neale

1734 School Court
Fort Pierce, Florida

Famed author Zora Neale Hurston (1891–1960) rented a room in this house — one of the few standing buildings closely linked with Hurston's life — in 1942. It was while living here that Hurston taught part-time at the Florida Normal and Industrial Institute and completed her autobiography, *Dust Tracks on a Road.* She also met novelist Marjorie Kinnan Rawlings, a St. Augustine resident and author of *The Yearling,* during this period. Earlier, in 1927, Hurston married Herbert Sheen, a Chicago medical student, at the St. Johns County Courthouse. Throughout her life, Hurston traveled the back roads of Florida collecting folk stories and songs which inspired her musical plays, short stories, and novels.

Ingalls, Laura

Historic Home and Museum
3068 Highway A
Mansfield, Missouri
1-877-924-7126

In 1932, Laura Ingalls Wilder published the first of her beloved *Little House* books, which described the pioneering of the Ingalls and Wilder families during the 1870s–1890s. All of the nine manuscripts for these cherished books were written here, and the publication of these stories made the Wilders well-known international literary characters and eventually led to the creation of the popular *Little House on the Prairie* TV series.

Interview with the Vampire

503 Divisadero Street
San Francisco, California

This ornate purple and green Victorian house is where author Ann Rice wrote *Interview with the Vampire.* (The fictional "interview" happened here, too.) She lived in the house's upstairs flat, and in the very first paragraph of the novel, Rice evokes the house: "He stood there against the dim light from Divisadero Street... a wash basin hung on one wall." *Interview with the Vampire* remains one of the best-selling books of all time.

Kerouac, Jack

Pollard Memorial Library

401 Merrimack Street
Lowell, MA
978-970-4120

A popular Kerouac haunt (when it was known as the Lowell Public Library) in the 1920s and '30s, this is where the writer would, as he detailed in *Maggie Cassidy* and *Vanity of Duluoz*, skip school "at least once a week" to read Shakespeare, Victor Hugo, William Penn, and scholarly books on chess. "It was how I'd become interested in old classical-looking library books," he writes in *Maggie Cassidy*, "some of them falling apart and from the darkest shelf in the Lowell Public Library, found there by me in my overshoes at closing time."

On the Road

29 Russell Street (between Hyde and Eastman Streets, south side of the street)
San Francisco, California

The phrase "The Beat Generation" was first used by writer Jack Kerouac in 1948. (John Clellon Holmes introduced the phrase to the wider public in 1952 in an article he wrote in the *New York Times Magazine* called "This Is the Beat Generation.") In 1958, noted San Francisco columnist Herb Caen coined the term "Beatnik." But of course Jack Kerouac came to epitomize "The Beat Generation" to the world.

A poet, a writer, a wanderer, a traveler, a storyteller, he traversed the country and the world, combining with Allen Ginsberg, Neal Cassady, and William S. Burroughs to produce some of the most radically timeless and inventive literature of the 20th century. He is certainly most famous for 1957's *On the Road*, written at this house (in the attic) in only three weeks. (Other works of note include: *The Dharma Bums, The Subterraneans, Desolation Angels* and *Big Sur*.) Jack Kerouac had arrived at this house, the home of his friends Neal and Carolyn Cassidy, in 1951, and it was also here where the three formed a well-documented love triangle.

Kerouac, Jack

Jack Kerouac Commemorative Statue

A few hundred yards from Kearney Square
Lowell, Massachusetts

Lowell honors its native son with a beautiful memorial featuring the opening passages from Kerouac's five "Lowell novels," as well as passages from *On the Road, Lonesome Traveler, Book of Dreams,* and *Mexico City Blues* in-scribed on eight triangular marble columns. Created by Houston artist Ben Woitena and dedicated on June 25, 1988, the artful creation is located on the site where a 12-story brick and concrete warehouse once stood – a building Kerouac described as "the great gray warehouse of eternity." Jack Kerouac died in Orlando, Florida in 1969 at the age of 47.

Kipling, Rudyard

Off Interstate 91 at exit 3
Brattleboro, Vermont

Rudyard Kipling lived here in a home he designed and built in 1892–93 called "Naulakha." It was an eclectic structure for its time and place, one part American shingle style, one part Indian bungalow, and it was tucked against a hillside, as Kipling described it, "like a boat on the flank of a distant wave." Every room in the house has a beautiful view across the Connecticut River valley to New Hampshire's Mount Monadnock, which breaks the horizon, Kipling recorded, "like a giant thumbnail pointing upward."

While living in this home for four years, Kipling wrote *Captains Courageous, The Day's Work,* and *The Seven Seas,* as well as starting on *Kim* and the *Just So Stories.* Most famously, though, this is where *The Jungle Books* were written, featuring Mowgli, the boy raised by wolves; Shere Khan, the ruthless tiger; and Bagheera, the fearless panther. Naulakha is not open to the public (except on several summer weekends), but it can be seen from the road and rented for private use. Call for details (802-254-6868).

London, Jack

2400 London Ranch Road
Glen Ellen, California (about 20 minutes north of Sonoma)
707-938-5216

Jack London State Historic Park is a memorial to legendary writer and adventurer Jack London, who made his home at the site from 1905 until his death in 1916. The park was once part of the famous writer's 1,500-acre Beauty Ranch, and contains the cottage res-

idence where he wrote books, short stories, articles and letters while he oversaw a multitude of agricultural enterprises. After London's death, his wife, Charmian, continued to live in the cottage until her death in 1955. It was her wish that the ranch be preserved in memory of Jack London and his work.

There is a museum in "The House of Happy Walls," which Mrs. London built in a redwood grove. A pleasant 3/4 mile walk takes you to a dam, lake, and bathhouse built by Jack London himself. Other hikes lead up through fir and oak woodlands to views of the Valley of the Moon. Another trail leads to Jack London's grave and to "Wolf House," London's legendary dream house, which was destroyed by fire in 1913.

London, Jack

Heinold's First and Last Chance Saloon
56 Jack London Square
Oakland, California
510-839-6761

Opened in 1883, this historic bar was originally called J.M. Heinold's Saloon and is built from the timbers of old whaling ships. Considered to be London's favorite saloon, he would sit here and listen to sailors' tales, many of which would later appear in his books.

London wrote at a favorite table, and Heinold and the saloon are referred to 17 times in his novels *John Barleycorn* and *The Tales of the Fish Patrol*. (Other former customers of the tiny saloon include President William Howard Taft and writers Robert Louis Stevenson, Robert Service, Ambrose Bierce and Erskine Caldwell.) Adjacent to the saloon is a portion of London's 1898 Yukon cabin which was moved here to Oakland in 1969.

Looking for Mr. Goodbar

**All State Café
250 West 72nd Street
New York City, New York
212-874-1883**

This is the bar where, in real life, a young teacher met a guy, took him to her apartment across the street and wound up being immortalized in the novel *Looking for Mr. Goodbar*. The book, written by Judith Rossner, was eventually made into a 1977 movie starring Diane Keaton and Richard Gere.

Melville, Herman

**780 Holmes Road
Pittsfield, Massachusetts
413-442-1793**

This was the home of Herman Melville from 1850-1863, and it was here at the place he called "Arrowhead" that he wrote his most famous work, *Moby Dick*. In addition, he wrote three other novels here, *Pierre, The Confidence-Man,* and *Israel Potter*; a collection of short stories entitled *The Piazza Tales*; all of his magazine stories; and some of his poetry. Arrowhead is now a house museum interpreting the life of the Melville family in the Berkshires. It is owned and operated by the Berkshire County Historical Society, a non-profit corporation, and welcomes visitors all year round.

Margaret Mitchell House and Museum

**999 Peachtree Street NE (Corner of Peachtree and 10th Streets)
Atlanta, Georgia
404-249-7012**

It was in an apartment in this building that Mitchell and her second husband, John Marsh, lived while she wrote her masterpiece, *Gone With the Wind*. The novel, completed in 1929, would remain unpublished until 1936. In 1932, Mitchell moved to a larger apartment, where she was living when her novel was actually published. Tragically, while crossing Peachtree Street (at 13th Street in downtown Atlanta) in 1949, she was hit by a drunken taxi-cab driver and died five days later from her injuries. (Mitchell and her husband were on their way to see *The Canterbury Tales* after stopping for a drink at the Atlanta Women's Club.) She is buried in Atlanta's Oakland Cemetery.

O'Henry

Pete's Tavern
129 East 18th Street (Irving Place)
New York City, New York
212-473-7676

Pete's Tavern first opened its doors in 1864 and has been open ever since. (Thus making Pete's Tavern both an official historical landmark and the longest continuously operating bar and restaurant in New York City – it even stayed open during Prohibition . . . disguised as a flower shop.) Pete's Tavern still looks exactly as it did when literary history was made here in 1902 when its most celebrated regular, the writer O. Henry, wrote the classic *Gift of the Magi* at his favorite booth by the front doors (which is marked today).

O'Neill, Eugene

Tao House
Danville, California
925-838-0249

Eugene Gladstone O'Neill, the only Nobel Prize-winning playwright from the United States, lived here at Tao House in the hills above Danville from 1937 to 1944. It was at this site that he wrote his final and most successful plays: *The Iceman Cometh, Long Days Journey Into Night,* and *A Moon For the Misbegotten.* In early 1937, he and his wife Carlotta had been living in a San Francisco hotel. "No roots. No home," Carlotta wrote as they searched for a place to live. The privacy and climate of this 158-acre San Ramon Valley retreat near Danville became the couple's sanctuary.

Since 1980, the National Park Service has been restoring Tao House, its courtyard and orchards, and telling the story of O'Neill, his work and his influence on American theater. Reservations are required to visit this site and the National Park Service provides a shuttle van for the short ride to the site.

Parker, Dorothy

8983 Norma Place
Los Angeles, California

Writer/humorist Dorothy Parker of Algonquin Roundtable fame lived here in the early 1960s (long after the glory days in New York), and it was here where Parker found her husband, Alan Campbell, dead on June 14, 1963. When a neighbor asked Parker what she could do to help, Parker famously responded, "Get me a new husband."

Poe, Edgar Allan

Edgar Allan Poe House

West 84th Street and Broadway

This is the "Edgar Allan Poe Street." At one time, Edgar Allan Poe lived at a broken-down farmhouse located smack in the middle of Broadway. It was here that he wrote "The Purloined Letter" (the last Dupin tale), "The Oblong Box" and "Thou Art the Man." Obsessed by a true murder case in New York, Poe twisted its events to form the two latter tales. Two plaques dedicated to Poe detail more of his life here; they are located on the northern buildings on either side of Broadway.

Edgar Allan Poe House II

532 North Seventh Street
Philadelphia, Pennsylvania
215-597-8780

This small brick house (now connected to 530 North Seventh Street) was home to Edgar Allan Poe from 1838-1844. During the entire six years that Poe lived in Philadelphia, he attained his greatest success as an editor and critic, and he published some of his most famous tales, including, "The Gold Bug," "The Fall of the House of Usher," "The Tell-Tale Heart," and "The Murders in the Rue Morgue." Of his several Philadelphia Poe homes, this is the only one that survives. The site became part of the National Park System on November 10, 1978.

Poe, Edgar Allan

Poe Park

Grand Concourse at Kingsbridge Road
Bronx, New York
718-881-8900

The tiny Poe cottage in the Bronx was the last home of Edgar Allan Poe. Set in a tiny park on the (once grand) Grand Concourse, it is the only house left from the old village of Fordham. In 1846, Poe and his wife Virginia leased the house for $100 a year. Virginia, who was 13 when she married her first cousin in 1836, had tuberculosis and was in failing health when Poe decided that the Bronx country air might help her feel better. Sadly, Poe was penniless despite his literary success, having lost his savings in a magazine venture that went bankrupt. Virginia's mother, who lived with them, had to forage in neighboring fields to feed the family.

During this difficult period, Poe wrote many soon-to-be-famous poems including "The Bells," "Eureka" and "Annabel Lee." Virginia finally died in 1847; and Poe himself died two years later during a trip to Baltimore. Their cottage was saved from destruction in the 1890s by the Shakespeare Society and moved from its original location on the other side of Kingsbridge Road in 1913. Today, the Bronx County Historical Society operates the house.

Sandburg, Carl

1928 Little River Road
Flat Rock, North Carolina
704-693-4178

"Connemara" is the 240-acre farm in the Western North Carolina mountains that was home to Pulitzer-prize winning poet, author, lecturer and Abraham Lincoln biographer, Carl Sandburg. The great writer lived and worked here for the last 22 years of his life. Though he was a Midwesterner most of his life, Sandburg and his family moved to North Carolina in 1945.

Today the site, managed by the National Park Service, preserves the Sandburg legacy for future generations. The historic site consists of the circa 1838 antebellum house, a dairy goat barn complex which is home to the Connemara Farms goat herd, sheds, rolling pastures, mountainside woods, walking/hiking trails, two small lakes, ponds, flower and vegetable gardens, and an orchard.

The Shining

Estes Park Stanley Hotel
333 Wonderview Avenue
Estes Park, Colorado
1-877-434-1212

Located 72 miles north of Denver, this beautiful grand hotel, opened in 1909 by F.O. Stanley, is just six miles from Rocky Mountain National Park. Late in the summer of 1973, author Stephen King, flush from the success of his first novel, *Carrie* (his second, *Salem's Lot* had been written by now as well), moved his family to Colorado. After discovering this hotel, he checked in for a stay with his wife and was immediately inspired. It was while staying in room 217 that the idea for *The Shining* was first realized. (Though in the chilling novel, the Stanley Hotel became a fictional hotel known as The Overlook, near a mountain town called Sidewinder.)

The book would eventually go on to become a movie starring Jack Nicholson, Shelly Duvall, Danny Lloyd and Scatman Crothers, but it was not shot here. Director Stanley Kubrick had wanted to use the hotel, but there was not enough snow, so he used exterior shots of Timberline Lodge on Mt. Hood, Oregon. (All of the interiors were shot in England.)

Steinbeck, John

John Steinbeck's Birthplace and Boyhood Home

132 Central Avenue
Salinas, California
831-424-2735

The beautifully restored Victorian house where John Steinbeck was born on February 27, 1902 is now a charming restaurant. It also includes the Best Cellar Gift Shop, a treasure trove of Steinbeck books (including first editions), Steinbeck House cookbooks and individual recipes, and wonderful gift items. You can also tour the home and view family heirlooms, precious mementos and photographs.

Steinbeck, John

Steinbeck Family Cottage

147 11th Street (between Lighthouse and Ricketts Row)
Pacific Grove, California

Built by John Steinbeck's father for use as a summer home, this pretty cottage features

a pine tree in the yard that Steinbeck planted himself as a child. In 1930, Steinbeck brought his wife, Carol, here to live with him (where they got by on a $25-per-month allowance provided by John Steinbeck, Sr.). Steinbeck worked with his dad to remodel the cottage and eventually Steinbeck even added a fish pond to the property.

After leaving the cottage, Steinbeck returned in the fall of 1932 when his mother suffered a stroke, eventually dividing time between this cottage and the family home in Salinas. During this period, he worked on parts of *The Red Pony, The Pastures of Heaven, Tortilla Flat* and *In Dubious Battle.* Steinbeck also began to write his classic *Of Mice and Men* at this cottage, but eventually moved out to Monte Sereno to escape the attention that his growing fame brought.

John Steinbeck Home

16250 Greenwood Lane
Monte Sereno, California

In May 1936, John and Carol Steinbeck purchased this 1.639 acre plot of land in what was then Los Gatos, California (now Monte Sereno). Carol designed a 1,452 square foot home, which was built in the summer of 1936. This small, one-story wooden structure was to become the first home owned by Steinbeck, and to protect his privacy, Steinbeck built an eight-foot grape stake fence around the property. At the entrance gate he personally placed a carved wooden plaque which read "Arroyo del Ajo" or "Garlic Gulch."

While living in this house, Steinbeck completed his classic *Of Mice and Men* and wrote another literary landmark, *The Grapes of Wrath.* While living here he also entertained many notable guests, but as other homes began to sprout up in the area, the Steinbecks decided to move to regain some privacy. They sold this house in September 1938, and in December 1989 it was added to the National Historic Registry.

Steinbeck, John

John Steinbeck's Cottage

425 Eardley Avenue (between Spruce and Pine Streets)
Pacific Grove, California

Steinbeck bought this cottage early in 1941 and lived here briefly with Gwen Conger, who later became his second wife. He wrote parts of *The Sea of Cortez* and *The Forgotten Village* here before moving to New York City in the summer of 1941.

Stevenson, Robert Louis

530 Houston Street
Monterey, California
408-649-7118

When Robert Louis Stevenson came to Monterey in 1879 to be closer to Fanny Van de Grift Osbourne (whom he would eventually marry), he lived in this adobe (then a hotel) which was built in the 1830s. In 1937, the building was purchased by Edith C. Van Antwerp and Mrs. C. Tobin Clark to save it from destruction, and they went on to present it to the State of California as a memorial (today it is part of Monterey State Historic Park). At the house you'll find lots of Robert Louis Stevenson memorabilia, including furniture, first edition books, manuscripts, keepsakes, and personal belongings of the famous writer donated by members of his family.

Stevenson, Robert Louis

608 Bush Street (above the Stockton Tunnel across from Burritt Alley)
San Francisco, California

This is where the famed Scotsman lived in early 1880. Once a rooming house, a plaque here at the San Miguel Barbershop explains that a miserable, down on his luck Stevenson wrote many poems, essays, etc. during the long, lonely winter he spent here.

Stowe, Harriet Beecher

63 Federal Street
Brunswick, Maine
207-725-5543

It was while her husband Calvin was teaching here in the early 1850s that Harriet Beecher Stowe wrote the classic *Uncle Tom's Cabin,* a book whose portrait of slavery had such a cultural impact that Abraham Lincoln is said to have greeted her with the words "so this is the little lady that made this big war." The rambling old house is now a motel; guests stay in modern rooms around the back, but can use the lounge of the original house.

Twain, Mark

Twain Home and Museum

208 Hill Street
Hannibal, Missouri
573-221-9010

Born in 1835, Mark Twain "came in with Haley's comet" and went out with it 75 years later in 1910 just as he had predicted he would. This small frame house was occupied by the John Marshall Clemens family from 1844 to 1853. Samuel Clemens grew up here and used many incidents from his real life as patterns for Tom Sawyer and other characters. From 1853 to 1911, the home was a rental property.

When the home was scheduled for demolition in 1911, the

local Hannibal Commercial Club started a campaign to purchase it, but progress was slow. A local attorney, Mr. George A. Mahan, purchased the home and gave it to the city of Hannibal on May 15, 1912. Today, the home is part of a complex which includes Twain's boyhood home, a museum, the Becky Thatcher house, the John M. Clemens Justice of the Peace Office, Grant's Drugstore/Pilaster House, and the new Mark Twain Museum.

Twain, Mark

Angels Hotel

Corner of Main Street and Bird Way
Angels Camp, California

Mark Twain's first major writing success was "The Celebrated Jumping Frog of Calaveras County," published in 1865. The amusing tale of an amphibian wagering scam can be traced to this hotel, where Twain first heard the origins of the story. On February 20, 1865, Twain visited the saloon where Ben Coon, the bartender, told him the tale about a man and a jumping frog. Back at the Gillis cabin, where Twain was staying, he turned this story into a "villainous backwoods sketch" entitled "Jim Smiley and His Jumping Frog."

Published later that year in newspapers throughout America and Europe, the story earned Twain worldwide recognition. Reprinted in 1867 in a collection of Twain's western writings, the story was re-titled "The Celebrated Jumping Frog of Calaveras County," by which it is known today.

Complete with a statue of its favorite son, Mark Twain, this town along Highway 49 is unofficially called "Frogtown" because of its yearly Jumping Frog Jubilee at the Calaveras County Fair. The event began in 1928 when local leaders decided to honor Mark Twain, who once lived near here. The international event, featuring thousands of frogs, is held annually during the third weekend of May during the Calaveras County Fair. (The cabin where Twain wrote the story atop Jackass Hill was destroyed by fire and rebuilt in 1922.) The hotel building still stands but now houses law offices.

Twain, Mark

Montgomery Block

600 Montgomery Street
San Francisco, California

Perhaps San Francisco's most recognizable building, the Transamerica pyramid is the site of a onetime literary landmark, as a brass plaque in the lobby attests. It was the city's prime literary and artistic crossroads, called the Montgomery Block. From 1853 until being razed in 1959, the four-story building was a haven for writers, bohemian poets, artists, and political radicals. Rudyard Kipling, Robert Louis Stevenson, Mark Twain, and William Randolph Hearst all rented office space here, and it was also here in the basement steam baths that Twain met a fireman named Tom Sawyer — who later opened a popular San Francisco saloon.

The Golden Era

732 Montgomery Street
San Francisco, California

This was the home of San Francisco's first literary magazine, *The Golden Era,* founded in the 1850s, which helped launch the careers of Bret Harte and Mark Twain. Twain later credited Harte with developing his talent. "He changed me from an awkward utterer of coarse grotesqueness to a writer of paragraphs and chapters that have found a certain favor in the eyes of some of the very decentest people," Twain said.

Mark Twain Home

351 Farmington Avenue
Hartford, Connecticut
860-247-0998

Today you can tour the 19-room, Tiffany-decorated mansion where, from 1874-1891, Mark Twain raised his family and wrote such classics as *The Adventures of Tom Sawyer, Adventures of Huckleberry Finn* and *A Connecticut Yankee in King Arthur's Court.* The

house contains many pieces of Clemens family furniture, including Mark Twain's ornate Venetian bed and a billiard table owned by the author. The Mark Twain House is a designated National Historic Landmark and the winner of a major award for restoration from the National Trust for Historic Preservation.

Wharton, Edith

The Mount
2 Plunkett Street
Lenox, Massachusetts
413-637-1899

This spectacular 29-room American classical mansion was designed and built by Edith Wharton in 1901-02 (in collaboration with architect L. V. Hoppin). Before moving to Europe, Wharton lived here from 1902 to 1911. Edith Wharton was born in 1862 into a tightly controlled society known as "Old New York" at a time when women were discouraged from achieving anything beyond a proper marriage. But Wharton broke through the stereotypes of the day to become one of America's greatest writers.

Her credits include *The Age of Innocence*, *Ethan Frome*, and *The House of Mirth*; in all she wrote over 40 books in 40 years, including important and elegant works on architecture, gardens, interior design, and travel (a lot of her writing was done here in this mansion). She was the first woman awarded the Pulitzer Prize for Fiction, an honorary Doctorate of Letters from Yale University and full membership in the American Academy of Arts and Letters. Group tours of the estate are offered, plus the grounds feature The Terrace Café and a bookstore located in the main house.

Pop Culture Landmarks by State

Alabama
Greyhound Bus Station – 77
King, Martin Luther – 105
Liuzzo, Viola – 78
Pettus, Edmund Bridge – 77

Alaska
Coldest Day Ever (U.S.) – 18
Klondike National Park – 108

Arizona
Bonaduce, Danny – 172
Close, Bill – 148
Discovery of Pluto – 124
Fort Bowie – 91
Monroe, Marilyn – 43
Vigiliotto, Giovanni – 170

Arkansas
Bates, Daisy – 74
Central High School – 75
Designing Women – 260
Presley, Elvis – 53
Rolling Stones, The – 250

California
10 – 221
48 Hours – 210
A Place in the Sun – 216
All About Eve – San Francisco
An American Family – 258
Austin, Mary – 274
Back to the Future – 203
Bad News Bears – 203
Band, The – 231
Barr, Roseanne – 47
Basic Instinct – 204
Beach Boys, The – 226
Bin Laden, Osama – 120
Blade Runner – 205
Blandick, Clara – 172

Blossom Room – 205
Bridgeville – 15
Browne, Jackson – 226
Buffy the Vampire Slayer – 259
Cagney and Lacey – 259
Cassidy, Jack – 174
Chasen's – 23
Chinatown – 206
Christo – 17
City Lights Bookstore – 276
Cobb Salad – 24
Creedence Clearwater Revival – 226
Crosby, Stills and Nash – 227
Dandridge, Dorothy – 179
Dean, James – 19-21
Dennis the Menace – 260
Devonshire Downs – 246
Dick, Andy – 179
Dirty Harry – 208
Divine – 180
Donner Party – 84
Doors, The – 227
Dr. John – 228
Dragnet – 261
Duck Soup – 209
Duel, Peter – 180
Egg McMuffin – 25
Entwistle, Peg – 181
Falcon Crest – 261
Father of the Bride – 209
First Air Show – 69
First Hollywood Movie Studio – 209
First Water-to-Water Flight – 135
Fitzgerald, F. Scott – 277
Fleetwood Mac – 253
Flores, Juan – 153
Forty Acres Backlot – 262
Friends – 263
Fugitive, The – 264
Gaye, Marvin – 46
Godfather II – 211

West Virginia
Battle of Point Pleasant – 124

Wisconsin
Gein, Ed – 155
Laverne and Shirley – 265
Roosevelt, Theodore – 130

Wyoming
Buffalo Bill – 16
Dubroff, Jessica – 175
Shane – 219
Starkweather, Charles – 169

Canada
Coldest Day Ever (North America) – 18
Dionne Quintuplets – 21
Earhart, Amelia – 85
Houdini, Harry – 30
Hughes, Howard – 31
Monroe, Marilyn – 38
Richards, Keith – 251
Roxanne – 219
Toronto Rock and Roll Festival – 248

St. Croix
Columbus, Christopher – 81

Acknowledgments

A project like this would be all but impossible without the assistance, support, and generosity of others.

Specials thanks to Alan Lombardi, Ann Vaughn, Anne Leighton, Brandi Stansbury, Catherine Reynolds, Dora St. Martin, Frank Brusca, Gary Axelbank, J. Larry Helton, Jr., Janet Menshek, Karen Smalley, Leanne Potts, Marcia Tucker, Michael Esslinger, Michael Stephens, Nina M. Hunt, Pauline Frommer, Scott Michaels, Steele Wotkyns, Steven Luftman, Timothy Brookes and Mark Sedenquist of www.roadtripamerica.com. As well, I'm grateful to The National Park Service for offering such thorough photographic and text resources.

To Dawn Verhulst, Emily Bradley, Erin Portman, Dani Dudeck, Dawn Wells, Allison Schwartz and Jeremy Baka at Cohn/Wolfe, Los Angeles; and Melissa O'Brien and Tori Walsh at Hampton Inn Hotels — thank you for the opportunity and privilege to be involved with Hampton Inn's "Hidden Landmarks" program.

Thanks to my publisher/editor/friend Jeffrey Goldman; his wife, Kimberly; and their son, Nathaniel. Also, once again, to Ken Niles for his smart design and ingenious cover idea, and to Amy Inouye for her extremely hard work on the production of this book.

I would also like to acknowledge my wife, Jean; daughter, Claire; and son, Charlie; along with my mom, Louise; sisters Margaret and Lee; brothers-in-law Ciro and Billy; and my nephew, Luca. (And my cousin, David McAleer!) I am blessed with a special family.

And of course, thank YOU, the reader, for your interest and time.

Photo Credits

Soeren Larsen, p. 14
© Christo 1983, Photo credit Wolgang Votz, p. 30 bottom
© Bettman/CORBIS, p. 19 bottom, p. 22 bottom, p. 39 bottom, p. 53 bottom
Gary Campbell, p. 31
Ballantines Hotel, p. 37 middle
Brandi Stansbury, p. 40 top left and right
Steve Luftman/Karen Smalley, p. 49 middle, p. 185 middle, p. 235, p. 277 top, p. 282
Todd/Brooke Olsen, p. 50 top left, p. 88 top, p. 95 bottom, p. 96 bottom, p. 137,
p. 181 bottom, p. 266 bottom
Tupelo Hardware, p. 51
Janet Menshek, p. 53 top
Dan Tanner, p. 68
National Park Service, p. 72, p. 75, p. 76, p. 77, p. 81 bottom, p. 92 top, p. 93, p. 108,
p. 123 top
Jimmy Carter Library, p. 73, p. 74
Amelia Earhart House and Museum, p. 85
J. Larry Helton, Jr., p. 87 top and bottom
Mike Oldham, p. 58
Patti Elsworth, p. 88 bottom two
David McAleer, p. 89 middle and bottom, p. 136, p. 148, p. 162, p, 190, p. 201, p. 214, p. 227
bottom, p. 237 middle and bottom, p. 238, p. 240, p. 244, p. 266 top, p. 273, p. 287 top,
p. 288 top
Lyndon Baines Johnson Library, p. 99, p. 100 top, p. 104, p, 107
President Lincoln and Soldiers' Home National Monument, p. 111
Library of Congress, Prints and Photographs Division, p. 112
Carthage Jail, p. 114
PDPhoto.org, p. 117
Eric Draper/White House, p. 120
Richard Nixon Library and Birthplace, p. 121 top, p. 122 bottom
Lowell Observatory, www.lowell.edu, p. 124
Library of Congress, p. 125, p. 130 top
F.D.R. Library, p. 127, 128
The Little White House, p. 132
Harry S. Truman Presidential Library, p. 133 top
Gold Coast Museum/Mike Hall, p. 133 bottom
Frank Ballinger, p. 141, p. 143
Jeff Maycroft, www.alcaponemuseum.com, p. 147
Coffeyville Chamber of Commerce, p. 150
Anne Gallo Morris, p. 151 top and bottom, p. 152
Timothy Brookes, p. 154 bottom
Gary Williams, El Paso County Historical Commission, p. 157 top and bottom

Dana Williams/www.totalescape.com, p. 161
Scott Michaels/www.findadeath.com, p. 180 top and middle, p. 189, p. 198 top
Alamo – Louis Villafranca, p. 191, bottom
Pollock-Krasner House and Study Center, p. 192 top and middle
Oheka Castle, p. 207
Bedichek Middle School, p. 208
Photo courtesy of www.PreservationDirectory.com, p. 219 top
© Aaron Leventhal, p. 224 top and bottom
E.J. Stephens. p. 229 middle
Sean Michael Styles, p. 232
Blues Museum, p. 234
Wade Wilkes, p. 242 bottom
Memory Motel, p. 250 top and bottom
Charlie Epting, p. 255
Mount Airy Visitors Center, 257
Geekphilosopher.com, p. 270
National Archives and Records Administration, p. 280
The Hemingway Museum/Linda Mendez, p. 281 bottom
Lowell Library, p. 284
Used by permission of Phil Chaput and Lowell Celebrates Kerouac!, p. 285
The Margaret Mitchell House & Museum, p. 287 top
Courtesy of the Berkshire County Historical Society, p. 287 middle
Tao House, p. 288 bottom
Connemara, p. 290
Michael Esslinger, p. 292, top, middle and bottom
The Mount, p. 297
Mark Twain Home, p. 296

All remaining photos were either shot by the author or culled from the author's personal collection. Any omissions or errors are deeply regretted and will be rectified upon reprint. Additionally, all appropriate lengths were taken to secure proper photo credit and permissions.

Like Marilyn? You'll *Love* James Dean!

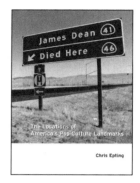

James Dean Died Here
The Locations of America's Pop Culture Landmarks
by Chris Epting

James Dean Died Here takes you on a journey across North America to the exact locations where the most significant events in American popular culture took place. It's a road map for pop culture sites, from Patty Hearst's bank to the garage where Apple Computer was born. Featuring hundreds of photographs, this fully illustrated encyclopedic look at the most famous and infamous pop culture events includes historical information on over 600 landmarks – as well as their exact location. *James Dean Died Here* is an amazing portrait of the bizarre, shocking, weird and wonderful moments that have come to define American popular culture.

Chapters and Sample Entries

Americana: The Weird and the Wonderful
• Bigfoot
• Groundhog Day
• McDonald's (First Location)

History and Tragedy
• The Hindenburg Crash
• Abraham Lincoln's Log Cabin
• Rosa Parks' Bus Ride

Crime, Murder, and Assassination
• Bonnie and Clyde are Killed
• Patty Hearst Bank Robbery
• O.J. Simpson

Celebrity Deaths and Infamous Celebrity Events
• John Belushi
• Hugh Grant
• John Lennon

Let's Go to the Movies
• The Casablanca Airport
• Diner's diner
• The "Field of Dreams"

R&B, Rock 'n' Roll, and All That Jazz
• The American Bandstand Studio
• Jimi Hendrix Burns His Guitar
• Sid & Nancy's Hotel Room

Channel Surfing
• The Brady Bunch House
• The Andy Griffith Lake
• The Seinfeld Diner

Play Ball!
• Wilt Chamberlain Scores 100
• Eddie Gaedel
• Willie Mays' Famous Catch

$16.95 • ISBN 1-891661-31-0 • Trade Paper • 312 pages
6 × 9 • Hundreds of Photos • Travel / Popular Culture

Call 1-800-784-9553 to Order

Books Available from Santa Monica Press

Blues for Bird
by Martin Gray
288 pages $16.95

The Book of Good Habits
*Simple and Creative Ways to
Enrich Your Life*
by Dirk Mathison
224 pages $9.95

The Butt Hello
*and other ways my cats
drive me crazy*
by Ted Meyer
96 pages $9.95

Café Nation
*Coffee Folklore, Magick,
and Divination*
by Sandra Mizumoto Posey
224 pages $9.95

Cats Around the World
by Ted Meyer
96 pages $9.95

Childish Things
by Davis & Davis
96 pages $19.95

**Discovering the History of
Your House**
and Your Neighborhood
by Betsy J. Green
288 pages $14.95

The Dog Ate My Resumé
by Zack Arnstein and
Larry Arnstein
192 pages $11.95

Dogme Uncut
*Lars von Trier, Thomas
Vinterberg and the Gang
That Took on Hollywood*
by Jack Stevenson
312 pages $16.95

**Exotic Travel Destinations
for Families**
by Jennifer M. Nichols and
Bill Nichols
360 pages $16.95

Footsteps in the Fog
*Alfred Hitchcock's
San Francisco*
by Jeff Kraft and
Aaron Leventhal
240 pages $24.95

**Free Stuff & Good Deals for
Folks over 50, 2nd Ed.**
by Linda Bowman
240 pages $12.95

**How to Find Your Family
Roots and Write Your
Family History**
by William Latham and
Cindy Higgins
288 pages $14.95

How to Speak Shakespeare
by Cal Pritner and
Louis Colaianni
144 pages $16.95

**How to Win Lotteries,
Sweepstakes, and Contests in
the 21st Century**
by Steve "America's
Sweepstakes King" Ledoux
224 pages $14.95

**Jackson Pollock:
Memories Arrested in Space**
by Martin Gray
216 pages $14.95

James Dean Died Here
*The Locations of America's
Pop Culture Landmarks*
by Chris Epting
312 pages $16.95

The Keystone Kid
Tales of Early Hollywood
by Coy Watson, Jr.
312 pages $24.95

Letter Writing Made Easy!
*Featuring Sample Letters for
Hundreds of Common
Occasions*
by Margaret McCarthy
224 pages $12.95

**Letter Writing Made Easy!
Volume 2**
*Featuring More Sample
Letters for Hundreds of
Common Occasions*
by Margaret McCarthy
224 pages $12.95

Life is Short. Eat Biscuits!
by Amy Jordan Smith
96 pages $9.95

Marilyn Monroe Dyed Here
*More Locations of America's
Pop Culture Landmarks*
by Chris Epting
312 pages $16.95

Movie Star Homes
by Judy Artunian and
Mike Oldham
312 pages $16.95

Offbeat Food
*Adventures in an
Omnivorous World*
by Alan Ridenour
240 pages $19.95

Offbeat Marijuana
*The Life and Times of the
World's Grooviest Plant*
by Saul Rubin
240 pages $19.95

Offbeat Museums
*The Collections and Curators
of America's Most Unusual
Museums*
by Saul Rubin
240 pages $19.95

A Prayer for Burma
by Kenneth Wong
216 pages $14.95

Quack!
*Tales of Medical Fraud from
the Museum of Questionable
Medical Devices*
by Bob McCoy
240 pages $19.95

Redneck Haiku
by Mary K. Witte
112 pages $9.95

**School Sense: How to Help
Your Child Succeed in
Elementary School**
by Tiffani Chin, Ph.D.
408 pages $16.95

Silent Echoes
*Discovering Early Hollywood
Through the Films of
Buster Keaton*
by John Bengtson
240 pages $24.95

Tiki Road Trip
*A Guide to Tiki Culture
in North America*
by James Teitelbaum
288 pages $16.95

	Quantity	Amount
Blues for Bird (epic poem about Charlie Parker) ($16.95)	_____	_____
The Book of Good Habits ($9.95)	_____	_____
The Butt Hello . . . and Other Ways My Cats Drive Me Crazy ($9.95)	_____	_____
Café Nation: Coffee Folklore, Magick and Divination ($9.95)	_____	_____
Cats Around the World ($9.95)	_____	_____
Childish Things ($19.95)	_____	_____
Discovering the History of Your House. . . ($14.95)	_____	_____
The Dog Ate My Resumé ($11.95)	_____	_____
Dogme Uncut ($16.95)	_____	_____
Exotic Travel Destinations for Families ($16.95)	_____	_____
Footsteps in the Fog: Alfred Hitchcock's San Francisco ($24.95)	_____	_____
Free Stuff & Good Deals for Folks over 50, 2nd Ed. ($12.95)	_____	_____
How to Find Your Family Roots . . . ($14.95)	_____	_____
How to Speak Shakespeare ($16.95)	_____	_____
How to Win Lotteries, Sweepstakes, and Contests . . . ($14.95)	_____	_____
Jackson Pollock: Memories Arrested in Space ($14.95)	_____	_____
James Dean Died Here: America's Pop Culture Landmarks ($16.95)	_____	_____
The Keystone Kid: Tales of Early Hollywood ($24.95)	_____	_____
Letter Writing Made Easy! ($12.95)	_____	_____
Letter Writing Made Easy! Volume 2 ($12.95)	_____	_____
Life is Short. Eat Biscuits! ($9.95)	_____	_____
Marilyn Monroe Dyed Here ($16.95)	_____	_____
Movie Star Homes ($16.95)	_____	_____
Offbeat Food ($19.95)	_____	_____
Offbeat Marijuana ($19.95)	_____	_____
Offbeat Museums ($19.95)	_____	_____
A Prayer for Burma ($14.95)	_____	_____
Quack! Tales of Medical Fraud ($19.95)	_____	_____
Redneck Haiku ($9.95)	_____	_____
School Sense ($16.95)	_____	_____
Silent Echoes: Early Hollywood Through Buster Keaton ($24.95)	_____	_____
Tiki Road Trip ($16.95)	_____	_____

Shipping & Handling:	**Subtotal** _____
1 book $3.00	CA residents add 8.25% sales tax _____
Each additional book is $ .50	Shipping and Handling (see left) _____
	TOTAL _____

Name _____

Address _____

City _____ State _____ Zip _____

☐ Visa ☐ MasterCard   Card No.: _____

Exp. Date _____ Signature _____

☐ Enclosed is my check or money order payable to:

Santa Monica Press LLC
P.O. Box 1076
Santa Monica, CA 90406